THE SIMON & SCHUSTER GUIDE TO
THE WINES OF
BURGUNDY
SERENA SUTCLIFFE

THE SIMON & SCHUSTER GUIDE TO
THE WINES OF
BURGUNDY

SERENA SUTCLIFFE

A Fireside Book

Published by Simon & Schuster Inc.

New York   London   Toronto   Sydney   Tokyo   Singapore

A Fireside Book
Published by Simon & Schuster Inc.
Simon & Schuster Building, Rockefeller Center,
1230 Avenue of the Americas, New York, NY 10020

Edited and designed by Mitchell Beazley International Ltd
Michelin House, 81 Fulham Road, London SW3 6RB

First published 1986 as *Serena Sutcliffe's Pocket Guide to the Wines of Burgundy*.
This edition, revised, updated and expanded, published 1992.

Editor: Anthea Snow
Art Editor: Paul Tilby
Illustrations: Madeleine David
Production: Sarah Schuman
Executive Editor: Anne Ryland
Art Director: Tim Foster

Typeset in Bembo by Servis Filmsetting Ltd, Manchester, England
Colour reproduction by Mandarin Offset, Hong Kong
Produced by Mandarin Offset, Hong Kong
Printed and bound in Hong Kong

10 9 8 7 6 5 4 3 2 1

Library of Congress Cataloging-in-Publication Data
Sutcliffe, Serena.
   The Simon and Schuster guide to the wines of Burgundy / Serena Sutcliffe.
     p.   cm.
  "A Fireside book."
  "A Mitchell Beazley book."
  Includes index.
  ISBN 0-671-79710-7
  1. Wine and wine making–France–Burgundy.   I. Title.
TP553.S87   1993
641.2'2' 0944714–dc 20   92-19087
                                                                  CIP

Contents

Foreword

Access to the personal files of a top professional is surely the most that any serious amateur of wine could ask. This latest generation of wine books represented by Serena Sutcliffe's *Guide to the Wines of Burgundy* and David Peppercorn's companion volume on Bordeaux amounts almost to such a privileged snoop.

The situation reports and critical opinions that form the basis of buying decisions are normally classified information. But wine literature has moved with quite startling speed from the phase of enthusiastic generalization to that of precise wine-by-wine commentary. In this book it drops its sixth, if not seventh, veil. Now we are allowed to know as much as the most experienced professionals.

Serena Sutcliffe has earned a formidable international reputation as a wine-taster of authority and decision. She is now a director of Sotheby's and heads their Wine Department. From London she travels constantly throughout the wine world, but Burgundy has always fascinated her – partly, one suspects, because it is such an enigmatic, volatile and controversial area. Everyone knows that Burgundy, both red and white, can be sublime. Yet it so often fails to meet expectations. What greater challenge for an unprejudiced taster and writer than to track down the authentic and commendable, and to warn us about the rest?

Serena Sutcliffe learned her impeccable French as a translator for UNESCO in Paris. She learned her wine in the London wine trade, being one of the first women to pass the stiff examination and become a Master of Wine. Her writing is a natural gift, which was made plain to the world in 1981 when she was responsible for a totally new edition of André Simon's *Wines of the World*.

These attributes together make her a highly qualified guide. Her day-to-day dealings with Burgundy and Burgundians give her an up-to-date insight such as none before her has tried to pack into the convenient compass of a book of this size. It is a remarkable privilege to be able, as it were, to look over her shoulder at the sometimes hypnotizing complexities of the most tantalizing of all the great wine regions.

Hugh Johnson

Introduction

The new edition of my book on Burgundy comes after a decade of exciting wines from this elusive region. The 1980s converted many Burgundy sceptics into Burgundy lovers and, if 1990 is a harbinger of what is to come in the next decade, devotees will remain faithful.

In updating a book with the density of information contained within these covers, it is always surprising to find so much that has *not* changed – the eternal truths of winemaking and wine lore. At the same time, and this is particularly Burgundian, some estates have splintered and spawned others (usually in a welter of hyphens), while others have become more relevant as they now sell all, or a larger part, of their production themselves and not through *négociants*. The encouraging trend is that virtually all those who made great wine in the mid-1980s still do, and there are many others who have improved immeasurably. Conversely, there are some disappointing instances where the quality does not match the hype.

I have been enormously helped in updating this book by Michael Schuster, for whom I have the greatest professional respect. He pulled it all together and made sense of the maze of names and web of information. It is a pleasure tasting with him as, happily, our views on intrinsic quality in a wine coincide.

Reading about Burgundy can never equal the frisson of drinking its best wines, but if this book leads you to some memorable bottles, from modest Mâcon to the grandiose Grands Echézeaux, it will have served its purpose.

How to Use this Book

The book has three main parts: first, an introduction; second, a section on wines and villages; third, an A–Z list of Burgundy producers.

Introduction to the Region

The Introduction to the Region gives a general picture of Burgundy and its wines and is an ideal starting point.

Wines and Villages

This section gives a briefing on each area and its *appellations* (including soil and topography) together with profiles of selected domains and their wines.

The five Burgundy areas (Chablis, Côte d'Or, Côte Chalonnaise, the Mâconnais, Beaujolais), and the *appellations* within them, are arranged in geographical order from north to south.

To look up a particular village/*appellation*, turn to the area section first and then to the village/*appellation* within that section (eg Beaujolais→Fleurie). The maps at the start of each area section show the principal ACs and can help with this.

For Chablis, Côte Chalonnaise, the Mâconnais and Beaujolais, each *appellation* briefing is followed by a listing of the area's principal producers with details of their holdings (where available), winemaking methods and an assessment of the wines.

In the case of the Côte d'Or, which is by far the largest and most diverse area, only a selection of producers, together with an assessment of their best wines, is included under Wines and Villages. For a comprehensive listing of the Côte d'Or producers, and details of their holdings and winemaking methods, consult the A–Z.

A–Z of Burgundy Producers

The A–Z section is a list of some 600 producers and provides an index to those recommended in the Wines and Villages section. It can be used when looking up individual producers.

To save space, a number of abbreviations have been used. Vineyard areas are expressed in hectares (shortened to ha), and yields are expressed in hectolitres (hl) or hectolitres per hectare (hl/ha). At the beginning of each area and village section, the symbols ● ○ ◑ indicate whether red, white or rosé wine is produced.

GAEC	Groupement Agricole d'Exploitation en Commun
AC (AOC)	Appellation d'Origine Contrôlée
km	kilometres
cm	centimetres
mm	millimetres
1 hectare (ha)	= 2·47 acres
1 hectolitre (hl)	= 22·02 gallons (Imperial)/ 26·45 gallons (US) = approx 11 cases of wine (12 × 75cl bottles per case)

Introduction to the Region

The Region and the Wines

To many people, French and foreigners alike, the word Burgundy is synonymous with wine and rollicking good living. It conjures up visions of gastronomy, bonhomie and rosy cheeks, berets and cellars and baggy trousers. Quite how this image came about is lost in the alcoholic fumes of time, but there is no doubt that it is there. Whether it has actually helped or hindered historic Burgundy to find its rightful place amongst the truly great wines of the world is another matter.

There is nothing homogeneous about the term Burgundy. 'Burgundy' is a good chunk of eastern France, and to many who live there its frontiers are often the limits of their travels. The region covers the area from Chablis down to Lyon, encompassing much beautiful, rolling countryside which will not be of immediate interest to the wine-lover. But what will attract anyone who has ever lifted a glass of good Burgundy to his or her lips is the diversity of tastes emerging from such a disparate landscape.

Viticultural Burgundy consists of the Yonne, chiefly known for its Chablis, the Côte d'Or, Côte Chalonnaise, the Mâconnais and Beaujolais. Chablis is an island, isolated from the rest and logically more a part of Champagne than Burgundy, but the other four defined areas form the Burgundian corridor which leads into the Rhône valley and on down to the Mediterranean.

History of the region

Camille Rodier, writing from the fastness of Nuits-St-Georges in 1920, pours a certain amount of scorn on the theories of Pliny and Plutarch as to the origins of the vine in present-day Burgundy. The ancients would have it that the Gauls invaded Italy for its wine (a somewhat chauvinistic point of view) and when they turned tail and returned over the Alps, they took Italian vinous habits with them. The Burgundians of our days have, incidentally, made a brave attempt to illustrate Gallo-Roman living conditions by erecting a model village of that era by the Beaune service station on the Autoroute du Sud. What does seem likely is that the vine came to Burgundy via the Greek settlement of Marseilles about 600 years BC, considerably predating the arrival of the Romans and their need for the grape. In the following centuries, in spite of Roman protectionism, safeguarding the Italian home product, and barbarian invasions in the 5th century, the vine flourished – so much so that in the 6th century Gregory of Tours was singing the praises of the wines produced near Dijon.

The history of the vine in Burgundy is unalterably linked with the Church. From the end of the 5th century, monasteries were established throughout Burgundy, and the rise of what are now some of the grandest *appellations* of the area became inextricably bound up with royal or aristocratic gifts to the abbeys. The vastly powerful religious centre of Cluny in the Mâconnais was founded in 910 and Cîteaux, on the plain near Nuits, followed in 1098. The harsh order of the Cistercians did much to discipline vine production and ensure the fame of the local wines, and they were, of course, the founders of the Clos de Vougeot. It is worth pondering the austerity of the Cistercian order as one dines now in Bacchanalian fashion with the Chevaliers du Tastevin at Vougeot.

Secular power in Burgundy was held from the 14th century for more than 100 years by the Valois Dukes. At their apogee, their empire and influence included large chunks of France and Flanders; and, in the absence of a competent King, Duke Philip the Bold of Burgundy was certainly the most powerful man in the whole of France. Four Dukes, Philip the Bold, John the Fearless, Philip the Good and Charles the Bold, presided over a state characterized by military strength, material wealth and artistic splendour, perfect conditions for the vine to flourish. It was at this time that the Low Countries became such good clients of Burgundian winemakers, a tradition which has continued to this day. A key figure was Nicolas Rolin, Chancellor to Philip the Good, who was able to amass considerable wealth while holding this post. In 1443 he atoned for his excesses by founding the Hôtel-Dieu in Beaune, later to be supported by the donation of vineyards.

However, in the end, the scattered nature of the Burgundian empire proved to be its downfall, and with the death in battle of Charles the Bold in 1477, Burgundy became truly French under the rule of Louis XI.

The first great Valois Duke, Philip the Bold, had in 1395 declared war on the Gamay grape by ordering that it be pulled up and replaced by the 'nobler' Pinot. This was a recurring theme in Burgundian viticultural history, and the first shot in what was to be a long battle between quality and quantity. But the pendulum always had a tendency to swing towards the 'generous' Gamay. In 1855, of the 26,500 hectares of vines on the Côte d'Or, 23,000 hectares were planted to Gamay, a state of affairs which needs no commentary. However, in mitigation, it must be said that yields varied between 15 and 20 hectolitres per hectare. It should also be remembered that Burgundy was ahead of Bordeaux in the selection of grape varieties.

Taking the Côte d'Or, it is interesting to note the fluctuations in the area under vine:

1816	24,000 ha	1955	8,825 ha
1875	33,745 ha	1982	8,600 ha
1929	12,112 ha	1990	8,549 ha

In 1929, hybrid vines were planted on 1,723 hectares of the region, while in 1955 there were 5,048 hectares of Appellation Contrôlée vines. The 1982 figure included 7,621 hectares of vines producing AC wine, with a mere 979 hectares producing *vin de table*. By 1990, the figure for *vin de table* was so small as to be negligible.

One of the keys to the whole enigma that is Burgundy is the multifarious ownership of the vineyards. This was originally brought about by the French Revolution of 1789, when the religious estates were broken up with all the ferocity of a zealous Henry VIII of England 250 years earlier. Aristocratic domains were also dispersed, rarely to come together again, whereas in Bordeaux returning emigrés were able to carry on as before. This fragmentation of vineyard area has been exacerbated by French laws of succession: all the children inherit, not just the eldest son.

Burgundy did not escape the two natural disasters which hit the whole of viticultural France in the 19th century. The first was oidium, or powdery mildew, which began seriously to affect yields until the remedy of dusting the vines with sulphur was discovered. This method has been used, in one form or another, ever since.

The second disaster, phylloxera, was to have far more devastating effects, as shown by the dramatic drop in the area under vine between 1875 and 1929. This vine louse, or aphid, came originally from the United States, and vines simply died under its attack. In the absence of accurate scientific methods growers often resorted to superstitious folk remedies, and much time and money were lost in experiment and deliberation. Flooding, one suggested remedy, was hardly practicable on the slopes, and injecting the soil with carbon bisulphide was not a permanent solution to the invasion. Only grafting on to American vine rootstocks, immune to the activities of the pest, guaranteed complete safety and gradually, as the 19th century turned into the 20th, this technique was adopted. But the economic ramifications were enormous. Many growers could not afford the cost and either gave up vine-growing or left the region, and the area under vines shrank irrevocably. It was the better sites on the slopes that survived and yields leapt forward, so the picture after phylloxera was in many ways a good deal healthier than in the past. At this time high-yielding Pinots made their appearance. It is a distortion, however, to attribute the increase in yields entirely to new clones. Better and more intelligent vineyard husbandry played a part. The comparatively tiny yields of the past were as often the result of disease as anything else.

The Geography

Burgundy is in eastern France, far away from maritime influence and 'enjoying' a continental climate (although sometimes that is perhaps not quite the word to use in the Siberian conditions of many a Burgundian January). What rivers there are do not make their mark on the microclimate in any significant way – the Serein in Chablis is far too tiny, and the Saône of the Côte Chalonnaise too far from the vineyard slopes. River and vineyard are closest in the Mâconnais, where the Saône breaks its banks with monotonous regularity – however, crops other than the vine usually bear the brunt of this.

Chablis, 136km (85 miles) to the north-west of Dijon, lies stranded on the way to Paris, only about 70km (44 miles) to the south of the Aube, the southernmost classified area of Champagne.

Chablis forms part of the Auxerrois, with the Yonne valley vineyards west of Chablis producing somewhat earthy wines from the communes of St-Bris-le-Vineux, Chitry, Irancy and Coulanges-la-Vineuse. Chablis' claim to fame is its subsoil of Kimmeridge clay/limestone, to which Chardonnay is ideally suited. Nowadays, Portlandian limestone, found in some of the outlying villages around Chablis, is considered by the authorities to be just as special. Unfortunately, this island of vines is subject to particularly severe winters, with spring frost a hazard right up to the end of May. The great hill of the Grands Crus, close to Chablis itself, is a particular frost trap, while the plateau areas of Chablis are often swept by snow during the winter. Indeed, in 1985 Chablis was hit by an isolated snowstorm as late as March 16, a final flurry after an especially bitter winter.

The Côte d'Or, or la Côte as it is known locally, stretches from Dijon 50km (31 miles) down to Dezize-les-Maranges in the department of Saône et Loire, in a southerly direction until Beaune, but then veering more to the south-west. The Côte is, in fact, the eastern edge of a calcareous upland plateau which ends with the Saône river plain. The 'Golden Slope' is so described because of the fiery colours of the vine leaves in autumn. When gazing at this splendour, it is easy to forget that only two percent of the agricultural surface of the department of the Côte d'Or is covered by vines, but this supports 2,300 growers and 30 percent of salaried agricultural labour.

The vineyard area of the Côte d'Or can be divided into three distinct parts: the Côte, which comprises the Côte de Nuits and the Côte de Beaune; the Hautes Côtes; and the plain of Beaune. The greatest wines come from the Côte and the vine here reigns supreme. The domains are very small, averaging five hectares, mostly family-owned and often with plots in several villages.

The Hautes Côtes, frequently ignored in the past but now worthy of serious consideration, are in the hinterland, with vines planted on the slopes of small valleys called *combes*. Here the vine is mixed with other fruit production such as blackcurrants and raspberries, but, as the growers find more economic ways to run their vineyards, confidence in wine is returning. The family properties in the Hautes Côtes tend to be 10–15 hectares in size and, for economic viability, the vines are mostly high-trained and wide-

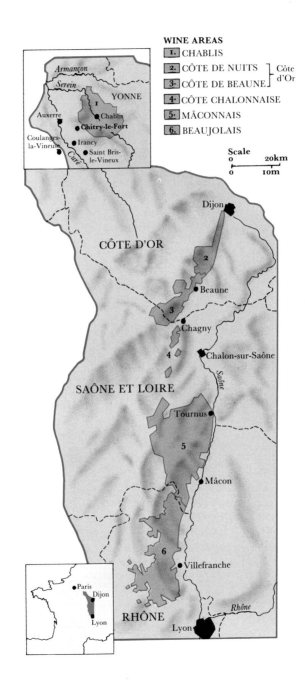

WINE AREAS
1. CHABLIS
2. CÔTE DE NUITS ⎤ Côte
3. CÔTE DE BEAUNE ⎦ d'Or
4. CÔTE CHALONNAISE
5. MÂCONNAIS
6. BEAUJOLAIS

Scale
0   20km
0   10m

YONNE

Armançon
Serein
1
Auxerre   Chablis
Coulanges-   Chitry-le-Fort
la-Vineuse   Irancy
Cure   Saint Bris-
                  le-Vineux

Dijon
CÔTE D'OR
2
Beaune
3
Chagny
4   Chalon-sur-Saône
SAÔNE ET LOIRE
Saône
Tournus
5
Mâcon
6
Villefranche

Paris
Dijon
Lyon
RHÔNE
Rhône
Lyon

spaced. Some of the slopes are not as well exposed here as on the Côte itself, so good weather is needed for optimum ripeness.

The plain around Beaune is, again, not specifically viticultural, but there are now some noble grapes, Pinot Noir, Chardonnay, Aligoté and Gamay, amongst the mixed farming.

The Côte Chalonnaise is not a continuous, visible escarpment, but a series of hills, stretching southwards from Chagny, with fine slopes ideal for vine-growing. The vines are usually grown at heights of 300–335 metres (985–1,100 feet), higher than the Côte d'Or and therefore usually vintaging three or four days later. The vineyards of Rully and Mercurey are close to each other, but Givry stands on its own to the south, and to the south-west of Chalon-sur-Saône, Montagny and Buxy are responsible for some fine white wines. The vineyards appear between fields and woods, not as predominantly eastward facing as those on the Côte d'Or.

Much of the Mâconnais vineyard area lies to the north-west of the town of Mâcon, but the finest area of the 'Pouilly satellites' is found to the south-west. To the north, where the 'bulk' Mâcon is made, the slopes are gentle and undulating, with patches of vineyard where the slope is favourably placed, and white cattle grazing on rich grass where the site is not so propitious to the grape. To the south, the slopes and escarpments become more dramatic, and this is where the grandest wines are made.

The Mâconnais runs into the Beaujolais – more accurately, into the granite hills which make up the ten Beaujolais *crus*, the best area. Vines here are intensively planted, to the virtual exclusion of anything else, making up about a half of the total AC surface area of viticultural Burgundy. The steep hills and peaks of northern Beaujolais give way to different soil and flatter land south of Villefranche; clay and limestone rather than sand over granite, Beaujolais rather than Beaujolais-Villages.

Soil in Burgundy is a geologist's dream, or a layman's nightmare. The Burgundian vineyards perch on the edge of the Massif Central and the Morvan. On the Côte d'Or, a limestone base is interspersed with marl, which is itself a calcareous mudstone, or clay and carbonate of lime, with admixtures of pure clay, sand and gravel. Of course, limestone varies considerably in consistency, from the exceptionally hard Comblanchien 'marble' to something much softer and less resistant.

The limestone scree from the top of the hills has, over the years, been regularly washed down over the surface of the slopes to mix with the marl. This is all to the good, for marl on its own is too rich for even the most powerful red wines. But there is no doubt that without this marl, great red wines could never be made in such a northerly area (for who but the most chauvinistic of protagonists would call Pinot Noir from Alsace or a Spätburgunder from Germany 'great'?).

The basic rule is that where the limestone is dominant and the soil chalky, the Chardonnay is planted for white wine. When the Pinot Noir is planted too near the top of the slope, where the soil is significantly more chalky, the resultant red wine is thin indeed. Over the last 20 years on the Côte d'Or, much scrub and forest land on the upper slopes has been cleared for vineyards. No one can pretend that the wine produced at these extremities is of top quality.

The Côte de Nuits is narrower and more sharply sloping than much of the Côte de Beaune. Most of its vineyards clearly face east, with variations of east-south-east and east-north-east. Rich alluvial deposits tend to be lower down the slope on the Côte de Nuits than on the Côte de Beaune, with the best growths correspondingly lower down. Alluvial deposits also gather in folds in the slope, or in *combes*, which can explain why there are sudden pockets of top *climats*. The wider Côte de Beaune faces east or south-east, according to the various valleys, with softer, rounder hills and vines growing closer to the summits. The marl 'strip' is wider here than on the Côte de Nuits, and higher up the slope.

All this soil has been worked for centuries, and it consequently suffers from erosion, countered at certain times by additions of earth from the foot of the slope or elsewhere. When comparing wines from the so-called New World with those from the Old, it is worth remembering the often meagre soil of historic vineyards, where the vine must delve deep for goodness, in comparison with the fertile, 'virgin' soil of American or Australian plantations.

Who is to say that an element of soil exhaustion does not contribute to finesse? On the other hand, really tired soil in Europe is now helped by judicious fertilizing or mineral additions. Drainage on the slopes is not a problem, and the process is facilitated by gravel and particles of broken-up stone, an important element in vineyards producing top quality wines.

Climate

The most vital month in the whole year, from a climatic point of view, is September. In Burgundy, the weather's performance in this crucial month can make or mar a vintage. Whereas the *size* of the crop is largely decided (with last-minute variations possible due to rain) either by the presence or absence of spring frosts, or by the relative success of the flowering, the *quality* of the crop is determined in September. Catastrophic rain in September ruined the 1975s on the Côte d'Or, whereas a superb September saved the situation in 1978 and thus made the wines great.

Clearly, making red wine in such a northerly region is something of a risk, and Burgundian white wines will always show less vintage variability than reds or, to be more accurate, they will plumb the depths less often than the reds. There is a basic north-to-south difference in temperatures, with Chablis cooler than the Mâconnais, especially in the summer months. However, during this period, the temperatures on the Côte Chalonnaise are lower than on the Côte de Nuits, while the Côte de Beaune suffers fewer extremes of cold and heat than the Côte de Nuits, so there is no straightforward pattern.

December, January and February are the coldest months, July and August the hottest. The strongest frosts are in January and February, but March and April frosts are usually more to be feared since the vegetation is further advanced. Snow cover is always a protection against frost damage, but unfortunately there was no snow in the severe cold of February 1985. One way to combat frost is careful selection of vineyard sites – facing east and south in the Beaujolais, Mâconnais and the Côte Chalonnaise, east-south-east (generally) in the Côte d'Or, and south-east and south-west in Chablis. A warm June is critical for flowering. August and September are always hotter in Bordeaux than in Burgundy, which goes a long way towards explaining the more consistent record of Bordeaux vintages compared with those of Burgundy.

Light and sunshine are also vital to successful grape-growing and Burgundy, situated around 47° latitude, enjoys long periods of daylight in the growing season. With its inland continental climate, Burgundy hardly lags behind Bordeaux in hours of sunshine. July is the sunniest month, followed by August, June and May. Humidity is remarkably similar in both areas as the vine develops.

Rainfall is often the cause of Burgundy's undoing. The crucial factor with rain is not so much the *quantity* which falls, but *when* it falls. Regular light rain is always more desirable than storms, and when rain is interspersed with sun, the earth can warm up relatively quickly. Persistent rain in summer brings with it the risk of grey rot, the Burgundians' bogey. However, even after a seemingly lethal bout of rain in August, a dry September and early October can completely save the situation. The Côte d'Or is drier than the regions to the south, and certainly less wet than the Hautes Côtes, partly because the climate is drier and more continental towards Dijon, and partly because the slope of the Côte affords a measure of protection from the rain-bearing winds from the west.

However, the drawback of this favoured position is that northern Burgundy is more susceptible to hail than elsewhere, and the Côte de Nuits seems particularly vulnerable, with significant damage in 1983, 1981, 1979 and 1971 (the Côte de Beaune was even worse hit in 1971). But hail is always highly localized, and part of a commune can be hit while the rest remains untouched.

As in every viticultural region, the microclimate of their own particular area (or plots, in the case of Burgundy) will concern growers far more than the general picture. Factors like position on a slope, proximity to woods and the neighbouring topography (for instance, a dip in the hill causing a current of wind) all serve to temper or aggravate an overall tendency, and can make the difference between wild success and only moderate performance.

The Appellations

To set the scene, it is as well to keep in mind the amount of wine produced in Burgundy which is covered by the Appellation Contrôlée laws. Shown opposite, by region, are the AC figures for 1990, both a very good and a generous year. Yields were as high in most of the 1980s, with the exception of 1981 and 1984.

The first known attempt to define Burgundy wines and guard their origins was made by King Charles VI of France in 1416. He defined the area of 'Vin François', by which he meant wine made in

The 1990 Crop in Burgundy

Area	White (hectolitres)	Red and Rosé (hectolitres)
Regional Appellations	132,763	279,796
Chablis	176,838	—
Côte de Beaune + Grands Crus	54,724	124,263
Côte de Nuits + Grands Crus	805	78,427
Côte Chalonnaise	20,974	39,252
The Mâconnais	251,563	58,807
Beaujolais	11,568	1,332,908
Total 2,562,688	**649,235**	**1,913,453**

the region of Paris, and that of 'Vins de Bourgogne', for wines made above the bridge at Sens, including the Auxerrois and the Beaunois, and transported on the Yonne river. Things have become a little more sophisticated since then. However, at the outset, it should be reiterated that the AC system in France (and not just in Burgundy, although this region seems to receive more criticism than most) is not a *guarantee* of quality, much as we would like it to be. For that to happen, controls would have to be more stringent and, in the case of Burgundy, the arrangements regarding tasting dramatically overhauled. But that would be Utopia. What could be realistically hoped for would be rules and regulations created by people of integrity with great practical knowledge of growing vines and making wine in a capricious area, rather than by desk-bound bureaucrats, however worthy their motives.

What the AC laws do endeavour to do is guarantee the geographical origin of the wines, and lay down viticultural and vinification precepts which *should* lead to better quality. The specifications cover:

Area of production
Grape varieties permitted
Minimum alcohol level before
    chaptalization (Page 26)
Maximum yield per hectare

Methods of planting, pruning and
    treating the vines
Vinification
Maturation and *élevage*

Four organizations carry out between them the work of controlling the quality and marketing of French wines:

The INAO (*Institut National des Appellations d'Origine*)
The ONIVIT (*Office National Interprofessionnel des Vins de Table*)

The SRFCQ (*Service de la Répression des Fraudes et du Contrôle de la Qualité*)
The DGI (*Direction Générale des Impôts*)

The basis for today's laws has been laid down during this century, with refinements and improvements at each stage, culminating in the 1974 revision, which offers the chance of real progress. The two 1974 Decrees stopped the 'cascade' quality rating system and ordered that all AC wines be analysed and tasted.

Before 1974, a grower who made well over the permitted yield from a Grand Cru site could obtain the Grand Cru AC for up to 30 hectolitres per hectare of what he had produced, and baptize the excess yield with more modest names (Premier Cru, straight or *village* wine, and right down the line to Bourgogne Rouge and *vin de table*) in descending (or 'cascading') order. All the wine was the same, but the prices changed. *Génial!*

Now the grower has to opt for the classification he wants for his entire crop at the time of the *déclaration de récolte*. The system starts with a *rendement de base*, or basic yield, which can be adjusted each year by the fixing of a *rendement annuel*, or annual yield for that vintage, to allow for fluctuating climatic conditions. After 1974, a *plafond limite de classement* (PLC), or classification ceiling, was also introduced, allowing a further quantity (usually 20 percent) to be accepted. As this involves obligatory tasting, and distilling of the entire production if the PLC is refused, many growers (especially in the Beaujolais) hold back from making this request, through a profound dislike of 'busybody' visits to their cellars.

In any case, it has to be said that, given the variable Burgundian climate, this kind of yield is often a pipe-dream. In many domains, especially where there is a good proportion of old vines, growers often do not achieve the maximum allowed for their Grands Crus. Consequently there is an argument for widening the gap between these very special wines and the Premiers Crus and *village* wines. These can stand an increase in the allowed production in good years, whereas the Grands Crus will not, and should not, be so prolific. A move towards a lighter hand on the rein was made in a Decree just before the prolific vintage of 1982, but perhaps at the wrong end of the quality scale, because red Grands Crus like Corton had their *basic* yield increased from 30 to 35 hectolitres per hectare, while the whites jumped further, Chablis Grand Cru from 35 to 45 and Le Montrachet from 30 to 40. Le Montrachet's 1982 *rendement annuel* was increased to 60 hectolitres per hectare, which, plus a further 20 percent PLC, gave a total of 72. In 1983, the comparable figures were 50 hectolitres per hectare plus 20 percent, giving 60. Large yields affect the quality of white wine less than that of red, especially with the sensitive Pinot Noir, but these very generous yields for Grand Cru wine must impair concentration and extract. But again I know of producers who did not reach these permitted yields, to their credit.

As an example of how the *rendement annuel* can alter the *rendement de base*, the tables overleaf show those fixed for 1983 and 1990. The latter was a problem-free year and there was therefore little need for the *rendement annuel* to alter the *rendement de base*. However, 1983 was an exceptional year. Certain Grands Crus such as Echézeaux, La Tâche and Romanée-Conti, and communes like Vosne-Romanée, had their basic yields greatly reduced by the *rendement annuel* – in this case because of hail damage. But at the same time they were given very high PLC limits, which allowed for more AC wine to be declared, after tasting.

The tasting requirement in Burgundy, supposedly operational since 1979, works quite well in the Côte Chalonnaise (with a certain amount of self-regulation) but not on the Côte d'Or. It has proved impossible in this immensely complex and fragmented area for every wine in every grower's cellar to be tasted every year. This, of course, does not worry the majority of growers, but logistically the scheme does pose genuine problems. In any case, the plan was to taste in growers' rather than *négociants'* cellars, meaning that an enormous amount of wine would have to be tasted in the few months after the vintage, before many wines 'disappeared' into blends. What happens in reality is that random sampling is done in growers' cellars, which acts as a mild deterrent.

But even if the tasting is done to the letter of the Decree, there is still room for switching and deception by a determined producer.

1983: Allowable Yields Per Hectare in Burgundy

Appellations	Rendement de base	1983 Rendement annuel	Plafond limite de classement
Côte d'Or			
Grands Crus Côte de Nuits Bonnes Mares, Chambertin, Chambertin Clos de Bèze, Clos de la Roche, Clos St-Denis, Clos des Lambrays, Clos de Tart, Clos de Vougeot, Musigny Rouge Chapelle-Chambertin, Charmes-Chambertin, Griotte-Chambertin, Latricières-Chambertin, Mazis-Chambertin, Mazoyères-Chambertin, Ruchottes-Chambertin	35 hl/ha 37 hl/ha	35 hl/ha 37 hl/ha	+20% +20%
Echézeaux, Grands Echézeaux	35 hl/ha	26 hl/ha	+60%
La Tâche, Richebourg, La Romanée, Romanée-Conti, Romanée-St-Vivant	35 hl/ha	15 hl/ha	+100%
Musigny Blanc	40 hl/ha	37 hl/ha	+20%
1er Cru Côte de Nuits Same figures apply as for communes below			
AC Communes Côte de Nuits Chambolle-Musigny, Côte de Nuits-Villages, Fixin, Gevrey-Chambertin, Morey-St-Denis, Nuits-St-Georges, Vougeot	40 hl/ha	40 hl/ha	+100%
Vosne-Romanée	40 hl/ha	24 hl/ha	+100%
Grands Crus Côte de Beaune Corton Blanc, Corton-Charlemagne, Charlemagne, Bâtard-Montrachet, Bienvenues-Bâtard-Montrachet, Chevalier-Montrachet, Criots-Bâtard-Montrachet, Le Montrachet	40 hl/ha	50 hl/ha	+20%
Corton Rouge	35 hl/ha	35 hl/ha	+20%
1er Cru Côte de Beaune Same figures apply as for Côte de Beaune-Villages			
Côte de Beaune-Villages Vins rouges: Aloxe-Corton, Auxey-Duresses, Beaune, Blagny, Chassagne-Montrachet, Cheilly-les-Maranges, Chorey, Côte de Beaune & Villages, Dezize-les-Maranges, Ladoix, Meursault, Monthélie, Pernand-Vergelesses, Pommard, Puligny-Montrachet, St-Aubin, St-Romain, Sampigny-les-Maranges, Santenay, Savigny, Volnay	40 hl/ha	40 hl/ha	+20%
Vins blancs: Aloxe-Corton, Auxey-Duresses, Beaune, Chassagne-Montrachet	45 hl/ha	45 hl/ha	+20%
Cheilly-les-Maranges, Chorey, Côte de Beaune, Dezize-les-Maranges, Ladoix, Meursault, Monthélie, Pernand-Vergelesses, Puligny-Montrachet, St-Aubin, St-Romain, Sampigny-les-Maranges, Santenay, Savigny	45 hl/ha	55 hl/ha	+20%

1990: Allowable Yields Per Hectare in Burgundy

Appellations Côte d'Or **Grands Crus Côte de Nuits** Bonnes Mares, Chambertin, Chambertin Clos de Bèze, Clos de la Roche, Clos St-Denis, Clos des	Rendement de base	1990 Rendement annuel	Plafond limite de classement
Lambrays, Clos de Tart, Clos de Vougeot, Musigny Rouge, Echézeaux, Grands Echézeaux, La Tâche, Richebourg, La Romanée, Romanée- Conti, Romanée-St-Vivant Chapelle-Chambertin, Charmes- Chambertin, Griotte-Chambertin, Latricières-Chambertin, Mazis- Chambertin, Mazoyères-Chambertin, Ruchottes-Chambertin	35 hl/ha 37 hl/ha	35 hl/ha 37 hl/ha	+20% +20%
Musigny Blanc	40 hl/ha	40 hl/ha	+20%
1er Cru Côte de Nuits Same figures apply as for communes below			
AC Communes Cote de Nuits Vins rouges: Chambolle-Musigny, Fixin, Gevrey-Chambertin, Morey- St-Denis, Nuits-St-Georges, Vosne- Romanée, Vougeot, Côte de Nuits- Villages, Marsannay	40 hl/ha	40 hl/ha	+20%
Vins blancs: Morey-St-Denis, Nuits- St-Georges, Vougeot, Côte de Nuits- Villages, Marsannay	45 hl/ha	50 hl/ha	+20%
Grands Crus Côte de Beaune Corton Blanc, Corton-Charlemagne, Charlemagne, Bâtard-Montrachet, Bienvenues-Bâtard-Montrachet, Chevalier-Montrachet, Criots- Bâtard-Montrachet, Le Montrachet	40 hl/ha	40 hl/ha	+20%
Corton Rouge	35 hl/ha	35 hl/ha	+20%
1er Cru Côte de Beaune Same figures apply as for Côte de Beaune-Villages			
Côte de Beaune-Villages Vins rouges: Aloxe-Corton, Auxey- Duresses, Beaune, Blagny, Chassagne-Montrachet, Cheilly-les- Maranges, Chorey, Côte de Beaune & Villages, Dezize-les-Maranges, Ladoix, Meursault, Monthélie, Pernand-Vergelesses, Pommard, Puligny-Montrachet, St-Aubin, St- Romain, Sampigny-les-Maranges, Santenay, Savigny, Volnay	40 hl/ha	40 hl/ha	+20%
Vins blancs: Auxey-Duresses, Beaune, Chassagne-Montrachet, Cheilly-les- Maranges, Chorey, Côte de Beaune, Dezize-les-Maranges, Ladoix, Meursault, Monthélie, Pernand- Vergelesses, Puligny-Montrachet, St- Aubin, St-Romain, Sampigny-les- Maranges, Santenay, Savigny Aloxe-Corton	45 hl/ha 45 hl/ha	50 hl/ha 45 hl/ha	+20% +20%

The INAO controls the amount of Burgundy sold in relation to what is harvested, but obviously there is room for manoeuvre, given the fact that major roads pass through Burgundy. The INAO reputedly tastes a producer's wines at least once every three years, but it is worth stressing that there is many an AC and VDQS wine from other regions in France that has jumped through all the tasting and analytical hoops and come out disgusting! Strict adherence to all the rules in the world will not ensure delicious wine at all times – it comes down to the integrity and intelligence of the producer and the demands of an enlightened consumer.

The Répression des Fraudes does make periodic prosecutions, which sometimes even bite, at least financially. Where the AC system falls down in Burgundy, at least as a credible institution, is in the hypocrisy of some of its edicts – for instance, in the case of chaptalization (the addition of sugar to the must, or grape juice, to increase alcohol). The legal limit is clear: 1·7 kilos of sugar added to 100 litres of must, increasing the alcohol in the wine by approximately one percent. It is not permitted to go over the addition of nine kilos of sugar per three hectolitres of must and 200 kilos per hectare. Above all, the wine must have naturally attained the minimum alcohol level for its AC before any sugar can be added to the must. It is widely known that in 1984, for example, many wines (especially reds) did not attain the minimum level and were consequently chaptalized way beyond the permitted amount – for they all finished up around 12·8–13 percent as usual.

Another aspect of the AC laws that indicates that they are somewhat removed from the realities of winemaking in Burgundy is the virtual banning of acidification. Many Burgundies need additions of tartaric acid in order to keep well. There is nothing wrong in this: low natural acidities are a problem in other parts of France, especially recently. A recognition of this would inspire more confidence that the AC system is designed to improve the wines rather than just to form rules and push paper.

The hierarchy of the ACs is as follows:

Grand Cru
Premier Cru
Village Wine (*AOC Communale*)★
Generic or Regional

★*Village* or commune wine is also described as 'straight', eg straight Meursault.

The last category includes Bourgogne and Bourgogne Grand Ordinaire, Bourgogne Rosé Marsannay, Bourgogne Passe-Tout-Grains, Bourgogne Aligoté, Bourgogne Hautes Côtes de Beaune and Bourgogne Hautes Côtes de Nuits.

Nomenclature

No one can be in Burgundy for long, or read a book on the subject, without noting the number of hyphens in the place names. The simple explanation is that the wily Burgundian, at some stage, tagged the name of the best-known local vineyard on to the name of his village – hence, Gevrey-Chambertin, Morey-St-Denis, Chambolle-Musigny and right on down the Côte.

Vineyard names, or *climats*, often give an indication of their soil: Les Chaillots (siliceous pebbles), Les Crais (pebbles), Les Grèves (small pebbles or gravel); or the vegetation once found there: Les Charmes (yoke-elms or hornbeams), Les Genevrières (juniper bushes), Les Chênes (oaks); or even of the wildlife one met there: Les Cailles (quails), Les Perdrix (partridges), La Combe aux Alouettes (the valley of the larks). The walls built from stones collected in the vines are even cited – Aux Murgers. Yes, Burgundian place names are picturesque, designed to lure and to allure.

Burgundian spelling is often what the French would call *facultatif* – you have a choice. Thus, Dominode and Dominaude, Véroilles and Varoilles, etc. They also seem uncertain as to whether to put an 's' on the end of Passe-Tout-Grains, and Chablisien spelling can appear positively anarchic. Similarly, the use of definite articles may vary. Thus, Beaune Les Grèves is often seen as Beaune-Grèves. This book endeavours to use the spelling and usage chosen by the domain and shown on its labels. (Mercifully, none of this affects the taste of the wine.) A vagary of Burgundian pronunciation is to say 'ss' for 'x', ie 'Fissin' (Fixin) and 'Aussey-Duresses' (Auxey-Duresses).

The Grapes

The grape scene is relatively simple in Burgundy although, given the difficult climatic conditions, continuous work is being done on clones in order to develop resistance to misfortunes such as grey rot. As a rule, the general density of planting of vines in the Côte d'Or is 10,000 vines per hectare, whereas in Chablis it is 6,000 per hectare. These are the principle varieties:

Red

Pinot Noir

This is perhaps the most tantalizing of the world's noble red grapes. In Burgundy, the Pinot Noir is the red grape of the Côte d'Or and the Côte Chalonnaise, with only a tiny amount grown in the Mâconnais. It achieves heights unsurpassed anywhere when at its best in Burgundy, but it travels only tentatively. The finest examples outside Burgundy seem to come from Oregon and Australia, with California (especially Carneros) and New Zealand (Martinborough and Canterbury) in the running; but these tend to be isolated cases, created by brilliant winemakers. It is also grown in Alsace, Austria, Germany (where the wines are light), Switzerland, Eastern Europe and north-east Italy, and is vital to classic champagne.

The Pinot Noir both buds and ripens early, and it is susceptible to spring frost and winter cold, as well as cold temperatures during flowering. It likes calcareous, marly soils, but dislikes unduly hot climates, where the wines lack finesse – hence its lack of success in the Napa Valley of California. The dark green leaves are thick and of medium size, with small, cylindrical bunches. The grapes are close together in the bunches, which facilitates the spread of rot, given the right humid circumstances. The berries are blue-black in colour, slightly oval, with relatively thick skins, although less thick than in the early part of this century due to clonal selection. All the colour in the wine comes from the skins, as the flesh and juice of the grape are colourless. It is encouraging that in a thin-skin year like 1984, many growers still managed to produce wines of good colour, showing improved vinification techniques.

Considerable experimentation on Pinot Noir clones is being done, especially at Echevronne in the Hautes Côtes de Beaune. The work is carried out under the auspices of the regional department of the Association Nationale Technique pour l'Amélioration de la Viticulture (ANTAV), which is composed of representatives from the INAO, the Syndicats et Associations Viticoles, the Coopératives, the Chambres d'Agriculture and the vine nurserymen. A vast array of Pinots is grown under controlled and identical conditions, and the resulting wines are tasted blind against each other. There are Pinots from the Côte Chalonnaise, the Jura, Champagne and Switzerland, the Pinots *fins*, *moyens* and *gros*, as well as the high-yielding Pinot *droit*. Some Pinots are named after villages on the Côte, some after growers.

Work is being done on resistance to grey rot and virus diseases such as fan leaf and leaf curl, and on the relationship between yield, alcohol and quality. It is difficult to see great red wines being produced at over 35 hectolitres per hectare, but good wines, in a healthy year, can certainly be made with a yield of 40 hectolitres per hectare. After all, not *every* village Burgundy should be made for lengthy laying down – just as not all Bordeaux should play the role of a classed growth. But growers should be persuaded to adopt the most successful quality clones, even if they have to renounce the highest-yielding examples. There is no excuse not to, with the prices their wines command nowadays. Good results have been seen on the Côte d'Or from three Pinot *fin* clones, numbers 113, 114 and 115, if they are not grafted on to excessively productive rootstocks.

Gamay

Although this is the grape *par excellence* of the Beaujolais, it probably originated in the hamlet of this name next door to St-Aubin on the Côte d'Or. It is at its best on the granite-based, sandy-schisty soil of the northern Beaujolais, where the ten *crus* are to be found. It is also successful on the richer clay and limestone soil of the southern Beaujolais (though the wines should be drunk very young). Here, over-large yields can make the wine a pale imitation of the 'real thing', but very good Beaujolais can be produced at 50–60 hectolitres per hectare.

The Gamay covers about one-third of the Mâconnais AC area, and is a significant grape in the Côte Chalonnaise, where it contributes to Bourgogne Passe-Tout-Grains, which is made of two-thirds Gamay and one-third Pinot Noir. It has very little importance on the Côte d'Or. The Gamay can be found scattered around France, in Savoie, the Loire and the Ardèche, as well as in California.

The Gamay Noir à Jus Blanc, or Gamay Beaujolais, yields well, even after spring frosts. Its juice is white, as the name implies, so the colour comes from the skins. The compact grapes are grouped in cylindrical bunches encouraging the spread of grey rot under humid conditions. The grape ripens early, but the optimum picking time must be judged carefully if the must is to have a good natural sugar content, especially if the yield is high. If rain swells the grapes near or at the vintage, it is difficult to get good colour and extract.

Two other grapes, the César and the Tressot, are allowed in the Yonne for Bourgogne, Bourgogne Ordinaire or Bourgogne Grand Ordinaire. They are earthy varieties, even a bit 'foxy'. The César has more merit than the Tressot, but both are rare and invariably mixed with Pinot.

White

Chardonnay

This is probably the most magic grape name in the whole world, eliciting cries of joy from consumers as they drink it, but often groans of pain as they pay the bill. The name Chardonnay may have come from a village of that name in the Mâconnais, or it could have been the other way round.

The Chardonnay makes all the best white wines from Chablis to the Mâconnais. It is one of the classic grapes of Champagne, and has recently been grown most successfully in the Ardèche, thanks to the efforts of Louis Latour. It also produces excellent results in California, Australia, New Zealand and a host of other countries, with Bulgaria and northern Italy knocking at the consumer's door at a more reasonable price.

The Chardonnay adores limestone soil and, in most cases, its wine ages beautifully in bottle. The vine has large thin leaves and the bunches are not so tight as other varieties, allowing air movement and reducing the risk of rot. The early budbreak makes spring frost a danger, but relatively early maturity makes it a good choice for areas with shorter growing seasons. It is a generous producer, but is susceptible to fan leaf, or *court noué*. It is not a member of the Pinot family, as was originally thought – the erroneous name is even enshrined in a Burgundian AC, Pinot-Chardonnay-Mâcon.

Two Chardonnay *moyen* clones which have proved successful on the Côte d'Or are 95 and 96.

Aligoté

This is the second white grape variety of Burgundy, but it is not in the same league as Chardonnay. However, it yields well and ripens early and, in sunny years, the wine can be most appetizing. In less ripe years the results are too acid. It has no potential for ageing in bottle and should always be drunk young. The best Aligoté wines tend to be produced in the northern part of the Côte Chalonnaise and in villages like Pernand-Vergelesses and St-Aubin on the Côte d'Or.

Pinot Blanc

For a long time this variety was confused with Chardonnay, and not only in Burgundy (north-east Italy often got it wrong also). It seems rather a waste to grow it in Burgundy in the place of Chardonnay, as it does not have the zest of Pinot Blanc in Alsace. The wines can be rather heavy and plain. It is probably a mutation of the

Pinot Noir. There are one or two good examples on the Côte de Nuits, but it is a rarity.

Pinot Beurot

This is the Pinot Gris, or Tokay d'Alsace. Although in the same Pinot family, the wine is really more stylish than the Pinot Blanc when planted in Burgundy. It is rare indeed, but occasionally appears in the Hautes Côtes de Beaune.

The Melon de Bourgogne is still allowed for Bourgogne Grand Ordinaire, but I have never consciously drunk it. It is the same grape variety as the Muscadet of the Loire, but that is another story. The Sacy is grown in the Auxerrois, where it is usually made into sparkling wine because of its high acidity and low alcohol, essential prerequisites for transformation into bubbly. The Sauvignon appears here too, in the VDQS wine Sauvignon de St-Bris.

Rootstocks

Since phylloxera the European grape varieties must be grafted on to American or American/French rootstocks. Vine and rootstock must be well matched. Just as research and experiment with grape clones has been improved and extended, so has work on rootstocks. A particular rootstock on unsuitable soil can cause the grafted vine to overcrop, produce unripe or low-sugar grapes, or create *coulure* (failed flowering).

Successful combinations have been Pinot Noir clones 115 and 114 on rootstocks SO4 and 161–49, but 115 is also recommended on another pure American *porte-greffe*, Téléki 5BB, on very dry slopes. However, some growers have found that 161–49 is particularly good on calcareous soil, giving grapes which ripen well, while SO4 can produce too much wood and grapes of less sugar content on the Côte de Nuits. A Franco-American hybrid is 41B, very good in high limestone soils and on high ground. Chardonnay clones 95 and 96 have done well on 161–49 on pebbly soil.

Most of these same rootstocks are found in Beaujolais, but there is also the Vialla on granite soils, probably of pre-phylloxera origin, and the pure American 420A, which thrives at high altitude in *crus* such as Chiroubles. In Chablis, with high lime and accompanying risk of chlorosis (a disease which causes loss of colour in leaves, due to lack of iron in calcareous soil), the most common rootstocks are SO4 and 41B.

Growers and Merchants

There is a tendency nowadays to 'pigeon-hole' growers and merchants into 'Goodies and Baddies'. Of course, like everything else in Burgundy, it is far more complicated than that. There are good and bad in both camps, and there are merchants (*négociants*) who are also important domain owners. The traditional role of the *négociant* was to buy a multitude of different lots of wine, blend them, bring them up (*élevage*) and bottle them. Now, even that is changing, with some merchants (notably Bouchard Père & Fils and Moillard, with others following or already doing it on a smaller scale) buying in grapes and making wine themselves.

Growers often sell part of their crop to *négociants*, in order to improve their cash flow, and 'domain-bottle' a proportion, which involves 18 months to two years of stock-holding on the Côte d'Or. The domain-bottling is done either by the grower himself or by a mobile bottling unit, such as Ninot of Beaune. There is also a good deal of *métayage* in Burgundy, a rather feudal practice which can work well. Basically, an owner who does not want to tend his vines or make wine passes this responsibility to a *métayer* or farmer, who divides the crop with the landowner. It is a system which can be successful, but naturally it further confuses the issue of wine identification in Burgundy, as two differently labelled wines can be made by the same person. It is also frustrating when long-term arrangements cannot be broken and a really fine winemaker cannot reclaim control of some of his vineyards due to *métayage* contracts. *Fermage*, on the other hand, means the vineyard is let to a winemaker who pays rent for it and so has no obligation to share the crop with others.

The *négociant* business first started to flourish in the first half of the eighteenth century; some of those companies are still well-known today. In 1990 there were 140 *négociant-éleveur* businesses in Burgundy, belonging to the Fédération des Syndicats de Négociants Eleveurs de Grande Bourgogne, with 74 of them in the Côte d'Or, 32 in Saône et Loire, 28 in the Rhône (which covers Beaujolais) and six in the Yonne. The export market took 60 percent of their output, France 40 percent. The *négociant-éleveur* is equally important in Bordeaux and Champagne, with near identical turnovers in terms of millions of francs. His role is therefore fundamental both to the health of the Burgundian economy and to the supply of large quantities of wine as required around the world. The small grower, with a handful of casks to sell, is not going to be able to supply chains of hotels or shops with enough Burgundy to win friends and influence people. There is a place in the mosaic of international customers for both the small grower, with 'hand-made' quantities of wine to sell, and the *négociant* with important lots available.

The Burgundian *négociants-éleveurs* sold 3.7 million hectolitres (or the equivalent of 490 million bottles) in 1990, of which 45 percent was AC wine from Burgundy, ten percent other ACs (mostly Côtes-du-Rhône), five percent VDQS wine and *vin de pays*, and a whopping 40 percent *vin de table*. It is this which gives the slightly dubious reputation to the Burgundian merchant. Here he is, in Beaune or Nuits, selling this vast amount of ordinary table wine. Is it never possible for him to mix his *ordinaire* with his AC names? Of course, nowadays the two categories of wines have different *acquits* (certificates of origin), as stipulated by the INAO, but it would be a hypocrite who did not admit that a well-known Burgundian house name on a label can given an impression of quality to a *vin de table*. The only answer is for the consumer to become more knowledgeable in reading a label – if there is no Burgundian Appellation Contrôlée on the label, then he is not drinking Burgundy. Of course, to the purist, it would be better if a Burgundian house did not combine the two functions of supplying Burgundy and *vin de table*, and certain respected houses have never been in the *vin de table* market (for example, Joseph Drouhin, Louis Jadot and Louis Latour). But there is the argument that healthy sales of *vin de table* can help to finance the costly business of buying and maturing fine Burgundy.

In 1979, 74 percent of the Burgundian harvest was sold by *le commerce bourguignon*, or the *négociant* houses, and 26 percent directly by the domains or properties. In 1988, the proportion bottled by the domains had increased to 36 percent. Among this category there are some who are very new to the business of maturing and bottling their own wine, and others (like Gouges, d'Angerville and Rousseau) who have been doing it for 60 years. Of course, even old-established domain-bottlers and direct sellers

The Burgundy Wine Industry

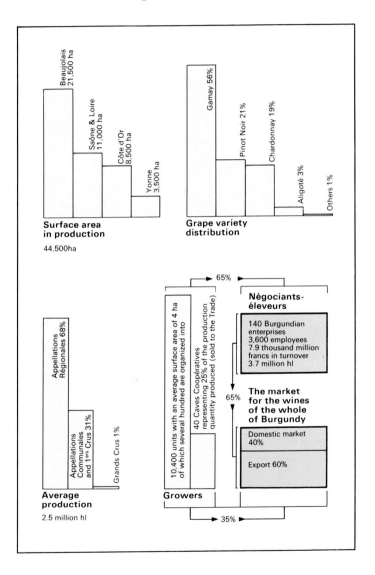

Surface area in production
44,500ha

- Beaujolais 21,500 ha
- Saône & Loire 11,000 ha
- Côte d'Or 8,500 ha
- Yonne 3,500 ha

Grape variety distribution

- Gamay 56%
- Pinot Noir 21%
- Chardonnay 19%
- Aligoté 3%
- Others 1%

Average production
2.5 million hl

- Appellations Régionales 68%
- Appellations Communales and 1ᵉʳˢ Crus 31%
- Grands Crus 1%

Growers

10,400 units with an average surface area of 4 ha of which several hundred are organized into

40 Caves Coopératives representing 25% of the production quantity produced (sold to the Trade)

65%

Négociants-éleveurs

140 Burgundian enterprises
3,600 employees
7.9 thousand million francs in turnover
3.7 million hl

65%

The market for the wines of the whole of Burgundy

Domestic market 40%

Export 60%

35%

sometimes sell part of their crop to the *négociants*, for fiscal or quality reasons, and occasionally they will take the really dramatic decision not to domain-bottle at all in a particularly poor year. In this case, the *négociant*, with his ability to blend from many, varied lots, has a far better chance of producing at least a palatable wine than a grower who can use only his own produce and who may have been particularly badly hit by, say, hail or rot.

There is no doubt that a fine domain wine, whether owned by a grower or a *négociant* house, can have all the individuality, excitement and character that we seek – among these are surely the best wines of Burgundy. Equally it is not in doubt that, just as there are some boring and lacklustre blends from *négociants*, there are some really appalling domain wines, individual only through their glaring faults. We, buyers and consumers, have to pinpoint the successes and lambaste (figuratively at least) the dismal failures until we raise the general standard and have a more happy 'strike rate'. We should be grateful to those who first encouraged domain-bottling, people like Frank Schoonmaker and Alexis Lichine, and support those Burgundians who do it really well.

With all the wine which passes between grower and *négociant* in Burgundy, brokers play a vital role. They submit the sample to the *négociant*, and row upon row of small bottles on the laboratory shelves of any merchant house is a familiar sight. Sometimes you wonder how long it takes for the samples to be tasted, but there is no doubt that the *négociant* who wants to get the best of a vintage has to make up his mind early. The broker, or *courtier*, will receive a two to three percent commission from the buyer and up to three percent from the grower. He never holds any stock, but it is his responsibility to ensure that the wine subsequently delivered is identical to the sample accepted.

There are also a few brokers in Burgundy who specialize in finding good domains, grouping them together and offering a choice to foreign buyers. This is especially useful to those who do not like to wrangle over price in the French language, and the best of this breed also act as a filter where wines of dubious quality are concerned. A few brokers fall into the trap of thinking that all domain wines are by definition better than *négociant* wines, and they could add to the already swollen heads of some growers, but the most responsible perform a valuable service.

There is one other category of participant in the Burgundian wine trade that is peculiar to the region – the *commissionnaire en vins*. He is somewhere between a *négociant* and a *courtier* in that he does engineer sales between domains and clients, but he also keeps stocks. He can hold a key position as a bridge between the somewhat hidebound and insular grower and the multifaceted export world, without being weighed down by the heavy corporate structure of a fully-fledged *négociant*. Hence his prices can be very keen for the relative quality of his wines – what the French would call a good *rapport qualité-prix*.

Cooperatives are singularly absent from the Côte d'Or scene apart from the well-run Coopérative des Hautes Côtes de Beaune et Nuits, one at Marsannay for making rosé and a small one at Nuits. There is a good cooperative at Buxy on the Côte Chalonnaise, a rather too powerful one in Chablis, others as dominant in the Mâconnais, and some reputable ones in the Beaujolais, particularly in the north.

Growing Grapes

There is nothing mysterious about growing grapes – it is just fruit farming. But healthy grapes are a prerequisite for making fine wine; they are the *matière de base*. They can only be achieved through the constant vigilance and presence of the vigneron and, if he is the owner, constant checking that his orders are being carried out effectively.

The planting of a new vineyard is costly indeed. The old vines are taken out, the ground is broken up, earth is moved and replaced with new earth (which *should* come from within the *appellation* area), the soil disinfected (vital in the prevention of *court noué*, or fan leaf), and the right organic and mineral balance established. Then there are grafts and stakes, posts and wire, which vary with the density of the planting – usually 8,000–10,000 vines per hectare. Of course, some grafts do not take, especially after a severe winter like early 1985, so in the second year there might be costly replacements to be made. All the time there are expensive treatments to be maintained against pests and diseases, as well as fertilizer to be added, and on top of all this are the labour costs. Not until the 'fourth leaf', or fourth year, can Appellation Contrôlée wine be made from the new vineyard.

Soil analysis is relatively new for some vignerons, and there is no doubt that there were periods, for instance, when too much potassium was added – one grower on the Côte de Nuits says he has not added any for over 20 years. Nitrogen must also be added with measured care, otherwise too much vegetation is produced, causing increased humidity around the vine and therefore increased risk of grey rot. Dehydrated manure is often used. As for weedkiller, some would not touch it, others insist on it, but what clearly emerges is that it should never be used over-enthusiastically – who knows what is being stored in the soil for the future?

Infectious degeneration of the vines, *court noué* or fan leaf, has been a problem in Burgundy, and the only cure is grubbing up a vineyard and disinfection, as well as the planting of resistant clones. Sometimes growers talk proudly of their small yields, but the tell-tale yellowish, deformed leaves give the game away. Not all small crops are healthy!

Grey rot is the bogey of Burgundy and it has by no means been mastered. It is ironic that this disease is welcomed under certain conditions in Sauternes/Barsac and in Germany, for it is none other than *Botrytis cinerea*. But it is a disaster when it spreads amongst Pinot Noir or Gamay grapes, destroying the colour cells and imparting an unpleasant taste to the resultant wine. Burgundian growers took to regular spraying against grey rot after the shattering experience of 1975, and for a few years it looked as if the situation was under control, but 1983 on parts of the Côte de Nuits proved that it was not. One answer seems to be to vary the chemical formula of the spray every two years, and certainly the grower has to be there to spray at *exactly* the right time. One spraying too few is often a false economy. Were the Septembers of that period more rainy than previous ones, or are there other factors, such as thinner grape skins and bigger grapes packed close together, which foster the conditions conducive to grey rot? Mildew, the downy variety, and oidium, the powdery type, are often now treated with fungicides, whereas in the past a copper sulphate and lime spray (Bordeaux mixture) effectively controlled downy mildew, or *peronospora*. This had the side-effect of hardening the grape-skins, probably making them more resistant to the spread of grey rot. It may or may not be significant that Beaujolais still widely uses Bordeaux mixture and suffers far less from rot than the Côte d'Or – but it is also less humid in summer in the Beaujolais, so it is not an entirely fair comparison.

Red and yellow spider and various kinds of moth all need careful and regular treatment at the critical times. The grape caterpillar which seems most to worry the Burgundian, especially in recent years, is the *ver de la grappe*, also known as *tordeuse de la grappe*, *cochylis* or *eudemis*. The most dangerous period is mid-July.

This is an outline of the Burgundian viticultural year:

January It is usually too cold and the ground too frozen to do much in the vineyard and, in any case, it is often unwise to prune too early. Those who had made a precocious start were caught by the extreme cold of 1985. Snow cover, of course, can act as protection for the vines if the temperature falls really low.

February February and March are when the main pruning takes place. This sets the whole scene for the eventual quality of the wine, because you can prune either for indiscriminate quantity or for reasonable cropping. It is the most skilled job in the vineyard, and good pruners are highly prized. Each vine must be treated individually, bearing in mind its strength, how it may have reacted to a previous big yield, hail or cold. Experienced pruners have a feel for each vine, something almost instinctive which guides their pruning clippers as they work.

The following types of pruning are used in the region:

Guyot pruning Single-Guyot is the most common form found on the Côte d'Or and the Côte Chalonnaise, with double-Guyot in Chablis. The main, fruit-bearing cane, pruned to six buds, is attached to the lowest of three wires supporting the shoots and vegetation. A short cane, with two buds, is also left to produce fruit but, more importantly, to grow the shoots which become the next year's two canes – hence, poor pruning can affect not only the current year's crop, but also the following one.

Vines are trained low in Burgundy, about 30 cm from the ground, so that any warmth in the soil from daytime sunshine can continue to help ripen the grapes at night. High training is practised in the Hautes Côtes, which is more economical and carries less risk of spring frost.

Gobelet pruning This is the classic method of pruning in the Beaujolais. The vine is really a free-standing bush, with three or four 'spurs' of wood, each producing a fruit-bearing cane cut back to two buds. The vigorous vegetation is tied up around a post, or occasionally trained between wires, resulting in a less bush-like appearance.

Cordon-de-Royat pruning This spur-pruning is found at the southern end of the Côte de Beaune, especially in Santenay and Chassagne-Montrachet. The vine is trained horizontally, with the spurs producing fruit-bearing canes pruned to one or two buds. Skill is needed to start off the horizontal training, but once set up, the vegetation is well spread out between wires.

Taille à queue This is what is seen traditionally in the Mâconnais, with the producing branch bent over in a semicircle.

One of the most evocative Burgundian sights in winter is the smoke from the wheelbarrow braziers where the vigneron burns the prunings as he works up and down the rows. The smoke mingles with the frosty mist and the effect is a blue haze. It also warms freezing fingers, and the soil is enriched by the ashes.

March The pruning is completed during this month, followed by bending the fruit-bearing canes under the lower wires, avoiding damage to the buds. If earth has been piled around the roots to protect them from severe frosts, it is dug up and spread out. This airs the soil and helps distribute fertilizer. The fertilizer options here are: manure (probably still the best choice), nitrogen for the vegetation, phosphoric acid for successful fruit development and healthiness, and potassium for increased yield, improved must and to help the vines resist disease and frost. Getting the recipe right is a difficult task. Tractors for ploughing have been used for 35 years in Burgundy now. This is also the month for grafting, using the *greffe anglaise*, a z-shaped cut which fits the French vine graft to the rootstock. In these northern climes, there is no such thing as grafting 'in the field', and these successful grafts will be planted in the vineyard the following year.

April Grafting continues, usually requiring about two to three weeks to take at a temperature of 20°C in sand or sawdust. The vigneron fears spring frost, as by this time the vine is really vulnerable and it is often this fear which causes him to prune 'generously'. The red spider can also make a first appearance at this time. The main cane is fixed to the lower wire and, now that the sap has risen, the wood is more pliable. New vineyards are planted out this month. There will be grapes after three years, but Appellation Contrôlée wine only after four.

May The frost threat continues during the first week. Weeds are dealt with by weedkillers or ploughing, and treatments against spiders, moths, mildew and oidium are applied – frequently these can be combined in one spray. The timing of these treatments is critical, and a *station d'avertissements agricoles* issues advice based on the meteorological conditions. It is a frightening thought that mildew fungi can remain incubated for several years – those of 1975 survived the dryness of 1976 to reappear alarmingly in 1977. The successful new grafts are planted out in the nursery for their year's sojourn there. In the vineyard, unwanted, non-fruit-bearing shoots are removed.

June This is the month when the vines flower. Ideal conditions include sun and warmth, with minimum rain and wind. Good, quick, regular flowering ensures a healthy crop, barring later calamities like hail-storms. However, if the weather is poor, *coulure*, or flower abortion, occurs, substantially reducing the size of the harvest. Any straggling branches are placed between the double wire in the middle and new shoots are attached to the upper wire by metal or plastic clasps or clips. Treatments continue, although preferably not during the actual flowering.

July Treatments continue as before, with growers totting up the cost. Ploughing along the rows is often effected, as well as the mechanical trimming of excess foliage at the end of the branches, which only takes away nutrition intended for the grapes. This is also the time when an altruistic grower might remove excess bunches in an effort to improve quality. This could give as much as a two percent increase in natural alcohol if a crop is reduced by a third. Understandably, growers are reluctant to do this, on the assumption that quantity equals cash (if not reputation) but if more had done so in 1982, we would not have seen the excessive yields and resultant over-chaptalized wines so often encountered in this vintage. Hail is a risk during this month, and both rockets and aircraft have been used to disperse clouds or to make the hail fall as rain. However, as hail often happens at night, disasters still occur – parts of the Côte de Nuits in 1983 bore witness to the fact that nature is still not completely tamed.

August There will be more foliage trimming, or *rognage*, plus general maintenance, such as repairing walls, and cleaning around the periphery of vineyards. This is the month of the *véraison*, or the process of the grapes softening and changing colour. In the nursery, any rootlets which have appeared on the graft are removed. All the equipment for the vintage is cleaned, with all wooden vessels being soaked and rendered watertight. Bacteria can take a real hold on equipment lying fallow for a year, and there is no doubt that the arrival of stainless steel or enamel-lined equipment has simplified this work.

September General maintenance and preparation for the vintage continues, with one eye on the heavens. Grape ripeness depends on so many things – the weather, the age of the vine, where it is planted, how much it has been asked to produce, how it has been cared for. The optimum moment for picking is when there is the right balance between sugar and acidity, but it is usually the former quality which is deficient in Burgundy, hence the need to chaptalize. But acidity has been on the low side if you take a general view of the past 20 years, a phenomenon noted also in Bordeaux, and considered to be due in part to excess use of chemical fertilizers. Pick early and the risks from inclement weather are reduced, but there is more sugar to make up. Pick late and the acidity can go even lower and the resultant wine can lack balance and be without much projection of fruit.

The Côte Chalonnaise usually picks a few days after the Côte d'Or, probably due to vineyards at a higher altitude, with the Mâconnais starting before them both, usually in company with the Beaujolais. To show how widely the start of the harvest can vary, here are the dates when the *Ban de Vendange* was called on the Côte de Beaune in recent years:

1973	22 September	1983	22 September
1974	23 September	1984	29 September
1975	25 September	1985	24 September
1976	30 August	1986	27 September
1977	9 October	1987	28 September
1978	7 October	1988	21 September
1979	25 September	1989	13 September
1980	6 October	1990	17 September
1981	23 September	1991	25 September
1982	16 September		

It can be seen at a glance that there is no neat correlation between date of picking and quality, with a fine year like 1978 being late, and another fine year, 1989, early.

Picking is still done almost entirely by hand in Burgundy, in sharp contrast to Bordeaux. In 1983 the Gironde topped the list with 1,050 machines, while the Yonne had 27, the Côte d'Or 25, the Saône et Loire 16, with the Rhône (Beaujolais) right at the bottom with just one. By 1986 the number of machines in the Gironde had risen to 1,500. By 1991 in Burgundy, the figure was only 400: 190 in the Saône et Loire (principally for Mâcon Blanc), 150 in Chablis and 60 in the Côte d'Or. The Gamay's Gobelet pruning is unsuitable for machine harvesting, and there is no advance on the 1983 figure of one for the Rhône (Beaujolais). Picking by machine in Burgundy will no doubt increase, above all for white grapes, but at the moment there is no pressing socio-economic need for it and much of the vineyard does not lend itself easily to machine picking, either on account of its topography or because of the way it is divided into small, often scattered, plots.

October The vintage finishes this month and the grower gets down to making the wine – unless he sells his grapes to a *négociant* or a cooperative. This is also when old vineyards are grubbed up, with deep ploughing, manuring and disinfecting.

November Winter deep ploughing is accompanied by replacing any earth which might have fallen to the foot of a slope. Pre-pruning starts, cutting off the fruit-bearing main cane and leaving two shoots on the short cane for the main spring pruning. Some growers plough a furrow of earth around the feet of the vines to protect them from winter frosts, but others aver that the process is detrimental to the vine's root system.

December This month sees a repetition of the activities of deep ploughing, pre-pruning, preparing new vineyard land and earth adjustments. Pre-pruning is held up if the temperature drops below freezing.

Making the Wine

Winemaking in Burgundy is as idiosyncratic as one would expect from a region of individualists. If you make a tour around any given group of winemakers, you will hear almost as many theories and views on the best way to make either red or white wine. A variety of different systems coexists, particularly with regard to procedure at vinification, or fermentation, and there is no absolute blueprint for success. However, the main themes are clear. It is also worthy of note that both a particularly brilliant maker of white wine and one of red have cited cleanliness as being the most important element in the whole process.

A brief look at the structure of the grape will give a clearer idea of the raw material. The stalk or stem accounts for three to five percent of the whole, the skin 10–20 percent, the pulp or fleshy part of the fruit 70–80 percent, and the pips two to four percent. Within these component parts are distributed water, cellulose, minerals such as sulphates, potassium phosphates, lime and soda, sugars (glucose and levulose), acids (tartaric, malic and citric) and tannin. The stalks contain tannin, which, in excess, can give a bitter taste, and water, which can dilute the alcohol level. A small quantity of stalks can, however, give a wine backbone. The pips contain even more tannin, so great care must be taken with crushing and pressing, or far too much astringence will appear in the wine.

But the flesh and the skins provide the basis of both the must (the unfermented juice) and the wine. The colourless juice which comes from the flesh contains the sugars and the acids, while, during fermentation, the colouring matter in the grape skins of both the Pinot Noir and the Gamay is dissolved by the alcohol and distributed in the must.

Red wines

The Pinot Noir grapes (for Gamay in the Beaujolais there is a different method) are brought into the *cuverie* and put through a crusher-stemmer. Many winemakers put back a proportion of stalks to strengthen the structure of the wine – perhaps 10–20 percent. Fermentation vats vary considerably, both in size and material. The traditional open wooden vats are still seen in many cellars and, whereas this type of vat poses problems in Bordeaux, the coolish Burgundian Octobers rarely result in temperature-control risks. Sometimes the temperature can go briefly over 30°C at the beginning of the fermentation, but it is usually not too dangerous and at night the temperature drops sufficiently for it to be a brake. In fact, it is much more usual to have to heat all or part of the must (in steam-heated, double-lined, copper bowls), in order to get things going, for a 'stuck' fermentation is dangerous – either because of the risk of oxidation (in spite of judicious addition of sulphur dioxide) or because of contamination by bacteria. Sometimes, when the must heating has been excessive, the wine can have a slightly 'jammy' taste.

Fermentation vats in Burgundy can also be of concrete or steel; some are lined with enamel or glass; and there is even a limited amount of stainless steel, especially with the largest houses. Nearly all vats, of whatever material, are open, but there are some advocates of closed vats. In many cases, the cap of skins is kept in contact with the juice, for good colour extraction, by means of wooden poles, or *piges*. There is also a certain amount of treading by men, which surprises those who think this practice is now confined to the Douro valley of Portugal. *Remontage*, or pumping the must from the base of the vat and spraying the top, is another means to the same end. There is a fair amount of tannin in the skins and the potential for aroma, so this process is vital if a quality wine is to be achieved. The yeasts are thus also spread well, essential when reliance is almost entirely on natural yeasts for turning the sugar into alcohol. Open vats can have a system of a permanently submerged cap, attained by the use of a perforated lid, but *remontages* are still necessary.

Chaptalization, or the adding of sugar to the fermenting must, can be effected with a *remontage*. There are those who like to do this at the beginning of the fermentation, and others who like to do it in small doses as the fermentation progresses, but great care has to be taken that no residual sugar remains at the end. For red wines, cane or beet sugar can be used, with cane sugar for white wines. Chaptalization, of course, raises the alcohol level, but it also slightly lowers the fixed acidity of a wine. The ratio of alcohol to extract is higher in chaptalized wines, and excessive chaptalization also tends to mask fruit and aroma. So, the conundrum remains – what to do in Burgundy when natural alcohol is deficient, owing to a sunless year. My own inclination is to settle for less alcoholic wines, destined for young drinking, and rigorously to declassify Grand Cru and Premier Cru wines to *village* level when the modesty of the year warrants such action. In poor years in Burgundy these grand-sounding names often fail to reflect the real nature of a top *cru*, so let us cease to pretend and simply say that, in some years, this level of achievement is not possible. Is it so shaming when we are the victim of nature? After all, there was hardly a single 1972 Bordeaux Cru Classé worthy of the name!

As for length of fermentation, or vatting time, this varies between winemakers, and it certainly varies between years. In an excessively tannic year like 1976 (an admittedly rare occurrence – but nevertheless an example), some meticulous producers actually *reduced* their vatting time so as to avoid an imbalance of tannin. Some people also believe in shorter fermentation when the grapes are less than healthy. On the other hand, the wines produced in a year of high production or only moderately sunny conditions can often benefit from a long fermentation.

However, all the main colour extraction is achieved in the first three or four days, although the extraction of tannin continues throughout the vatting. Increased body and extract can be added to a wine which is perhaps light owing to high yields (as in 1982) through the process of drawing off a quantity of juice during the fermentation, thereby increasing the ratio of solids to liquids. This results in a good deal of non-AC rosé wine, but it is a financial sacrifice which can pay off by greatly enhancing the quality of the remaining red wine. So, vatting times in the Côte d'Or generally vary between eight and 14 days, and there is no set of rules in this respect which will guarantee automatic perfection each time.

When the wine is run off the lees the remaining skin and pips are pressed and the first pressing is almost always added to the free-run wine. Nowadays, horizontal presses are in use – Vaslin, Mabille and Willmes. More press wine can be added if the vintage is completely healthy. The solid matter left after the pressings is later distilled into the spirit called *marc*. The malolactic fermentation follows, either in vat or barrel. The malic acid is transformed into lactic acid and carbon dioxide gas by this process, softening the wine and preventing a later fermentation in bottle, a misfortune which sometimes happened in the past in Burgundy. Often a cellar has to be warmed to about 17°C to enable the malolactic fermentation to take place – very cold Burgundian cellars create difficulties. I would go so far as to say that some growers' wines are bottled too late, way after the optimum point, just because they have had to wait so long for the malolactic fermentation to be completed.

Red wine is then taken off its lees and aged in oak barrels of approximately 225 litres for anything between one year and two, depending on the type of wine, the nature of the vintage and the whim of the producer – judgement might be a kinder word. Every type of oak seems to be in service, with wood from the Allier and the Vosges often favoured for red wine, as well as that from the Jura and the Limousin. However, oak from the Tronçais and the Châtillonnais, the plateau of the Côte d'Or north of Dijon at Châtillon-sur-Seine, is also seen. The proportion of new wood in a cellar varies with the financial strength of a house and the needs of a year, although that is difficult to judge since the new casks have to be ordered well in advance of the harvest. In 1992, a new oak barrel, or *pièce*, cost 2,700 francs. The Pinot Noir cannot take excessive new oak, with its overpowering tannin and vanilla flavours, so the balance of new oak against old has to be just right. New casks can be seasoned, often using water, to remove excess astringence.

Racking, or the periodic transfer of wine from one barrel to another, thereby separating it from any stale solid matter which may have fallen to the bottom of the cask, is usually done three times before bottling – in the spring after the vintage, before the following vintage, and before bottling. The tendency is for less rather than more, as excessive racking can tire and dry out a wine. Burgundian cellars are usually cold and humid, so less evaporation takes place here than elsewhere in France. Nevertheless, topping-up is a regular operation, especially as in Burgundy the bung-hole is always on top, thereby leaving room for personal expression. Of course, the wine used for topping-up should be similar, but often I suspect it might be inferior. If done too enthusiastically, it could contribute to the 'house style' of certain *négociants*' wines, but, as usual, conscientious winemakers will do their honest best.

A fining to clarify the wine is usually carried out before bottling, using whites of egg, gelatine, casein (a milk protein), isinglass (a fish product) and bentonite. Whites of egg seem to be favoured for red wines, but gelatine can be used to remove excess tannin (as in 1976). These substances bring about a coagulation of any suspended matter, which then falls to the bottom of the barrel or tank, leaving the clear wine to be racked off. Usually, the wines receive a light filtering before bottling, but some domains feel this can affect quality (less flavour, body or extract?) and avoid filtering, often signifying this by a small slip label to warn the consumer that there might be some haze or deposit in the wine. Personally, I feel that super-clarifying can detract from maximum character in a wine, but when wine is shipped around the world, deposit is disliked. However, it is ironic to note that it has always been more accepted in a Bordeaux than in a Burgundy, for no valid reason, unless it is that sediment in Burgundy can be more hazy and less solid than it is in Bordeaux.

Bottling is of vital importance, because it is tragic when a wine-maker falls at the last hurdle, and there are still too many bottling faults in Burgundy – oxidation and uncleanliness being the two chief culprits. Nowadays, the wine is assembled in tanks before bottling so as to achieve homogeneity and avoid the cask-to-cask differences of the past. Nearly all Burgundy is cold-bottled, although a few houses pasteurize. It seems to me that absolute hygiene, a great deal of running water in the cellar, and limited but sensible use of sulphur dioxide should provide all the precautions needed by a careful winemaker.

White wines

With these wines the whole process takes place in a different order, with pressing before fermentation. The stalks are not removed, and they help 'drain' the juice from the horizontal presses, which can be pneumatic or screw type. Oxidation is a great enemy of white wine, so a speedy but gentle pressing and a judicious use of sulphur dioxide are both desirable. The murky juice is then immediately run off into vats to stand and clarify – the *débourbage*. In large concerns, centrifuges are sometimes used, as the aim is to start with a very clean must.

Fermentation then takes place, either in barrel or vat. Nearly all fine Côte d'Or wines are fermented in oak, often new – Limousin oak often seems to be very successful. The ideal temperature is 15–20°C and the fermentation should be lengthy in order to extract maximum flavour and bouquet, with periodic rousing of the lees and yeasts to keep the process moving regularly. The cask also needs to be filled to the right level, to allow some air for the yeasts to work, but not too much to cause oxidation. The wine stays on its lees until completion of the malolactic fermentation, which could be late spring, but is then run off into clean barrels for the rest of its ageing. Here again, Limousin oak is often used.

Chaptalization is usually effected right at the beginning of fermentation. The most usual finings for white wine are casein, isinglass and sometimes bentonite for excess protein. For fine white wines only a light filtering should be necessary because fermentation in *barriques* has a 'fining' effect itself, and the wines tend to fall bright naturally from their long *élevage* in cask. Some of the best wines are bottled at 18 months of age, others before that time. Some Côte Chalonnaise wines are bottled in the spring after the vintage. In the Mâconnais, the more modest wines are kept in tank and bottled when needed, usually a matter of months after the vintage, and the wines are cold-stabilized by refrigeration to avoid tartrate deposit. On the Côte d'Or, allowing very cold air into the cellars usually brings this about naturally, and it would be a travesty to overtreat very fine white wines intended for ageing. A few tartaric crystals are a sign that a wine has been treated gently, which brings joy to the heart of a committed Burgundy-lover.

Rosé wines

Rosé does not mean much in Burgundy, except for the Rosé of Marsannay. The *vin gris* method is to press the red grapes in order to give a light colour, and then to ferment as for white wine. Or the grapes can be macerated for a day or two and the juice drawn off when the colour is right – fermentation follows.

Sparkling wines

Ever since 1822, *méthode champenoise* wines were made in Burgundy, but in 1975 a superior *appellation*, Crémant de Bourgogne, was created. Pinot Noir or Pinot Blanc, Chardonnay and Aligoté grapes are used and very gently pressed, with only the first pressings being retained for Crémant de Bourgogne. Fermentation is carried out and a *cuvée* is made which must be approved by a commission chosen by the INAO before it can be admitted for bottling and the *prise de mousse*, which is a secondary fermentation in bottle created by adding a dose of sugar and yeast to the wine. The wine has to age for nine months and goes through riddling, or *remuage*, and then *dégorgement* to eliminate the dead particles of yeast which have settled out.

This is now done by freezing the necks of the bottles to solidify the sediment, which can then be removed easily. The bottles are then topped up, their sweetness adjusted to correspond to the type of *crémant* required (Brut or Demi-Sec), recorked and 'dressed', and rested before sale. *Crémants* can be *blanc*, *blanc de blancs* (made from white grapes only) or rosé.

It is a pity that Crémant de Bourgogne is not better known and distributed, because the wines are fruity and fine, and of a generally very high standard.

Bourgogne Mousseux Méthode Champenoise does not have such strict conditions as *crémant* with respect to the base wine (grape varieties, which can include Gamay and Sacy, ripeness at vintage, yields, methods of transport, pressing and vinification), but the wines are still most honourable, be they white, rosé or red, the last one being rather a Burgundian speciality.

The Trade in Burgundy

Historically, Burgundy was at a disadvantage in comparison with Bordeaux when trying to sell its wines abroad, as there was no port and no direct river to the sea. The Yonne was used to some extent, and wine was also taken both to Paris and Rouen for onward transportation on the River Seine. Nowadays, road tankers and container lorries leave Burgundy for destinations all over Europe, and France's fine system of autoroutes provides speedy travel. The hold-ups occur at frontiers, and even more so at Channel ports, but that is the fault of bureaucracy, not transportation. Wine for the United States is usually taken to Le Havre, while exports to the Far East and Australia are usually sent via Marseilles.

AC exports in Burgundy in 1990 reached a value of 3,050 million francs and 1·65 million hectolitres in volume, of which 96 percent was in bottle and four percent in bulk. This total is steadily rising, with bottle sales on the increase and bulk exports falling. In 1984 the exports were to the value of 2,730 million francs and 1·14 million hectolitres in volume, of which 77 percent was in bottle and 23 percent in bulk.

The principal customers for AC Burgundy around the world are broken down as follows:

White Burgundy		Red Burgundy		Beaujolais	
UK	28%	Switzerland	25%	Switzerland	23%
USA	24%	UK	17%	Germany	19%
Germany	14%	Belgium & Luxembourg	13%	UK	14%
Japan	8%	Germany	10%	USA	11%
Belgium&Luxembourg	7%	USA	9%	Japan	9%
		Japan	7%	Netherlands	7%
				Belgium&Luxembourg	7%
(Others	19%)	(Others	19%)	(Others	10%)

It can be seen that the USA and UK are taking a large share of white wines, whereas the red wines are more evenly distributed around the world.

Who is drinking Burgundy? Both in France and in the export markets, much of the wine is eventually sold in hotels and restaurants, especially the high quality, very expensive wines. Here, the original cost of the wine is somewhat masked by the high mark-ups, and if the hospitality is classed as entertaining, the whole thing is more easily swallowed. There is a degree of resistance to the high prices of much Burgundy when it comes to the 'take home' trade, and top Burgundy is more likely to be sold by a fine wine merchant than a high-volume supermarket.

The upward trend in exports shows signs of continuing steadily, but only if unacceptable price increases are avoided. America, particularly, can fall out of love with a region just as fast as it can become enamoured of it, and the Burgundians should take care that they do not kill the golden goose. Many of the larger houses and domains are aware of this, but some estates, relatively new to exporting, might feel that the trend can only go upwards and that the market will absorb any wine at any price. This is not so, as numerous defections have shown in the past.

As long as Burgundy really delivers the quality behind the bottle, at a price which is not exorbitant for what the customer is getting, it will continue to keep old friends and find new ones. But greed and inconsistent quality are a certain route to failure in the long term.

Enjoying Burgundy

Bottles, labels and glasses

All Burgundy is in sloping-shouldered bottles, never the square shoulders of Bordeaux. The traditional colour is a yellow-green, which the French call *feuilles mortes*. It is especially pleasing with white wines when matched with a yellow capsule – for red wine, the capsules are red. It is very rare to find magnums in Burgundy, in spite of the fact that this is the ideal size for laying down: Burgundians should be encouraged to use this large format in great years. There was a brief experiment in the early 1980s with a 'Burgundian bottle' for AC wines, with 'AOC de Bourgogne' imprinted in the glass under the neck label. It was an aesthetic disaster and, happily for all, it died an early death.

Labels are comparatively simple in Burgundy:

Joseph Drouhin

PULIGNY-MONTRACHET

Appellation Contrôlée

Mis en bouteille par
JOSEPH DROUHIN
Négociant à Beaune, Côte d'Or

13·5%   75cl

Wine from a *négociant*
The name of the *négociant*.
The name of the wine.
Confirms AC status.
Bottled by Joseph Drouhin.
Address of the firm.
75cl, the standard EEC and USA content.
13·5%, the alcoholic content of the wine.
The vintage in this case appears on the neck label.

Mis en bouteille au Domaine
GEVREY-CHAMBERTIN

1ᵉʳ Cru Aux Combottes

Appellation Gevrey-Chambertin

1ᵉʳ Cru Contrôlée

1982 DOMAINE DUJAC
Morey-St-Denis (Côte d'Or)

13%   75cl

Wine from a domain
Bottled at the domain.
Name of the wine.
The fact that it is Premier Cru is mentioned in this case.
Confirms AC status.
Vintage and name of the domain.
Address of domain owner.
13%, the alcoholic content of the wine.
75cl, the standard EEC and USA content.

All the folklore and drinking songs of Burgundy might lead one to believe that the *tastevin* is the only vessel from which to drink its wine! But in reality, this dimpled, silver tasting cup (actually, it is more like a small saucer) is only useful for seeing if a wine still in cask is clear of haze. With the *tastevin's* wide surface, the bouquet of a wine is immediately lost, and gaining a true impression of a wine's taste is difficult against metal. So, for serious tasting and assessing, a glass is better.

The classic tulip-shaped glass is suitable for all wines, whether red or white, as is the approved tasting glass created by the INAO. But there are a few shapes widely used in Burgundy which seem to suit the particularly heady nature of the wines. It is as if Burgundy needs more room in a glass to breathe and develop than Bordeaux; great Burgundy has something slightly unrestrained about it, requiring space to express itself.

(a) The shape most favoured by Burgundians, both for red and white wine, is the *ballon*, a Cognac-type squat glass, with a short stem and a huge bowl narrowing at the top to catch and hold the bouquet. It is extraordinarily reassuring to grasp a *ballon* in the hand, swirl the wine around, deeply inhale and then, finally, take a good mouthful and let it roll in over the palate.

(b) In restaurants in Burgundy, particularly, you are quite often given a kind of elegant goldfish-bowl, on a long stem. Provided the size is not too exaggerated, this can be extremely effective in showing off the qualities of red Burgundy.

(c) There is another shape which I have not seen elsewhere, a large glass with a long stem and a generous bowl which tapers in only slightly towards the rim. This is a very traditional glass, and can allow a red wine to expand and open out.

The quality of the glass should be as fine as you can afford as it enhances the enjoyment of a wine. Riedel, the Austrian glass specialists, make beautiful examples in perfect Burgundy shapes. For all red Burgundy Riedel's Vinum 416/7 is wonderful, while for mature red Burgundy, in particular, the Sommelier 400/16 is unequalled. For all white Burgundy try the Vinum 416/5, and for mature white Burgundy I would suggest the Sommelier 400/0.

Serving Burgundy

Burgundians almost never decant their wines. Their attitude is usually one of great simplicity: bring up bottle from cellar, draw cork, pour into glass. As their cellars are very cool this eliminates the need for a refrigerator for the whites, and the reds are left to do their developing in the glass. There is much to be said for this approach. Decanting is a controversial subject anyway, and experiments do not seem to have proved conclusively that the process is beneficial or otherwise. However, I have had young Burgundy poured into a glass carafe and served soon afterwards, with delicious results. The perfume seemed to be even more heady than usual. With old wines it can also be sensible to separate wine from deposit, but the particles in suspension can be tricky to handle and decanting needs a steady hand and a keen eye; decant just before drinking.

Outside Burgundy, the most common fault associated with the serving of its wines is to offer the red wines too warm and the white too cold. Over-warm reds can be 'soupy' and really disappointing, while white Burgundy, over-chilled or left too long in a refrigerator, can completely break up, taste flat and lose its flavour. Red Burgundy is at its best served at 15–16°C (about 60°F), with young Beaujolais cooler, at about 13°C (55°F). White Burgundy can have a bigger variation. The very finest, especially if they have some bottle age, can be served at around 13°C (55°F), but a simple Mâcon-Villages could be served a great deal cooler, at around 9–10°C (just under 50°F). But even then, don't kill it with cold – you will miss so much.

Tasting Burgundy

To unlock the flavours and smells of fine Burgundy is to attain a hedonist's nirvana. Trying poor Burgundy is a deadening experience, with no impression of clean fruit on the palate, and either a tainted or over-alcoholic 'mask' preventing you from seeing something true and frank.

Both red and white Burgundy possess a multitude of perfumes and tastes, and the more you find, the better the wine is likely to be. More modest wines should be attractive, straightforward and fruity, while wines from fine sites, in ripe years and made by gifted winemakers will keep you searching for adjectives to describe them until the last drop has disappeared from the glass.

All the following flavours have been ascribed to Burgundy, more especially to the bouquet of fine bottles – they are not fanciful, just an attempt to try to pinpoint those heady, sensual aromas which assail the lucky drinker of good Burgundy:

Cherries, Raspberries, Strawberries, Redcurrants, Cassis, Apricots, Peaches, Figs, Prunes, Plums, Greengages, Quinces, Apples, Loganberries, Blackberries, Hazelnuts, Vanilla, Cinnamon, Acacia, Mayblossom, Hawthorn, Blackthorn, Honey, Liquorice, Laurel, Truffles, Chocolate, Tar, Grilled almonds, Roses, Violets, Hay, Toast, Wet fur, Wet leaves, Farmyards, Leather, Cocoa, Honeysuckle, Hung game, Oatmeal.

This is by no means a definitive list: the more Burgundy tasted, the greater the experience and vocabulary to express it. In addition, individual tasters differ in the qualities that impress them and the similarities that they perceive. There are other aromas, occasionally fleetingly encountered in Burgundy, but which seem to me to occur more frequently in Bordeaux – tobacco and mint are examples (the influence of Cabernet, as opposed to Pinot Noir, or is it more complicated than that?).

Some descriptions are used far more often with reference to white wine than to red. Mayblossom, acacia and hazelnuts are more often associated with Meursault than with Pommard, for instance, while cherries, farmyards and raspberries are firmly in the red camp. But it would be misleading to categorize all these descriptions rigidly into red and white columns, because they do overlap and surprises have a habit of creeping up on even the most experienced taster – this is one of the joys of wine.

When starting to taste Burgundy, it might be less confusing first of all to try to impress the basic scent and flavour of Chardonnay and Pinot Noir on the mind and senses. Then treat this as a canvas upon which to splash all the other sensory perceptions which present themselves. Let us hope that most of them will be positive, attractive and appetizing, but inevitably there will be some less appealing odours and tastes too – maybe dirty wood, vinegar or nail varnish. Discard those wines, but not without complaining to the supplier, and concentrate on finding those Burgundies which astonish with their range of bouquet and savour. They are easy to recognize and difficult to forget!

Burgundy with food

There is a Burgundy to go with virtually every type of food, with the exception of the dessert or pudding course, as there is no sweet white wine of the region. However, some of the most perfect meals finish with cheese and nuts, and this gives great scope.

Burgundian red wines, particularly the great growths of the Côte de Nuits, are superb with game, especially if it is well hung. One of the greatest gastronomic partnerships I ever experienced was in the company of that respected Burgundy man, Harry Yoxall, at what was to be our last dinner together. We had roast grouse, *bien faisandé*, with a bottle of Grands Echézeaux 1952 from the Domaine de la Romanée-Conti. What was incredible was that the Grands Echézeaux had the rich, gamey smell of the grouse! Venison, hare and wild boar are also magnificent with ripe Burgundy from a good year.

The combinations, of course, are infinite – mixed *charcuterie* with Beaujolais, Chablis with *andouillettes*, Meursault with *jambon persillé*, that splendid green-speckled Burgundian ham galantine. It was in Burgundy that the myth that eggs 'do not go with wine' was finally put to rest – what is better than a young Côte de Beaune with *oeufs en meurette*, lightly poached eggs with a red wine sauce? With the garlicky snails of the region, an Aligoté is ideal, while something like a plain sole or piece of turbot deserves a Chevalier-Montrachet or Corton-Charlemagne.

Robust dishes like *boeuf bourguignon* or *coq au vin* are more than welcome after a morning's tasting in cold cellars (or pruning on a February day), and a vibrant, even earthy Burgundy is best here – perhaps a Santenay or a Mercurey. Unfortunately, some regional recipes which require a long cooking time are rarely found in restaurants, such as *potée bourguignonne* (ham, pork and sausages cooked together with vegetables), or *pouchouse*, made from fresh fish from the Saône simmered in white wine (if red wine is substituted it becomes a *matelote*, and the colour of the accompanying wine changes accordingly).

Two dishes often found in the Mâconnais are refugees from the Ain, across the Saône. *Quenelles de brochet*, or flaked-pike moulds, should really only be eaten in restaurants of impeccable reputation, otherwise you might come up against a floury, 'ersatz' version, while poached *poularde de bresse* is a dish of great subtlety, which is equally happy with either red or white Burgundy.

At last people have realized that not all cheese has a miraculous effect on wine and, while the soft, creamy little goat cheeses of the Mâconnais and *fromage blanc* floating in cream are delicious with chilled Beaujolais, Epoisses and even Cîteaux often seem to be too strong and tangy for fine Côte d'Or wines. I prefer the Gruyère-related Comté or the Savoyard Beaufort, one of the great, unsung cheeses of the world.

Vintages

As with any wine area, there is a general picture for each vintage, on which there is over-painting by individual growers. A poor winemaker will not suddenly produce tremendous wine in a fine year, and a skilled winemaker can make surprisingly attractive wine in a poor one. With older vintages, the assessments really only apply to Grands Crus and the top Premiers Crus.

1991: The weather was good right up to the harvest, and Burgundy was very little damaged by the frost which had affected so much of the rest of France on April 22nd. Some parts of the Côte de Nuits had suffered from hail in June, but the main problem was that the heavens opened on the date of the *Ban de Vendange* (25 September). It is early days yet: the reds are very variable, though there were some good wines in cask; the whites look better in general, but neither will be exceptional. Results from the Mâconnais and Beaujolais, on the other hand, look much more successful, for the harvest in these areas was completed before the rains.

1990: Picking took place in ideal conditions after a long, hot, dry summer. The yield was large for both red and white wines but acidities were generally better than in 1989. Chablis made excellent wines for the second year running and the Côte de Beaune whites were better balanced than many of their respective '89s, if not as exciting as the best of the earlier vintage. Although a few growers claim to have made better red wines in 1989, most of the '90 reds are more concentrated in all respects. They have a wonderful richness of fruit and an opulence of flavour similar to the '85s. Like that vintage, they will probably drink well early on, but they have the structure to keep well too. Once again, there were delicious wines from Beaujolais and the Mâconnais, though the Mâconnais' can be dizzily alcoholic.

1989: A very promising early vintage was diluted somewhat by rainfall in the fortnight before picking. Acidities were on the low side overall and – in contrast to 1988 – the yield was higher for the red wines than for the whites. As a result, the reds suffered from some dilution, but they are ripely flavoured wines with considerable charm, for relatively early drinking. The best Chablis are outstanding as are the best Côte de Beaune whites; but some of the latter can be over-alcoholic and seriously lacking in acidity. Excellent quality in the Mâconnais, Côte Chalonnaise and, especially, in Beaujolais.

1988: After a mild winter, wet spring and hot, dry summer, the harvest took place in ideal conditions. The crop was large, unexpectedly so for the white wines, and consequently some Chablis and Côte de Beaune whites tend to lack depth; others are textbook. The best reds will be excellent: concentrated, firm and tannic – aromatic, flavoury wines for the long haul, with less of the lush, ripe fruit that is found in the '85s, '89s and '90s. Some very good whites from Pouilly-Fuissé that will benefit from keeping.

1987: One of the rare years when the natural sugar level of the reds was higher than the whites. Much depended on whether people harvested before or after the rain. Picking was late and there was some rot, but good domains sorted out the affected grapes. Most of the wines lack concentration (except when yields were very small), but there are softly attractive reds which are already drinking well in the early 1990s, and whites are fresh and forward, if without a great deal to say for themselves.

1986: A good late flowering promised well, but late summer storms encouraged rot on the plain. However, most of the vintage took place in glorious weather and the crop was nearly as big as 1982's. As a result, some reds lack concentration and definition – others appear charming, but the beauty and consistency of the '85s is not there. The whites have style and elegance. The Côte Chalonnaise, the Mâconnais, the Beaujolais *crus* and Chablis were all most successful.

1985: The particularly severe winter hit the headlines: in January, the temperature fell to $-25°C$, while in February it hit a mere $-15°/20°$. The worst damage was in Chablis and the lower parts of the Côte de Nuits, forcing considerable replanting. However, in the vital three months between the flowering and the vintage, temperature and sunshine were above average and rainfall below. September and October were glorious, and as there was so little rain, the grapes were incredibly healthy. The wines are beautifully clean, radiantly fruity and attractive, with the rich texture and seduction of a really ripe vintage. This is a luscious vintage, which will appear delicious relatively young, but which will undoubtedly produce great bottles for the future. The whites gave great pleasure when quite young; the best have the balance and fat to last well.

1984: Cold weather in September prevented the spread of rot, but inevitably it also precluded real ripeness, and the wines were very low in natural alcohol. As a result, chaptalization came into its own, and there are undoubtedly unbalanced wines as a result. But it is also a pleasant surprise to see how successful some wines appear, with clean, fruity qualities. However, they do not have depth and many are past their best. The Chablis have typical *nervosité*, and the problem here is one of quantity, not quality.

1983: The best wines will confirm that this is the finest vintage since 1978. But there was rot, and hail in parts of the Côte de Nuits has stamped its imprint on a fair number of wines. Where these twin scourges were avoided, there are remarkable wines of power and concentration, with a good deal of tannin of a kind which is more penetrable than it was in 1976. This is a vintage to lay down, something for those who say that modern Burgundy is 'too light'. However, in the early 1990s almost all the reds have advanced colours and some have a tell-tale dry mousiness when tasted. The white wines have great body and power, although a few seem to have too much (natural) alcohol on the nose. It would be a tragedy to drink the top wines too young.

1982: A record harvest, which had the unhappy side-effect of overcropping from the Pinot Noir. Consequently some red wines were mere shadows of their normal selves, and others were given too much of a helping hand or suffered from heating processes to extract colour. There were many fruity, gulpable wines for young drinking, and where a winemaker ran off a good deal of surplus juice during the vinification process, there was more structure. The whites were relatively forward, but delicious and easy.

1981: Hail tainted many wines, while others just had a dry finish. A few, somewhat miraculously, tasted good and concentrated, partly due to the small yield. The white wines have firm acidity and the grandest of them can still be kept.

1980: A controversial vintage, which unfortunately masked the reality of the situation. Where the grower treated wisely against rot, there were some very creditable wines, especially at reputed domains and particularly on the Côte de Nuits. These were reds of style and fine flavour, but most should probably have been drunk by now. The whites did not have much character.

1979: A large vintage, which inevitably brings an element of variability to the scene. Many wines had most attractive fruit and charm with an infinitely enticing taste, and the grandest wines are drinking splendidly now. The top Grand Cru and Premier Cru whites share these qualities.

1978: An exceptional vintage, where both red and white wines have concentration, complexity and real interest – they can still be splendid. There is fruit on a sound structure, giving wines which are perfect candidates for long-term cellaring. It is the flavour and individuality of each *cru* and *climat* which really impresses.

1977: The wines were not marvellous, but could have been a lot worse – only the fine September weather saved the vintage from disaster. The reds are now old and dry – only the very best wines are not marked by this characteristic. The whites were better, everywhere, but they had no real pretensions.

1976: These wines are really atypical Burgundy, overloaded with tannin which sometimes succeeds in masking the fruit. Where the fruity character can break through, there are some exotic wines which have kept well, and there is nearly always a concentrated 'roasted' character to them. The whites were rich and low in acidity, and many were flat or blowsy at ten years old. The top Chablis can be better balanced, although their fat character makes them closer to the Côte de Beaune in style.

1975: A year all but ruined by rot, and the reds consequently had an unhealthy brown colour and a tainted taste. The whites on the Côte d'Or were slightly better, although now most have maderized. But Chablis produced wines of breed and balance, many of them gems.

1974: Fairly firm reds, with some body to them, but many were rather dull-tasting and lacked individuality. The whites had more interest, and some improved in the bottle.

1973: A very large vintage which produced lightish wines of charm and fruit. The whites had low natural acidity, and were generally at their best young.

1972: The best reds developed surprisingly well throughout the 1970s and 1980s, and now many are firm and well structured, with good fruity character. Occasionally, they are a little green. The whites also suffered from lack of ripeness, but some have recovered well. However, this might be one of those rare years in Burgundy where the reds eventually turned out better than the whites.

1971: A very ripe vintage, in some instances overripe, with lovely richness and opulence. The best are a heady experience, while some are too full-blown. Patches of hail on the Côte d'Or affected a few wines. Most of the whites are blowsy now, although the best balanced, including Chablis, still amaze.

1970: A large vintage of soft, fruity wines. They were most attractive up to the mid-1980s, but both red and white should now have been drunk, except in the case of certain Grands Crus.

1969: A superb vintage, stamped by the 'breed' of the wines. The underlying acidity ensured that they lasted well, and they have that quality of great *appellation* character which is the hallmark of a fine vintage. All the whites, including Chablis, were exceptionally good.

1967: When the reds were not over-chaptalized, there were some attractive bottles, and the whites had breed. All should have been drunk by now.

1966: A highly successful year, with quantity and quality.

1964: Very good, definite-tasting wine, both white and red.

1962: Very good wines, with the fine balance giving them longevity. Extremely elegant whites.

1961: A small crop of excellent wines, with the concentration to taste magnificent at 25 years old and more.

Some older vintages of distinction:
1959 (especially for reds), 1957, 1955, 1953, 1952 and 1950 (both better for whites than reds), 1949, 1948, 1947 and 1945.

Wines and Villages

In this section, detailed information is given on each of the five Burgundy areas and their villages/*appellations*, setting the accompanying profiles of selected domains and their wines in context in terms of soil, topography, climate and history.

The areas and the villages/*appellations* within them are arranged in geographical order from north to south. The maps at the beginning of each area section show the principal villages/*appellations* and can be a quick source of reference.

For **Chablis**, **Côte Chalonnaise**, the **Mâconnais** and **Beaujolais**, the area's principal producers are profiled. Their wines are listed in the following order: Grand Cru, Premier Cru, *Village* and Regional, with each category divided by a full stop. Figures for holdings *en métayage* or *en fermage* (shown in brackets) are in addition to the main holdings figure. In the case of the **Côte d'Or**, because of its sheer size and the variety contained within it, a personal selection of each village/ *appellation's* producers has been included, with a discussion of their best wines.

Fuller details and a more comprehensive listing of Côte d'Or producers can be found in the A–Z of Burgundy Producers.

See also How to Use this Book.

Chablis

○

Chablis produces stupendous wines and contentious people. They can never quite agree amongst themselves which villages and slopes should fall within the *appellation* and which should not, whether Portlandian limestone is as good as Kimmeridgian, whether or not to use wood in the *élevage* of the wines, and even whether the aspersion method of frost protection (*see* page 71) is ultimately beneficial – the man who, in my view, makes the best Chablis today has serious reservations about the practice.

The one aspect of the Chablis saga that has never been in dispute is the status of the Grands Crus, which have remained inviolate since the creation of the AC in 1938. The seven Grands Crus are all on the slopes of the huge hill over the little Serein river from Chablis itself. They are:

Blanchot	*12·72 ha*	**Preuses**	*11·44 ha*
Bougros	*12·63 ha*	**Valmur**	*13·20 ha*
Les Clos	*26·05 ha*	**Vaudésir**	*14·71 ha*
Grenouilles	*9·38 ha*		

The name La Moutonne is used for wine from a 2·35 ha parcel of Preuses and Vaudésir, so it is considered as a Grand Cru.

The Premiers Crus area is currently being expanded, and here there is serious contention. It is difficult to judge these new plantings until the vines are older, although interested parties already think the quality is of sufficient standard. The nomenclature of Premiers Crus in Chablis has always been complicated, with a mass of alternative names. The principal Premiers Crus are listed overleaf and, below them, where applicable, are the vineyards which have the right to call themselves by the better-known name. It is worth remembering here that Chablisien spelling is notoriously idiosyncratic. Nowadays, the majority of wines are gathered under the main Premier Cru titles, which certainly makes for ease of marketing.

Premiers Crus
Vineyards

Mont de Milieu

Montée de Tonnerre
Chapelot, Pied d'Aloue,
Côte de Bréchain

Fourchaume
Vaupulent, Côte de
Fontenay,
l'Homme Mort,
Vaulorent

Vaillons
Châtains, Séchet,
Beugnons, Les Lys,
Mélinots, Roncières, Les
Epinottes

Montmains
Forêt, Butteaux

Côte de Léchet

Beauroy
Troesmes, Côte de Savant

Premiers Crus
Vineyards

Vau Ligneau

Vau-de-Vey
Vaux Ragons

Vaucoupin

Vosgros
Vaugiraut

Les Fourneaux
Morain, Côte de Prés
Girots

Côte de Vaubarcusse

Berdiot

Chaume de Talvat

Côte de Jouan

Les Beauregards
Côte de Cuissy

Naturally, there is far greater disparity of quality between the Premiers Crus than between the Grands Crus, which are in another category as far as richness and concentration are concerned. The Premiers Crus are scattered over a clutch of villages, some of them outlying. These villages include Fyé, Fleys, La Chapelle-Vaupelteigne, Poinchy, Fontenay, Maligny, Milly, Chichée and Beines, as well as the town of Chablis itself. Vau-de-Vey in the commune of Beines is, in fact, a new Premier Cru.

The villages which stand to gain most from the extension of the vineyard area are Maligny, Lignorelles and Villy; at Maligny, particularly, much vineyard area hitherto defined as Petit Chablis has been upgraded to Chablis, contributing to the decline of the former name. While most people with some knowledge of soil types would agree with the Institut National des Appellations d'Origine that Kimmeridgian and Portlandian clay are very similar, the importance of microclimate and site of a vineyard are vital, especially in a viticultural area as far north as Chablis, with its constant problems of frost and ripeness.

The danger of spring frost exists from the end of March until the middle of May. Two main methods of protection are now in use: aspersion, or spraying the vines to give a protective coat of ice, and burners in the vineyard. The timing of spraying must be perfect, starting the moment the temperature reaches zero, and it must be uninterrupted, continuing until the temperature rises above zero again – a blocked sprinkler can be disastrous. Wind, also, can blow the water off course. The installation of such a system is expensive, but labour costs are low. Spraying equipment can easily be seen on the hill of the Grands Crus and over large parts of Fourchaume, but the two methods of protection often exist side by side. The oil burners can now be filled automatically but they still have to be lit manually, so fuel and labour costs are the main disadvantages here. In both cases, efficacy is increased by accurate frost forecasts from the nearest Station Météorologique – the most dangerous moments are usually in the early hours of the morning.

The risk of frost has also been lessened by the use of weedkillers (fewer weeds mean less humidity and therefore less frost and, as the soil does not need to be worked, it exudes less humidity). Also, there are not so many isolated vineyards as in the past – both frost and birds seem to descend with greater frequency when vines are interspersed with uncultivated land. But no one would pretend that frost in Chablis has been conquered; its effects have, however, been mitigated. To people who knew the region in the 1950s, the change is nothing less than dramatic.

Most growers now ferment in stainless steel or lined cement vats, but opinion varies as to the best material for ageing Chablis. There are advocates of both new and old oak, and others who prefer that their wine sees no wood at all. In general, it appears to me that Grands Crus and Premiers Crus from ripe years, particularly the former, benefit enormously from some wood ageing (and the age of the wood seems, on tasting, to matter less than the absolute cleanliness of the casks), while straight Chablis can be delicious bottled younger and straight from the vat. Some more traditional winemakers keep their wine in vat until the spring following the vintage, when it should have finished its malolactic fermentation, and then age the wine in barrel for about a year. These casks, now, are more likely to be 225-litre *pièces* than the traditional smaller Chablis *feuillettes* of 132 litres. Naturally, new oak barrels are expensive, but that should probably not be a consideration where Grands Crus are concerned. However, care should be taken that no oxidation occurs when ageing in wood, which entails rigorous topping up, or *ouillage*, and that the wine does not take on too strong a taste of oak. Chablis supports this much less than a richer, fatter Meursault or California Chardonnay – even in a Grand Cru from Chablis there should be some underlying 'nerve' or steel, the true *appellation* character.

Fresh, youthful, straight Chablis need not see any wood – this is the kind of delicious *grande brasserie* wine one chooses with a dozen oysters. But just as winemakers should guard against over-heavy Chablis, they should also take care not to produce wines that are too neutral and that fade away a year or two after their birth. As with most things, a judicious mixture of the two methods, a winemaking compromise, probably produces the most memorable Chablis.

Commercially, the most significant change in Chablis has been in the greater control of its own destiny apparent during the last 25 years. Although Chablisiens still like to blame the *négociant* houses of Beaune for the wild fluctuations in price and the unsatisfactory balance between supply and demand too frequently encountered in the region, the fact remains that they now have more control over their own affairs than ever before. *Négociant* houses sold 65 percent of the Chablis produced in 1988, with the growers selling the remaining 35 percent. And as the producers of Chablis have a commodity which is in worldwide demand, they can very much call the tune as to the prices they charge. Obviously, it is difficult to

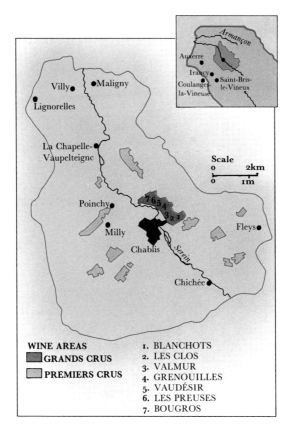

WINE AREAS
■ GRANDS CRUS
■ PREMIERS CRUS

1. BLANCHOTS
2. LES CLOS
3. VALMUR
4. GRENOUILLES
5. VAUDÉSIR
6. LES PREUSES
7. BOUGROS

have a stable situation when annual production figures vary as much as they do in Chablis, but the region has always been known for allowing prices to soar when there is little wine to sell, of whatever quality, and for selling its wine too quickly and too cheaply when there is a prolific vintage, such as 1982. If only some of the stock could be sensibly blocked until the result of the following vintage is known, and the sale spread over a longer period of time. Many people shunned the wonderful '78s because the prices were too high initially, whereas in 1985 there was a critical stock and price situation that was almost bound to spill over into 1986. Chablis has always made a speciality of lurching from one crisis to another!

The following table gives an indication of the unreliable nature of the yields in Chablis. Unusually low yields are almost always the consequence of severe spring frosts or poor flowering.

Yields of Chablis *(hectolitres)*					
Year	Grand Cru	Premier Cru	Chablis	Petit Chablis	Total
1978	3,850	17,731	25,179	2,332	49,092
1979	6,124	33,988	66,126	7,989	114,227
1980	5,113	25,491	46,601	5,359	82,564
1981	2,864	15,686	22,749	1,723	43,022
1985	2,693	25,650	65,294	6,218	99,855
1986	4,676	32,339	65,602	5,811	108,428
1989	5,149	36,623	95,293	10,688	147,753
1990	5,223	40,138	114,609	14,209	174,179
1991	5,072	39,870	102,670	11,325	158,937

As an illustration of how the number of hectares under vine is increasing, here are comparable figures showing the ten year difference between 1982 and 1991.

	1982 hectares	1991 hectares
Chablis Grand Cru	92.13	97.75
Chablis Premier Cru	476.94	691.95
Chablis	989.11	2,140.43
Petit Chablis	109.48	304.83

The Principal Chablis Producers

Cave Coopérative La Chablisienne

8 boulevard Pasteur, 89800 Chablis. 834 ha. Chablis Grands Crus. Chablis 1ᵉʳˢ Crus. Chablis, Petit Chablis, Bourgogne Blanc and Aligoté, Bourgogne Rouge Epineuil, Bourgogne Grand Ordinaire, Bourgogne Passe-Tout-Grain, Crémant de Bourgogne.

This is the somewhat coy name for the omnipresent cooperative at Chablis. It has great influence on the pricing policy each year, for it swallows nearly a third of the total production of the *appellation* and has just under 200 *adhérents* who bring must, not grapes, to the cellars. The policy of sometimes using the growers' names on the labels is justifiably criticized in some quarters, as it gives the impression of being domain wine although it came out of a cooperative vat. But La Chablisienne also sells in bulk to *négociants* in Chablis and Beaune, as well as abroad in both bulk and bottle. As with any cooperative, selection is the key to success in buying, but there is no doubt that some of the top wines are excellent, including some memorable Grands Crus, Grenouilles for example.

Domaine Jean Collet & Fils

15 avenue de la Liberté, 89800 Chablis. 21·5 ha (3·6 ha *en métayage*). Grand Cru: Valmur. 1ᵉʳˢ Crus: Mont de Milieu, Montée de Tonnerre, Montmains, Vaillons, Chablis.

Fine quality, well-constituted Chablis with the distinctive 'stony' imprint of the *appellation* and great depth of flavour too. The wines are fermented in stainless steel with Valmur, Montée de Tonnerre and Mont de Milieu usually being *élevés* in one-third new wood. An irritating problem for the consumer however is that there is no reliable pattern for what is aged in new wood and what is not. Montmains is sometimes quite 'oaky' and some *cuvées* of the Grand Cru Valmur see no new wood at all, but as there is no indication on the label there is no way of knowing. That said, Collet's wines are often a revelation.

Domaine Jean Dauvissat

3 rue de Chichée, 89800 Chablis. 8 ha. Grand Cru: Les Preuses. 1ᵉʳˢ Crus: Montmains, Vaillons.

Good quality Chablis, stainless steel-fermented and aged using a very small proportion of new wood (ten percent maximum).

Domaine René & Vincent Dauvissat

8 rue Emile Zola, 89800 Chablis. 9 ha. Grands Crus: Les Clos, Les Preuses. 1ers Crus: La Forest, Séchet, Vaillons.

Here is a gifted winemaker! These Chablis are really exemplary, combining the fruit and 'nerviness' we should find in this *appellation*, and the kind of flavour which just makes you go 'mmmm'. This is how M Dauvissat does it: pressing; *débourbage* or clarifying of the must; slow fermentation at low temperature (achieved by cooling) in vat, where the wine stays until after the malolactic fermentation. However, 10 percent of the must is fermented in oak barrels. The wine is aged in oak casks from April to November, and then bottled from December to March after refrigeration and light filtration. The wines keep beautifully. They go to Parisian and provincial restaurants, private customers and all around the world. Since 1950, the property has quadrupled in size, and there have been modern innovations alongside the traditional methods. These are wines of great beauty, perfectly balanced, with just the right amount of oak. Luscious Les Preuses and Les Clos, elegant La Forest and Vaillons. The epitome of all that Chablis should be about. I only wish the Dauvissats could expand even further, and then there would be more wine for us devotees!

Domaine Jean Defaix

Milly, 89800 Chablis.

Clean, unoaked and well-made wines; light but good.

Jean-Paul Droin

16 bis, rue Jean Jaurès, 89800 Chablis. 4 ha (16 ha *en métayage*). Grands Crus: Blanchot, Les Clos, Grenouille, Valmur, Vaudésir. 1ers Crus: Côte de Léchet, Fourchaume, Montée de Tonnerre, Montmains, Vaillons, Vaucoupins, Vosgros. Chablis, Petit Chablis.

Prior to 1986 no new wood was used at this domain. Currently the Grands Crus are fermented in a mixture of new and one-year-old wood and the Premiers Crus in one to four year-old wood; both are then aged for six months

in casks that are not new. Chablis and Petit Chablis are
made entirely in vat. Well-made, pretty and flowery wines.

Maison Joseph Drouhin

7 rue d'Enfer, 21200 Beaune. 35.3 ha in Chablis.

The firm of Drouhin is both owner in Chablis and *négociant*
in Beaune. Splendid wines, very much influenced by wood,
and often fat and concentrated. Consequently, they last
very well in bottle. *See also* A–Z.

Domaine Duplessis

89800 Chablis. 5 ha. Grand Cru: Les Clos. 1ers Crus: Fourchaume,
Montée de Tonnerre, Vaillons, Montmains.

These wines are fermented in vat and aged for up to 18
months with about six months' wood ageing in old *fûts*.
Very austere and angular '86s, but a lovely '85 Montmains:
warm, ripe and honeyed on the nose, good strong flavour
and typical '85 breadth and *rondeur*.

Jean Durup/Domaine de l'Eglantière

Domaine de l'Eglantière, Maligny, 89800 Chablis. 150 ha. Vines in
communes of: Maligny, Villy, Beines, Fyé, Chablis. 1ers Crus:
Fourchaume, Montée de Tonnerre, Montmain, Vau de Vey.
Chablis, Petit Chablis.

A highly efficient domain, which is just as well, given its
size. M Durup has been at the forefront of the Chablis
policy of expansion, although his family has been in
Maligny for five centuries. There is no oak in the cellars
here, but the vinification is '*la plus proche possible de la
nature*'. There are pneumatic presses, which are very gentle
on the grapes, and the vats are concrete lined with fibreglass
or enamel. The result is wines that are pretty and floral,
rarely deep in flavour but always elegant, and totally
uninfluenced by oak. The wines can be labelled Château de
Maligny, Domaine de l'Eglantière, Domaine de Paulière
and Domaine de Valéry.

Domaine William Fèvre/Domaine de la Maladière

Domaine de la Maladière, 14 rue Jules Rathier, 89800 Chablis. 50
ha. Grands Crus (16 ha): Blanchots, Bougros, Les Clos, Grenouilles,
Preuses, Valmur, Vaudésir. 1ers Crus (12 ha): Beauroy, Fourchaumes, Côte de Léchet, Les Lys, Mont de Milieu, Montmains,
Montée de Tonnerre, Vaillons, Vaucoupin, Vaugiraut, Vaulorent.

Chablis (20 ha), Petit Chablis (2 ha).

> A very important domain, with more Grand Cru Chablis than any other grower. The wines have finesse and style, the best being lanolin-smooth from ageing in new oak barrels. Until 1987 all Fèvre's wines used to spend some time in wood, but since 1988 his Petit Chablis, Chablis and Premier Cru wines from the west bank of the river Serein have received no wood contact at all. The Grands Crus, and Premiers Crus Vaulorent, Montée de Tonnerre and Fourchaume are vinified and matured in oak, 25 percent being new. In 1989 and 1990 he made outstanding wines, combining all the minerally flavours and keen backbone of acidity that should characterise good Chablis. They have closed up in bottle and should be given at least five to ten years to develop their exceptional potential. In addition to the two names above, the wines are also sold under the name Ancien Domaine Auffray.

Vincent Gallois/Domaine de la Vallée aux Sages

Lignorelles, 89800 Chablis.

> Excellent, unoaked, straight Chablis and Petit Chablis; concentrated, pure and vivid.

Domaine Alain Geoffroy

4 rue de l'Equerre, Beines, 89800 Chablis. 35 ha. 1ers Crus: Beauroy, Fourchaume, Vau-Ligneau. Chablis.

> Alain Geoffroy is a great supporter of the expansion of the vineyard area at Beines, and he himself certainly proves that fine Chablis can be made there. The winemaking is quite orthodox for Chablis, but includes no wood. The wines are sold young, but keep well in bottle for those who have the foresight to lay some down. I like the stylish, fresh character, which is instantly recognizable Chablis. Judges at competitions must like them too, as they scoop up medals with great regularity. I am not always in accord with the verdicts of these august juries, who often see wines when they are very young and miss the faults that develop later in the bottle, but in this case, I approve! If I did not, it probably would not worry them greatly.

Domaine Thierry Hamelin
Lignorelles, 89800 Chablis.
> Pretty '89 Premier Cru Vau Ligneau; very correct, no
> highlights, but bang-on.

Lamblin & Fils
Maligny, 89800 Chablis. Grand Cru: Valmur. 1ers Crus: Beauroy,
Fourchaume, Mont de Milieu. Chablis.
> *Négociants* and vineyard owners, with all the trappings of
> modern vinification. Clean wines; but a touch too neutral?

Domaine Laroche
L'Obédiencerie, 22 rue Louis Bro, 89800 Chablis. 76 ha (21 ha *en
métayage*). Grands Crus: Les Blanchots, Les Bouguerots, Les Clos.
1ers Crus: Côte de Léchet, Les Beauroys, Les Fourchaumes, Les
Montmains, Les Vaillons, Vau de Vey. Chablis, Petit Chablis.
> This is a big operation, with over 90 hectares of vines as
> well as the *négociant* business of Bacheroy Josselin. There is
> also the Domaine Laroche and its *sous marque* Domaine La
> Jouchère. The winemaking is of the most modern, with
> some limited new oak for the Grands Crus only. There are
> some fine separate bottlings of Vieilles Vignes such as
> Fourchaumes and Blanchot, but some of the wines seem a
> might too neutral in comparison with the very best.

Domaine Long–Depaquit
45 rue Auxerroise, 89800 Chablis. 45 ha. Grands Crus: Les
Blanchots, Les Clos, La Moutonne, Les Preuses, Les Vaudésirs. 1ers
Crus: Beugnons, Les Lys, Vaillons, Vaucopins. Chablis.
> The Beaune *négociants* Bichot are behind this well-run
> domain, which has a large part of La Moutonne, Grands
> and Premiers Crus as well as straight Chablis – some of the
> latter is bottled in Beaune. Impressive wines on the whole,
> the Grands Crus in particular.

Domaine des Malandes
63 rue Auxerroise, 89800 Chablis. 7 ha (15 ha *en métayage*). Grands
Crus: Les Clos, Vaudésir. 1ers Crus: Côte de Léchet, Montmains,
Fourchaume, Vau de Vey. Chablis, Petit Chablis.
> Wines made entirely without wood; they seem to be
> getting better if the lovely '89s are anything to go by.

Domaine des Maronniers

Préhy, 89800 Chablis.

Straight Chablis with a clear-cut mineral flavour and vivid acidity; taut and racy Montmains, both mouth-wateringly good and typical. Bernard Legland created this domain in 1977 from AC land his father had planted with cereals. He has a very clear idea of what good Chablis should taste like and he knows just how to make it. Most of his wine is unoaked, but he puts a small amount in 10–30 percent new wood for a year ... and indicates that it is oaked on the label. He started without any inherited *bagage* and seems to have absolutely the right ideas. I can see why his '90 Chablis won a gold medal at the 1991 Mâcon fair!

Domaine Louis Michel/Domaine de la Tour Vaubourg

11 boulevard de Ferrières, 89800 Chablis. 20 ha. Grands Crus: Grenouilles, Les Clos, Vaudésir. 1ers Crus: Les Forêts, Fourchaume, Montée de Tonnerre, Montmain, Séchets, Vaillons. Chablis.

This is a very fine, fourth-generation domain founded in 1870. The must goes through *débourbage* and fining, leaving absolutely clean material to be worked on. Fermentation takes place in vats at low temperature (18–20°C), and the malolactic fermentation is prolonged as long as possible, ie no measures are taken to speed it up. The wines are bottled in September. There is no wood in the process, but the slow, natural winemaking, plus yields which are not exaggerated, mean that the wines remain young, fresh and full of bouquet for years, always with that yellowy-green light to them which is so characteristic of Chablis. 80 percent of the production is exported, with the remaining 20 percent going to private clients and restaurants in France. There is a fine array of elegant, fruity Premiers Crus, wines almost with a sheen to them, as well as the Grands Crus and straight Chablis. These are beautifully-balanced, stylish Chablis wines, a tribute to what can be achieved by ageing in stainless steel alone.

J Moreau & Fils

Route d'Auxerre, 89800 Chablis. 73.7 ha. Grands Crus: Blanchot, Clos des Hospices, Les Clos, Valmur, Vaudésir. 1er Cru: Vaillons. Chablis.

This remarkable domain is family-owned, although half of the important *négociant* business is owned by Hiram Walker. Moreau & Fils are the largest *négociants* and vineyard proprietors in Chablis. Wood has no part in the vinification, and after the fermentations the wines are kept for three to six weeks on healthy lees before being racked. The pride of the pack is the Chablis Grand Cru Clos des Hospices (within Les Clos) which, they say, combines a bouquet of hazelnuts with a steely or flinty quality coming from the soil and a vanilla or lemony nose from the Chardonnay – and no wood influences these aromas. The other family-owned Grands Crus can also be serious wines, but good rather than great. The *vin de table* Moreau Blanc has nothing to do with Chablis but, as with Mouton Cadet, there is sometimes confusion in the public mind, not helped by the fact that the labels and the wording of the advertising are so similar.

Chablis in winter

Société Civile de la Moutonne
89800 Chablis.

Bichot owns most of the Société Civile. La Moutonne is majestic wine, enormously concentrated in great years.

Baron Patrick
89800 Chablis.

Baron Patrick is one of the brand names under which Patrick de Ladoucette – best known for his Comte Lafond Sancerre and Ladoucette Pouilly-Fumé – markets Chablis. Straightforward, unoaked Chablis. *See* A Régnard & Fils.

André Philippon
Fleys, 89800 Chablis.

Quality straight Chablis and Premier Cru Mont de Milieu, stainless steel-fermented and briefly aged in wood, very little of which is new.

Domaine Pinson
5 quai Voltaire, 89800 Chablis. 5 ha. Grand Cru: Les Clos. 1ers Crus: Forêts, Montmains, Montée de Tonnerre.

Wines that are fermented in vat and aged in old wood. Some very good Chablis, concentrated and minerally, but sometimes the taste of 'old wood' intrudes.

Domaine François & Jean-Marie Raveneau
9 rue de Chichée, 89800 Chablis. 2 ha (5 ha *en métayage*). Grands Crus: Blanchot, Les Clos, Valmur. 1ers Crus: Butteaux, Chapelot, Montée de Tonnerre, Vaillons.

Classic Grands and Premiers Crus, wood-aged and built for long life in bottle. They have style and enormous interest. Stupendous examples of the genre.

A Régnard & Fils
28 boulevard du Docteur Tacussel, 89800 Chablis. *Négociants* specializing in: Grands Crus: Vaudésir, Valmur; 1er Cru: Fourchaume.

This purely *négociant* house, bought by Patrick de Ladoucette in 1984, is still run by Michel Rémon, and the wines are still also sold under Rémon's own name as well as that of Albert Pic. The wines are stainless steel-fermented and have very little oak-ageing, but a later bottling than some. In spite of limited wood-ageing, a few Premiers Crus and Grands Crus in the mid-1980s had more than a hint of

old wood in their flavour. That said, consistent quality
should improve under the eye of M Ladoucette. The
complete range of Chablis is covered by this house, and if
you tasted no other you would have a very good idea of
the *appellation*.

Domaine Guy Robin

89800 Chablis. 10 ha. Grands Crus: Blanchot, Valmur, Vaudésir.
1ers Crus: Butteaux, Montée de Tonnerre, Vaillons.

A little wood is used in the winemaking for the Grands
Crus; the Premiers Crus see no wood at all. Difficult to
judge here, as form has been so erratic.

Domaine Ste-Claire

Préhy, 89800 Chablis. 50 ha (16 ha *en métayage*). 1er Cru: Chablis.
Chablis, Sauvignon de St-Bris, Bourgogne Irancy, Bourgogne
Rouge, Blanc and Aligoté.

Most of Jean-Marc Brocard's production is Chablis *tout
court* (35 ha), stainless steel-fermented and with no wood-
ageing. It is honest, straightforward wine. The Sauvignon
de St-Bris lacks a little breadth, even for St-Bris, but the
Chardonnay de St-Bris has a zesty northern freshness to it.

Simonnet-Febvre

9 avenue d'Oberwesel, 89800 Chablis. 4 ha. Grand Cru: Preuses. 1er
Cru: Mont de Milieu. Chablis.

This is a small domain, but Simonnet-Febvre is an
important *négociant-éleveur* who buys in must and vinifies it
for young bottling. The house was founded in 1840 and
Jean-Claude Simonnet is the fifth-generation member of
the family now in charge. The firm also makes a speciality
of other Yonne wines, such as Irancy and Coulanges. The
wines, bottled under several other labels, see no wood at all
and are straightforward in flavour – at best.

Domaine Philippe Testut

89800 Chablis.

Philippe Testut had virtually to begin all over again after
his family had sold nearly all its large estate. However, a
small part of Grenouilles was kept and the domain also has
fine Premiers Crus and straight Chablis. The wines are
archetypal Chablis, with both vat- and barrel-ageing
preserving harmony, fruit and balance.

Domaine Gérard Tremblay/Domaine des Iles
12 rue de Poinchy, 89800 Chablis. 28 ha (5 ha *en métayage*). Grand Cru: Valmur. 1ᵉʳˢ Crus: Beauroy, Côte de Léchet, Fourchaume, Montmains. Chablis, Petit Chablis.

Full, fruity Chablis which now sees no wood-ageing at all.

Domaine de Vauroux
Route d'Avallon, 89800 Chablis. 28 ha. Grand Cru: Bougros. 1ᵉʳˢ Crus: Montée de Tonnerre, Montmains. Chablis.

Jean-Pierre Tricon specialises in straight Chablis, which accounts for nearly 25 of his 28 hectares. His wines are stainless steel-fermented with the Grand Cru and Premiers Crus aged for a few months only in wooden casks. Fruity wines with attractive definition and pure Chablis character.

Domaine Robert Vocoret & Fils
40 route d'Avallon, 89800 Chablis. 30·4 ha. Grands Crus: Les Clos, Valmur, Blanchots. Chablis 1ᵉʳˢ Crus. Chablis.

Here, the more usual process is reversed, because the wines are fermented in large oak barrels but aged in stainless steel vats. The wines are textured and full, and there is a generous span of them in all categories. They benefit from time in bottle and age well.

Other Wines of the Yonne

No one would pretend that these wines are much sought after on export markets, but they are fun to track down while on holiday in the area and rewarding to drink in local restaurants at some of the most modest prices in the whole of Burgundy.

Irancy
By far the best known of the Yonne red wines, it has had its own *appellation* since 1977 and is now made mostly of Pinot Noir, with small quantities of César. Undoubtedly, the Pinot Noir contributes finesse, while the César is more rustic. The soil is Kimmeridgian, and the vineyard area is prey to the twin dangers of frost and hail, although Irancy has a favoured microclimate. Some Bourgogne Rosé is also produced here. The individual vineyard Palotte is, in fact, in the neighbouring village of Cravant and therefore can only

be called Bourgogne Rouge; it is the same for the wines from the commune of Vincelottes. The best growers are Léon Bienvenu, Bernard Cantin, André and Roger Delaloge, Gabriel Delaloge, Jean Renaud and Jean Podor, whose Irancy Les Mazelots is probably the top wine of the *appellation*. Much Irancy goes to the Chablis *négociants*, with Simonnet-Febvre making a speciality of the *appellation*. There is also the Domaine de Pérignon, run by the Nuits-St-Georges firm of Chauvenet, which produces Passe-Tout-Grains from Pinot Noir and Gamay.

Coulanges-la-Vineuse

Wine from Coulanges is only classed as Bourgogne but, rather strangely, Coulanges-la-Vineuse may appear on the label. The wine is similar to Irancy, although usually lighter, and it is made entirely from the Pinot Noir. The principal growers are Raymond Dupuis, Serge Hugot, André Martin & Fils and Pierre Vigreux, while the Chablis *négociants* of Bacheroy Josselin and Simonnet-Febvre also sell Coulanges.

St-Bris-le-Vineux

Although it is the Sauvignon de St-Bris which has the regional denomination *Vin Délimité de Qualité Supérieure*, the Aligoté is really the better wine and the one with the more optimistic future. Pinot Noir, Gamay, a little César, Chardonnay and Sacy are also grown, which gives scope for the production of Bourgogne Rouge and Blanc, Passe-Tout-Grains, Bourgogne Grand Ordinaire and Crémant de Bourgogne. The best growers, whose wines can also sometimes be seen abroad, are Louis Bersan & Fils, now run by the two sons, Jean Brocard, Robert Defrance, Michel Esclavy and Luc Sorin.

Chitry-le-Fort

Chitry has the same array of grape varieties as St-Bris, with especially good Aligoté, and Bourgogne Blanc made from Chardonnay, which shares the Kimmeridgian soil of Chablis and some of its characteristics. Very good Aligoté Côtes de Chitry comes from Léon Berthelot, Jean-Claude Biot, Paul Colbois (much better than his Sauvignon) and Gilbert Giraudon. Joel Griffe and Roland Viré are other reliable names. Many of the growers of Chitry and St-Bris belong to the agricultural collective of the SICAVA, which makes Crémant de Bourgogne. Wine is also made at Tonnerre, Epineuil and Vézelay.

● ○ ◑ Côte d'Or

The Côte d'Or is the heart of Burgundy, golden in name and in reputation. Although historic Dijon is by far the largest town on the Côte, the pivotal centres for the wine trade are Beaune and Nuits-St-Georges. As with any wine area, there is a complex web of *négociants*, growers and brokers who make and sell the wines, each jealously guarding his or her position in the line of supply. But the Côte d'Or is the most democratic of wine regions, its vineyards divided up into hundreds of small plots which are either inherited or acquired by a diplomatic marriage. Some growers see their job as suppliers of grapes, leaving the *négociant* houses to do their own vinifications, while others like to control the whole process right up to the sale to the customer. There is a large number of growers who both make their wine, and sell a part of it to the *négociants*, via the brokers, to finance the proportion they wish to mature and bottle themselves. Somewhere in all this lurk magnificent winemakers who have made Burgundy the most show-stopping word in wine vocabulary. Others, who are less skilled or less caring, unfortunately have access to the same labels.

The greatest red and white Burgundies are made on the Côte d'Or, particularly if you take a wine's ability to age as a criterion of quality. It is awesome to remember this if you drive from Dijon to Beaune, with the slope of the Côte on your right, an imposing presence all along the way. Do this in autumn, when the leaves are changing colour, and let the vineyards create their magic. This is the Côte d'Or, and this is where some of the most intoxicating taste sensations in the world are created.

Marsannay

● ○ ◑

1990 production: Marsannay
AOC Communale ●   *6,547 hectolitres*
Marsannay
AOC Communale ○   *345 hectolitres*
Marsannay
AOC Communale ◑   *1,500 hectolitres*

In 1987, the new *appellation* of Marsannay was created, covering 250 hectares in the communes of Chenôve, Marsannay-la-Côte and Couchey. It applies to white, red and rosé wines. Two *climats* in Chenôve, formerly very famous, Le Clos du Roi and Le Clos du Chapitre, are now part of the new *appellation* Marsannay. Bourgogne Aligoté, Bourgogne Blanc and Bourgogne Passe-Tout-Grains are also produced on a small scale. Much less rosé wine is produced now, with only about 15 percent on offer, but this quantity does vary with the quality of the vintage – in good years, growers tend to opt for making red. The cooperative at Marsannay is less important than it was, responsible now for about 1,500 hectolitres of wine. On the better slopes, growers concentrate on making red wine, which has improved as the plantings have aged. The rosé should be drunk young, when it has a hint of strawberries, and is excellent in hot weather, when a red Burgundy tastes flat and 'soupy'. Red Marsannay is frank and gamey, slightly earthy in character, with good concentration if the year is propitious and the vines old.

A Personal Selection of Marsannay Producers

Domaine Bruno Clair
Perfumed rosé and Bourgogne Rouge with a bouquet of 'wet dog' (which is very pleasant, I assure you) and a taste of redcurrants.

Fixin

● ○

1990 production: Fixin
           AOC Communale
           & Premiers Crus ●   *3,956 hecto-*
       Fixin   *litres*
           AOC Communale
           & Premiers Crus ○   *negligible*

It is interesting to see how a 'marginal' *appellation* on the Côte de Nuits is divided between the ACs with regard to vineyard area:

     Côte de Nuits–Villages and Fixin   *128·04*   hectares
       (the two are interchangeable)
     Fixin Premiers Crus   *20·00*   hectares
     Appellation Bourgogne   *56·84*   hectares
     Bourgogne Grand Ordinaire   *37·91*   hectares

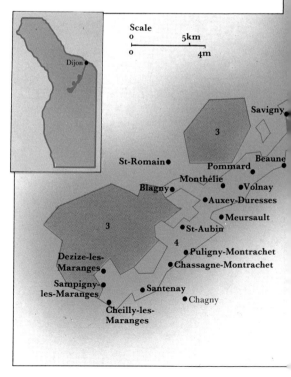

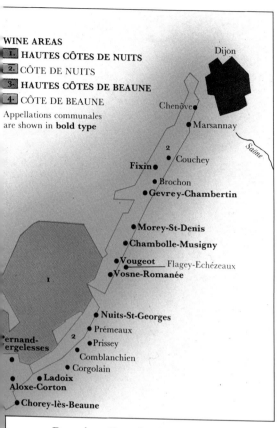

Premiers Crus Les Meix-Bas (part), Le Clos du Chapitre (part), Aux Cheusots (part), La Perrière (part), Les Arvelets (part), Les Hervelets (part).

The Premiers Crus are on the upper part of the slope, which goes up to 350 metres (1,150 feet), on a base of Bajocian limestone. Le Clos du Chapitre is on a marked slope, with Bathonian brown soil very rich in pebbles. La Perrière is above it, on a 12–14 percent gradient, with its share of pebbles. Aux Cheusots, within which lies the Clos Napoléon, is virtually without a slope. Les Hervelets and Les Arvelets, once the same *climat*, lie between Fixin and Fixey on Bajocian limestone and, in spite of only a mild slope, there is in places barely 25 cm (10 in) of soil over the base. Where limestone is predominant, the wines have more finesse, but deeper soil with more clay content gives tougher, more tannic wines.

La Perrière and Clos du Chapitre fight for front ranking at Fixin. Both can be kept safely for a decade, from good years. In youth the taste is somewhat *sauvage* and gamey, with blackcurrant flavours. Les Hervelets and Les Arvelets are thought more 'feminine', although in these days of *égalité* one should say that the fruit is softer. Aux Cheusots should have some finesse, although in the past I have been treated to some hefty Clos Napoléons which perplexed me somewhat. I think things are a little more *sain* nowadays.

A Personal Selection of Fixin Producers

Domaine Bruno Clair
White Fixin from the Pinot Blanc, vivacious when young, heavier after a few years in bottle – but I still wonder whether Chardonnay would not be better. Excellent red Fixin, partly from 40 year-old vines so the yield is not big – pure raspberries.

Domaine Pierre Gelin
Fixin which has that *sauvage* character, even at five years old. Big, gutsy Burgundy, without being 'blackstrap', so the fruit holds it own against the weight, but often it could take a decade in bottle.

Domaine Philippe Joliet
Clos de la Perrière which has improved in recent years – the '83 is certainly a *vin de garde*.

• Gevrey-Chambertin

1990 production: **Grands Crus**

Chambertin	*599*	*hectolitres*
Chambertin Clos de Bèze	*505*	*hectolitres*
Chapelle-Chambertin	*224*	*hectolitres*
Charmes-Chambertin/	*1,254*	*hectolitres*
Mazoyères-Chambertin		
Griotte-Chambertin	*106*	*hectolitres*
Latricières-Chambertin	*228*	*hectolitres*
Mazis-Chambertin	*382*	*hectolitres*
Ruchottes-Chambertin	*132*	*hectolitres*
Gevrey-Chambertin		
AOC Communale		
& Premiers Crus	*18,824*	*hectolitres*

Premiers Crus Les Véroilles, Village St-Jacques known as Le Clos St-Jacques, Aux Combottes, Bel-Air, Les Cazetiers, Combe aux Moines, Etournelles, Les Gémeaux, Lavaux, Poissenot, Champeaux, Les Goulots, Issarts, Les Corbeaux, Cherbaudes, La Perrière, Clos Prieur-Haut, Fonteny, Champonnet, Au Closeau, Craipillot, Champitenois known as Petite-Chapelle, En Ergot, Clos du Chapitre (part).

No commune in Burgundy has more Grands Crus than Gevrey – it could be compared to Pauillac boasting three First Growths, only more so. A peculiarity is that Chambertin Clos de Bèze may be called Chambertin, but not the other way round. Charmes-Chambertin can also be styled Mazoyères-Chambertin – the two names are interchangeable. Spelling runs riot at Gevrey – Les Véroilles alternates with Les Varoilles, Griotte sometimes sports an 's' at the end, and Etournelles can become Estournelles. But behind a certain disorganization in nomenclature, lies an array of some of the most seductive tastes in Burgundy.

The vineyard rises to 350 metres (1,150 feet), although the line of Grands Crus is below 300 metres (980 feet) on a gentle slope. They lie on a base of Bajocian limestone covered with thin debris, brown chalky soil with clay particles. Small pebbles play an important part, especially in the top section of Chambertin. Griotte and Chapelle-Chambertin have very thin soil, with the rock base even coming through in some places. Mazoyères and Charmes have gravelly soil of no more than 30–35 cm (12–14 in) in depth, a poor covering over the rock. Latricières and Ruchottes are on white oolite and everywhere there are outbreaks of the hard geological foundations. The Grands Crus shelter under the woods of the Montagne de la Combe Grisard, a good barrier against the winds from the north and also helping against hail. There are woods above the Premiers Crus, with Les Véroilles, one of the very best, right amongst them and possessing a microclimate of its own. The vines are picked later here than in the Grands Crus. Clos St-Jacques, often the equal of the Grands Crus, and Les Cazetiers share a very similar situation, but Champonnet has the unusual distinction of facing north to north-east.

Unusually for the Côte, the *village appellation* extends quite considerably over the Route Nationale and towards the railway. There is barely any slope, so good drainage depends on the subsoil. Here, there are layers of pebbles, so this aspect is satisfactory. I have come to the conclusion that when I have had mediocre wines from this part of the commune, it was not because of the soil, but due to over-production or bad winemaking.

The whole palette of aromas and flavours can come into top Gevrey. When the wines are young there are strawberries and raspberries, violets, undergrowth, and game in the rich wines. As they mature, flavours of liquorice develop with some intensity. Amazingly enough, Griotte really can be marked by cherries! Chambertin combines finesse with power, needing years to develop – the best-bred is never too generous with itself in youth. If there is a difference between Chambertin and Clos de Bèze, it is difficult to spot, as often winemaking techniques or the respective age of the vines override any innate variation. Then, there is the one-way interchangeability of the two names, so you have to be sure of what you are tasting – the best way to do this is when the wine is still in barrel and the winemaker himself describes the origin of each 'lot'. Latricières seems to have the most exquisite lacy quality, long and lingering but hardly ultra-powerful. Charmes-Chambertin can be less tannic and ready sooner than the other Grands Crus, while Chapelle-Chambertin can be very fruity.

Amongst the Premiers Crus, Clos St-Jacques has wonderful 'animal' scents and sturdy attack when young, while Clos des Varoilles (the whole six hectares of the Premier Cru is composed of this *clos*) is tannic when young, mouth-filling when more mature. Liquorice is a feature of many of these wines, especially in years of overripeness. Straight Gevrey should be silkily soft and perfumed, and easy to recognize.

A Personal Selection of Gevrey-Chambertin Producers

Domaine Bachelet
> Denis Bachelet is doing splendid work here, right up to Charmes-Chambertin level. There is finesse, class and great perfume.

Bouchard Père & Fils/Domaines du Château de Beaune
> Chambertin of great finesse, all silky violets. They do not own in Clos de Bèze, but buy grapes – it sometimes seems more powerful and more backward than the Chambertin at the same time.

Domaine Alain Burguet
> Straight Gevrey-Chambertin and Vieilles Vignes, both with a lovely bouquet, but sometimes a trifle too 'big' on the palate for the seductive style of the *appellation* to dominate. The Vieilles Vignes is usually a keeper.

Domaine Bruno Clair
> Rich Clos St-Jacques of great elegance and aromatic persistence.

Domaine Joseph Drouhin
> Griotte which is always very good indeed, a mixture of breed and balance . . . and those cherries.

Domaine Pierre Dugat
> Very pretty Premier Cru Champaux and supple, scented Charmes-Chambertin with a gentle *goût de terroir*.

Domaine Dujac
> Aux Combottes which shows that Jacques Seysses is as at home here as in Morey-St-Denis. Usually only a medium-keeper.

Domaine Faiveley

La Combe aux Moines Premier Cru has a true Gevrey bouquet, violets and warm earth, and a taste of redcurrants, cherries and violets.

Domaine Geantet-Pansiot

Attractive '87 Premier Cru Le Poissenot with a cherry fruit bouquet and some richness on the palate. The '90 Charmes-Chambertin is fabulous, but all their '90s are superb.

Labouré-Roi

This is not a domain wine, but their straight Gevrey is all juicy red fruit and the wines remain youthful in bottle – a good buy.

Domaine Ponsot

Chambertin, Griotte and Latricières which tend to be big and rich, sometimes jammy – most last well.

Domaine Philippe Rossignol

Straight Gevrey-Chambertin which is exemplary, if you want to know what the *appellation* is about at a non-grandiose level.

Domaine Joseph Roty

A small domain, but where the Charmes usually lives up to expectations, as does the rich and spicy Gevrey-Chambertin Premier Cru Les Fontenys.

Domaine Georges Roumier

Ruchottes which can be quite splendid, amongst the stars of the Côte de Nuits.

Domaine Armand Rousseau

The Clos St-Jacques always needs time, with its tight kernel of fruit – *une splendeur*! Also excellent Cazetiers, Ruchottes, Charmes, Mazy-Chambertin and Clos de Bèze. No serious Burgundy cellar should be without them.

Domaine Jean Taupenot-Merme

Lovely Charmes, with breed and style. This grower resists the temptation to 'bump up' in lighter years, like 1982; as a result the wines are delicious and not artificially 'big'.

Domaine Tortochot

Wines which are usually very big, sometimes impressive, sometimes a mite clumsy.

Domaine Louis Trapet (ceased to exist in 1990)
The colours were never dark here, and indeed could brown early, but the lingering flavours... There were ups and downs, but my greatest Latricières wines have come from this domain – sheer, lacy delicacy and breed – including, most recently, a wonderful '85.

Domaine des Varoilles
A range of Gevrey wines; lasting, classy bottles. There is velvety fruit intermingled with the structure. Clos des Varoilles is superb and concentrated.

● ○ # Morey-St-Denis

1990 production:

	Grands Crus ●	
Clos de la Roche	*572*	*hectolitres*
Clos de Tart	*298*	*hectolitres*
Clos St-Denis	*307*	*hectolitres*
Clos des Lambrays	*294*	*hectolitres*
Bonnes Mares	*523*	*hectolitres*
Morey-St-Denis AOC Communale & Premiers Crus ●	*3,922*	*hectolitres*
Morey-St-Denis AOC Communale & Premiers Crus ○	*134*	*hectolitres*

Premiers Crus Les Ruchots, Les Sorbés, Le Clos Sorbés, Les Millandes, Le Clos des Ormes (part), Meix-Rentiers, Monts-Luisants, Les Bouchots, Clos de la Bussière, Aux Charmes, Les Charrières, Côte-Rôtie, Calouères, Maison-Brûlée, Les Chabiots, Les Mauchamps, Les Froichots, Les Fremières, Les Genevrières, Les Chaffots, Les Chénevery (part), La Riotte, Le Clos Baulet, Les Gruenchers, Les Façonnières.

Morey-St-Denis considers that it is not sufficiently well known, sandwiched as it is between Gevrey and Chambolle – in 1985, a delegation of growers from the village even went to Japan to 'spread the word'. It is not very well publicized that there are two small cooperatives at Morey, which now vinify their grapes and sell the results to the *négociants*. But some of the greatest tastes in the whole of Burgundy can come from Morey-St-Denis, and luckily for us there is a handful of vineyard owners in the commune who are interested in achieving perfection, in spite of what the elements sometimes do to thwart them.

It is a considerable feat to have five Grands Crus in one commune, although only 1·5 hectares of Bonnes Mares lies in Morey – the remaining 13·5 hectares fall in the commune of Chambolle-Musigny. Clos des Lambrays was made a Grand Cru in 1981; in 1979 the estate had been sold to new owners after considerable time in the doldrums. Both Clos des Lambrays and Clos de Tart are in the hands of a single proprietor, which is a rare occurrence on the Côte d'Or. Clos de Tart and the Premier Cru Clos de la Bussière are typical abbey *clos* of the Middle Ages, completely surrounded by walls and with the buildings attached.

The slope of Morey-St-Denis lies next to that of Gevrey and shares the same geological makeup. The base is Bajocian limestone for the Grands Crus. The highest part of the Morey vineyard is Monts–Luisants at 350 metres (1,150 feet) on Bathonian limestone, with very poor, gravelly soil – the lack of clay and iron content makes it suitable for making the unusual white wine of the same name. The limestone rock is very evident, although Clos de la Roche probably refers to one rock which may have existed between Latricières-Chambertin and Clos St-Denis and which was used in Celtic or druidical rites. The calcareous vein comes from Bonnes Mares, crosses east-facing Clos de Tart and goes to the upper part of Clos des Lambrays, which is a little more sandy. Clos de Tart and Bonnes Mares have a very visible topsoil of calcareous debris, while Clos de la Roche and Clos St-Denis are on brown limestone soil with few pebbles, but benefiting from a good, sheltered microclimate.

These Grands Crus lead us into the realm of truffles, wild cherries and redcurrants. Clos de Tart may be the most tannic wine when young, but that derives as much from the winemaking techniques of no destalking and long vinification with the skins immersed as from anything else. Clos de la Roche has perfect structure and composition, the 'bonework' covered by rich fruit, which makes it ideal for ageing.

The breed in this *cru* is again evident in Clos St-Denis, which combines finesse and charm with a certain chewy quality, *mâche*. It is difficult to place Clos des Lambrays at this precise moment, as about a third of the vineyard was replanted in 1980 and gradually a proper rotation of new plantations will have to be created – under the previous owners nothing had been done for decades, and the average age of the vines was 70 years, a most unhealthy state of affairs. The wines are already fruity and attractive, but we hope they will gain in depth in future years, depending also on what selections are made. Bonnes Mares from Morey is very limestone influenced, and can appear quite hard and taut when young, full of breed, and opening out with age.

Most of the Premiers Crus are on the northern side of Morey; they share characteristics with the Grands Crus, but lack their richness and staying power, while offering immense flavour and earthy scents. It is said that the taste is of almonds and cherrystones. The straight Morey *appellation* even tips over a little on to the eastern side of the Route Nationale – the wines can be delicious and redolent of red fruits.

A Personal Selection of Morey-St-Denis Producers

Pierre Amiot

Clos de la Roche with vibrant fruit, tastes of plums and lingering flavours.

Bouchard Père & Fils

Their Clos de la Roche is not a domain wine, but they are important buyers of grapes. The wine has finesse and structure, and is somewhat austere when young, which is how it should be.

Domaine Georges Bryczek

Morey-St-Denis from this domain is always highly seductive and full of smokiness and all the red fruits.

Domaine Dujac

A domain run with the greatest intelligence by Jacques Seysses who, not being born Burgundian, perhaps finds it easier to try out innovations in his quest for quality. The Morey-St-Denis Premier Cru is always splendid, strawberries and redcurrants, while the Clos de la Roche has glorious projection of fruit and complexity – farmyards and violets! Sometimes the colours are not deep, but the flavours will overwhelm and there is never excess alcohol. Also fine Clos St-Denis and Bonnes Mares.

Domaine Robert Groffier
Rich and ample Bonnes Mares with the austerity and earthiness that come from the Morey side of the *appellation*.

Domaine Georges Lignier
This domain very often produces the 'essence of the grape' taste – beautiful, clear, breedy wine. The Clos des Ormes is always a fine bottle, full of liquorice flavours, and there is also Clos St-Denis, Clos de la Roche and Bonnes Mares.

Domaine Hubert Lignier
Elegant, textured Clos de la Roche, combining great richness of fruit with distinct minerally spice.

Mommessin/Clos de Tart
Solely owned by the Mommessin family, this *clos* produces remarkable wines. When young, they have a nose of violets, later a fascinating mixture of leather, humus and spices. The taste is redcurrants and vanilla when young (100 percent new barrels are used) and spicy concentration when mature. Only occasionally has there been a certain clumsiness and perhaps an excess of alcohol. These are Burgundies to lay down.

Domaine Ponsot
Clos de la Roche which always needs many years to develop; one-dimensional in youth, but a lovely scent and distinction when mature. Occasionally there has been oxidation, perhaps a bottling fault.

Domaine Georges Roumier
Clos de la Bussière which takes its time to develop as it is all raw fruit when young.

Domaine Armand Rousseau
Charles Rousseau's magic touch rarely deserts him – the wines are brimming with scent and class and luscious fruit. Clos de la Roche which is really superb, especially if given

five to ten years, even in good to moderate vintages, and then swirled in the glass.

Domaine Bernard Serveau

Premier Cru Les Sorbets which needs time in good years, but there is texture to match the framework.

Domaine Comte Georges de Vogüe

See Chambolle-Musigny.

● ○   Chambolle-Musigny

1990 production: **Grand Cru**

Musigny ●   *428   hectolitres*
Musigny ○   *0   hectolitres*
                            (*usually approx 20 hl*)

Chambolle-Musigny
AOC Communale
& Premiers Crus ●   *6,623   hectolitres*

Premiers Crus Bonnes Mares (part), Les Amoureuses, Les Charmes, Les Cras (part), Les Borniques, Les Baudes, Les Plantes, Les Hauts-Doix, Les Châtelots, Les Gruenchers, Les Groseilles, Les Fuées, Les Lavrottes, Derrière-la-Grange, Les Noirots, Les Sentiers, Les Fousselottes, Aux Beaux-Bruns, Les Combottes, Aux Combottes, Les Chabiots, Les Carrières, Aux Echanges (part), La Combe d'Orveaux.

The Grands Crus are Musigny, of which there is a tiny amount of white wine, and Bonnes Mares, 13·7 hectares of which fall in this commune. The vineyards of Chambolle-Musigny lie at between 250 and 300 metres altitude (820–980 feet) on a variety of debris materials, from red alluvial soil to brown limestone. Musigny itself is on an important gradient, varying between 8 and 14 percent, necessitating frequent replacing of earth from the bottom to the top of the slope. The subsoil is white oolite on the upper parts and Comblanchien limestone farther down. There is up to 20 percent pebbles, permeable limestone (giving good drainage and finesse) and some red clay, which gives richness. Musigny is, of course, on the southern, Vougeot side of Chambolle, while Bonnes Mares borders Morey-St-Denis to the north. Les Amoureuses, which lies just below Musigny, has a subsoil which is full of geological faults, so that some of the roots reach a depth of ten metres (33 feet).

The top wines of Chambolle should have supreme scent and lacy delicacy. The light soil should lead to perfume, elegance and 'femininity', rather than Nuits-type power and earthy splendour. The great complexity of the tastes should creep subtly up on you, not knock you for six with a sledgehammer. Of course, the fascinating comparisons are between Musigny and Bonnes Mares, or Musigny and Les Amoureuses, especially when they are made by the same person. Musigny combines a well-constructed framework, underlying body, with enormous subtlety and silky finesse. Bonnes Mares tends to have the more visible body and fat, while Les Amoureuses should be the epitome of elegance. Bonnes Mares has a bouquet which veers entrancingly from violets to the scent of undergrowth, a very Burgundian trait. Overall, in the wines of Chambolle-Musigny, raspberries and spices are often intermingled. The wines should never be robust (if they are, you have reason to be suspicious), but they should have both projected scent and tenacity of flavour.

A Personal Selection of Chambolle–Musigny Producers

Bernard Amiot
Straight Chambolle with all the bouquet and charm which one should get from this *appellation*.
Domaine Barthod–Noëllat
Straight Chambolle and Les Charmes which are floral, spicy and well worth buying.
Château de Chambolle–Musigny/JF Mugnier
Scented, lacy Les Amoureuses, and wonderfully fine-textured Musigny with a glorious 'peacock's tail' finish.
Maison Delaunay
Particularly delicate, refined selections in Les Chabiots.

Domaine Robert Groffier

Perfumed, spicy, elegant Les Amoureuses; the '87 has a remarkable concentration of fruit for the year.

Domaine Alain Hudelot-Noëllat

Straight Chambolle and Les Charmes which can be explosively good, with great breed and long finish. Just occasionally, there has been too rapid oxidation of the wine after opening, which could indicate a bottling problem (sulphur dioxide level too low). Everything else with these wines is absolutely lovely.

Domaine Mugneret-Gibourg/Domaine Georges Mugneret

An amazing '86 Premier Cru Les Feusselottes; classy, delicate and lingering.

Domaine Georges Roumier

Straight Chambolle which is pure fruit and shows great style. There is also a particularly floral Musigny and Bonnes Mares as well as stylish Amoureuses.

Domaine Bernard Serveau

Really excellent Les Chabiots which are infinitely silky. Other producers might learn from this little-vaunted domain.

Domaine des Varoilles

Bonnes Mares which is rich, fat and glossy – exemplary wine which ages in grand style.

Domaine Comte Georges de Vogüé

Les Amoureuses which is floral and sometimes ethereal. On occasions the Musigny is not so very much better, which it should be for the price; at other times, it is magical. Bonnes Mares can combine voluptuousness with backbone. The Musigny Blanc, made from Chardonnay, is good, but the rarity justifies the price more than anything else. However, I do not agree with those who say you could think it was a red wine if blindfolded!

Vougeot

● ○

1990 production:

Grand Cru ●

Clos de Vougeot   1,965 *hectolitres*

Vougeot
    AOC Communale
    & Premiers Crus ●   532 *hectolitres*

Vougeot
    AOC Communale
    & Premiers Crus ○   114 *hectolitres*

Premiers Crus Les Petits Vougeots, Les Cras (part), Clos de la Perrière.

The Grand Cru is Clos de Vougeot, and this can only be red, whereas the modest quantity of Premiers Crus and *appellation* Vougeot wine includes a small amount of white.

The Grand Cru dominates the commune, both by reputation and through its sheer size. It covers 50 hectares and accounts for more than four-fifths of the land under vines in Vougeot. Except for the fact that historically it is a *clos* surrounded by walls, all this land would almost certainly not be classed as Grand Cru, for the soil types and positions on the slope are amazingly disparate. The other drama is that if the Clos were in Bordeaux, it would almost certainly be in the hands of one owner, not of just under 80. The single proprietor could then select the best *cuvées*, from the *real* Grand Cru parts of the Clos, and make a genuine *grand vin*, perhaps creating a second wine for the rest. However, this is not to be.

The Clos lies at an altitude of 240–270 metres (785–885 feet), with a gentle three to four percent gradient. The vineyards go right down to the Route Nationale, making it the only Grand Cru to be so low on the Côte. It is this part that is especially worrying for those who *do* concern themselves about genuine Grand Cru status in Burgundy, because the soil here is deeper, on alluvial deposits, and not particularly well drained. It is impossible to make wines of intrinsic breed from soil of this composition, but it is just that quality which one seeks in a Grand Cru.

The top part of the Clos is on Bathonian oolitic limestone, with a covering of pebbles and little clay. In the middle of the slope it changes to Bajocian limestone with much more clay, but the pebbles help provide good drainage. There is no doubt that to have a hope of an element of real 'class' in your Clos de Vougeot it would be as well to choose proprietors with vineyards in the upper part of the Grand Cru. Unfortunately, however, it is not as simple as that. The hand of man counts, as always, for a great deal, and much also depends on the size of the parcel owned, as vinifying a small amount of wine is always difficult and a certain 'mass' is necessary for really satisfactory results. To this end, people with several plots in various parts of the Clos will put their grapes together to make one *cuvée*. This is sometimes beneficial when all the plots are well placed, but in other cases it 'dilutes' the 'real' Grand Cru plot by mixing it with grapes from a piece of land which would barely merit Premier Cru status in another commune.

Locally the difference between the upper and lower parts of the Clos has always been recognized; apparently, before World War II, there was even talk of taxing the two parts separately, but the idea was not followed through. Certainly, the most reputed *climats* (Musigny de Vougeot and Grand Maupertuis are examples) are in the higher part of the Grand Cru, although judicious blending between complementary plots of land can produce wines of great interest.

Clos de Vougeot should be rich, sometimes even chocolatey, with a powerful background. Some wines have violets on the nose and a liquorice finish, while the very ripe vintages can be redolent of roasted pecans. There should be good 'flesh' and generosity, and a long, long finish. However, the wine should not be 'massive' in the overwhelming sense – no Burgundy should. The aim is to overpower with flavour and texture.

The Premiers Crus share some similarities with Chambolle-Musigny, with finesse and attraction, but without the body of the Clos. The Clos Blanc de Vougeot produces white wines and is in the hands of one owner – for this reason it is difficult to judge if its lack of excitement is due intrinsically to the plot or to the winemaking.

Straight Vougeot does not show style, but can be pleasant – many a beginner has mistaken it for Clos de Vougeot.

A Personal Selection of Vougeot Producers

Domaine Robert Arnoux

Clos de Vougeot of a very high standard, and which does justice to its favoured position in the Clos. Rich, truffley and textured.

Domaine Bertagna

Recent vintages seem to be on the up – really lovely Vougeot Premier Cru, with wonderful bouquet and fruit, and good Clos de la Perrière, with cocoa and chocolate overtones. About half of this vineyard was replanted in the mid-1960s, so it has now 'come of age'.

Domaine Jean Grivot

Clos de Vougeot of fine quality and real Grand Cru character. I have been unlucky with the '80 though.

Domaine Jean Gros

Really superb Clos Vougeot, classic and rich. Impressive.

Domaine Mongeard-Mugneret

Beautifully placed in the Clos, the wines are usually most honourable, although I did find the '79 somewhat clumsy, a characteristic this vintage should not display.

Domaine Daniel Rion & Fils

Clos de Vougeot which can be really good. The excellent '80 was still youthful in 1990.

Domaine Georges Roumier

Beautiful, long-lasting wines worthy of the highest acclaim. I shall always remember the '76, which must be one of the best wines of this slightly neurotic vintage.

Domaine des Varoilles

These are classic Clos Vougeots, big, rich and needing time to develop – a prime example of the improvement in the quality of the wine since the decision to vinify with another owner holding a complementary plot – the 'mass' of wine became more important, and the wine immediately took on body, flesh and 'gloss'.

● Flagey-Echézeaux

1990 production:	Grands Crus	
	Echézeaux	*1,350 hectolitres*
	Grands Echézeaux	*279 hectolitres*

There are no Premiers Crus as such, although the two Grands Crus can be declassified, and the *village* wine from Flagey is sold as Vosne-Romanée. But the glory is in the two Grands Crus. These are really *lieux-dits* which are above Clos de Vougeot and not near the village of Flagey at all. The upper part of Echézeaux is certainly the best section of the vineyard, but the very size and disparity of this large area means that it sometimes does not reach the standard of the more homogeneous Grands Echézeaux.

The rock structure which underpins Echézeaux is immensely complicated, with lower Bathonian and upper Bajocian limestones in constant interplay. The vineyard of Echézeaux is placed very high for a Grand Cru, but the soil has good pebbles, and is deep enough, for the classification to be justified. However, there is great diversity, with excessive limestone in places, but rich clay and brown chalk in others. There is an enormous difference in gradient between the two Grands Crus, with the upper part of Echézeaux between 13 and 14 percent and Grands Echézeaux only three to four percent.

When tasting a number of Echézeaux against Grands Echézeaux, you tend to think that the difference between the two is overstated. As always in Burgundy, the hand of man counts for so much, and I have had many Echézeaux which were better than their grander brother. In principle, Grands Echézeaux should live longer, with the power and structure to outlast the more elegant Echézeaux. But judicious new wood can give both wines body and, as for finesse, that really can be gained or destroyed forever in the fermenting vat. You should find a touch more complexity of bouquet in mature Grands Echézeaux.

A Personal Selection of Flagey-Echézeaux Producers

Maison Joseph Drouhin
Grands Echézeaux and Echézeaux which have always impressed; earthy, spicy, superb and long-finishing.

Domaine René Engel
Grands Echézeaux to covet.

Domaine Henri Jayer
Wonderful unfiltered Echézeaux, which is difficult to resist in comparative youth because of its glossy fruit and structured balance, but you know you should keep it!

Domaine Jacqueline Jayer
Echézeaux of glorious scent and lovely full fruit – chewiness even – but you probably would not keep them as long as those of the above estate. What an exercise in comparison to contemplate for the future!

Domaine Mongeard-Mugneret
Both the Grands Crus are found at this domain, and very fine they are too – not ultimate breed, but big wines.

Domaine Mugneret-Gibourg/Domaine Georges Mugneret
Bang-on Echézeaux: the '89 has bitter cherry flavour in abundance and terrific persistence.

Domaine de la Romanée-Conti
Echézeaux usually matures faster than Grands Echézeaux. Both the '89s are fabulous; the Echézeaux red fruits, the Grands Echézeaux truffley, with more glycerol and fat. Echézeaux '84 is gamey and very good value. Both wines can last very well (Echézeaux '62 drunk recently), if you can resist them young (ie the '82s).

Domaine Robert Sirugue
Remarkable Grands Echézeaux – a small grower to watch.

● Vosne-Romanée

1990 production:	**Grands Crus**		
	Romanée-Conti	58	*hectolitres*
	La Romanée	33	*hectolitres*

La Tâche	*212 hectolitres*
Romanée-St-Vivant	*319 hectolitres*
Richebourg	*282 hectolitres*
Vosne-Romanée AOC Communale & Premiers Crus	*7,107 hectolitres*

Premiers Crus Aux Malconsorts, Les Beaux Monts, Les Suchots, La Grand'Rue (a Grand Cru awaiting ratification), Les Gaudichots, Aux Brûlées, Les Chaumes, Aux Raignots Le Clos des Réas.

There is an element of shared vineyards between Vosne and Flagey-Echézeaux, as the straight *appellation* Vosne-Romanée comes from both communes. But the splendour of Vosne is its Grands Crus, a matchless yardstick by which to measure other great wines from the Côte de Nuits. However, it sets itself a tough task, since now that the potential of these great growths is known, they are also measured against the best that they themselves can do. If we find them lacking, we have every right to say so, just as the producers feel they have every right to charge very high prices.

The Grands Crus are on the middle part of the slope, where the limestone/clay/pebble mixture is at its most balanced. The ideal size of these pebbles, or small broken stones, is between 2 mm and 1 cm in diameter. Their presence facilitates good drainage, and the larger ones store heat during the day and help to stop the temperature descending too far at night. Romanée-Conti has brown chalky soil, with clay and irony content – giving wines of finesse, depth and complexity. Romanée-St-Vivant has far deeper soil, with clay but also rich in limestone. Aux Raignots, above La Romanée, has sandier soil, but the limestone rock is close to the surface, so much so that 25 years ago they used explosives to break it up and prevent chlorosis of the vines.

The degree of slope changes, with La Romanée having a gradient of about 16 percent and Aux Raignots and the top part of Aux Malconsorts between 14 and 15 percent. The lower part of La Tâche is not on such a marked slope, but the pebble/small stone content ensures perfect drainage. The Vosne vineyard goes up to about 350 metres (1,150 feet).

The tasting differences between the five Grands Crus are, naturally, studied at length – decision-making of this sort is one of the least painful parts of the wine business even if it may hurt financially. Romanée-Conti and La Tâche seem to change positions according to the year – in one vintage Romanée-Conti runs away with the honours, in others it is La Tâche which sails straight to the top. What you find in both, in good years, is an explosive array of sensations on the nose and great persistence on the palate. Truffles, undergrowth, wet earth, sheer voluptuous texture and flavour are all hallmarks of these two Grands Crus. There are also extraordinarily rich Richebourgs, velvet come to life, and astonishing La Romanée and Romanée-St-Vivant, but they may not possess quite such a *brutal* amount of aromas and tastes. If you like your senses assailed, these are the wines for you – ascetics stay away. Rubens would have loved them.

La Grand'Rue lies between La Tâche and the Romanée wines, but does not display such depth and breed. As it is in the hands of one owner, it is difficult to say if it has the potential to rise higher – maybe it could. Aux Malconsorts can have great finesse, and Les Suchots and Les Beaux Monts hints of violets. Overall, the top wines of Vosne have an element of *spiciness* which is perhaps unique in Burgundy. It must be that irony, reddish soil. Straight *appellation* Vosne is usually perfumed and elegant – it should not be clumsy and thick. There is often a smell of cocoa and chocolate.

A Personal Selection of Vosne-Romanée Producers

Domaine Robert Arnoux

Romanée-St-Vivant and Les Suchots which mix oak, red fruits and violets – much seems to be going right here.

Bouchard Père & Fils

The family does not own land in the Grand Cru Richebourg, but its selections are absolutely impeccable and I have had very great bottles of this wine.

Domaine Jean Grivot

My tasting notes are somewhat mixed on their Vosne wines – some of the weaker years seem a bit too alcoholic. But there are good wines here.

Domaine Jean Gros

Clos des Réas with a stunning bouquet, a real mouthful of flavour. I always seem to strike lucky with this estate.

Domaine Alain Hudelot-Noëllat

Some formidable wines emerge from this domain, including juicy, fat Les Suchots, Romanée-St-Vivant with a spicy, cocoa nose and a taste of toast – an exotic spice bazaar wine with great length – and incredible, rich, velvety Richebourg. *A ne pas manquer.*

Domaine Jacqueline Jayer

Les Rouges always has a splendid bouquet – I like these wines when the violets come through the alcohol.

Domaine Lamarche

Les Malconsorts can be very good, but it needs time.

Maison Louis Latour

Romanée-St-Vivant Les Quatre Journaux has always been a favourite; some wonderful, flavour-packed wines to keep.

Domaine Manière-Noirot

Les Suchots which is earthy and *sauvage* – lots of spicy *appellation* character. The wines can age well.

Domaine Méo-Camuzet

Rich, scented Les Brûlées, and Cros Parentoux that I feel is Grand Cru quality in fine vintages, so great is its depth of flavour and aromatic complexity. 100 percent new wood makes these wines enticing even when young, for there is always enormous fruit extract as well.

Domaine Moillard-Grivot

Les Malconsorts which has pleased me more than any of their wines, because it has that Vosne minerally taste and balance and is not just 'big'.

Domaine Mongeard–Mugneret

There is a rustic side to these wines, but Les Suchots has spiciness on the nose and definite quality on the palate.

Domaine Daniel Rion & Fils

Patrice Rion does make very good wines, with a wonderful trio of vintages in '88, '89 and '90. The charm is in comparing Les Chaumes with Les Beaux Monts. The Chaumes often has a classier bouquet, but the Beaux Monts is so long and seductive on the palate.

Domaine de la Romanée-Conti

Superlatives abound here, and most of them are justified.
When these wines are on form, they do have that
'something' extra. The '80s and the '82s are very pretty
right now; Richebourg '79 is a recent stunner. Avoid the
'75s (which are no worse than any one else's); the '69s are
good but could have been even better. Romanée-Conti '78,
'66, '61, '55, '53, '52, '29, '28 and '21, all tasted at the
domain, could be the greatest Burgundies ever made. If a
wine could have a soul, it would be a Romanée-Conti. La
Tâche '62 and '52 are of those experiences made in heaven.
Romanée-Conti was replanted in 1947 – previous vintages
were on ungrafted vines – and '52 was the first vintage after
the replanting. The '85s are undoubtedly great, as are the
'88s, '89s and '90s.

Domaine de la SCI du Château de Vosne-Romanée

This estate is owned by the Liger-Belair family, but the
élevage, bottling and distribution is done by Bouchard Père
& Fils. Les Raignots and La Romanée are the wines and
they have the flavour and body to last beautifully.

● ○   # Nuits–St–Georges

1990 production: Nuits–St–Georges
                      AOC Communale
                      & Premiers Crus ●   *13,211 hectolitres*
                      Nuits–St–Georges
                      AOC Communale
                      & Premiers Crus ○   *83 hectolitres*

Premiers Crus (in the commune of Nuits) Les St-Georges, Les
Vaucrains, Les Cailles, Les Porets, Les Pruliers, Les Hauts Pruliers
(part), Aux Murgers, La Richemone, Les Chaboeufs, Les Perrières,
La Roncière, Les Procès, Rue de Chaux, Aux Boudots, Aux Cras,
Aux Chaignots, Aux Thorey (part), Aux Vignes Rondes, Aux
Bousselots, Les Poulettes, Les Crots (part), Les Vallerots (part), Aux
Champs Perdrix (part), Perrière-Noblot (part), Les Damodes

(part), Chaines-Carteaux (part), Aux Argillats. (Premiers Crus in the commune of Prémeaux) Clos de la Maréchale, Clos Arlot, Les Argillières, Les Grandes Vignes, Aux Corvées, Les Forêts, Les Didiers, Aux Perdrix.

Nuits-St-Georges may be the most evocative name in Burgundy. It certainly is for me. A Nuits-St-Georges Les Argillats ensnared me for ever, led me to realize what wine and taste could be, and taught me to link the brain with the senses. It also made me love Burgundy, the whole blend of landscape and people and history. Perhaps most important of all, it helped me to reject wines which do the region no honour.

The top *crus* are on the southern side of Nuits towards Prémeaux, but that should not overshadow those other good vineyards on the northern side towards Vosne-Romanée.

The nuances of taste between the most exciting of the Premiers Crus (which some would class as Grands Crus should there ever be a 'reshuffle') follow the subtle shifts in soil makeup. The overall picture is marl, intermingled with sand and pebbles which have come away from the hard calcareous summit of the slope. Mid-slope is where the silt and scree over marl formula works best, so here lie the best growths. In the Nuits-Prémeaux area, the subsoil is Bathonian limestone with outcrops of Bajocian limestone covered with clay. The two vineyards nearest the outskirts of Nuits, Rue de Chaux and Les Procès, have significant clay content and are also pebbly. La Roncière is on lighter, more gravelly soil, leading to earlier ripening (clay is a cold soil). The subsoil here is composed of a vein of Comblanchien hard limestone. Les Porets and Les Cailles have deep clay soil with few pebbles; Les Perrières is higher with more pebbles. Les St-Georges has more sand in the mixture, less heavy soil than at Les Porets, while Les Vaucrains combines heavy, rich soil with considerable sand and pebbles for balance.

The northern Nuits vineyards veer more to Vosne in soil type. There are outcrops of Bajocian limestone with some alluvial soil. La Richemone has lighter, pebbly soil, while Aux Chaignots possesses more clay with the pebbles – this is further accentuated as you go towards Nuits and the soil becomes heavier. Les Damodes looks towards Vosne in the type of wine it produces. Aux Argillats faces due south, while the general exposure of this area is south-east.

This, then, is the nursery of those great, rich, intoxicating Nuits wines. They have a severe backbone to them, an 'irony' structure and a minerally gaminess which makes no compromises. That is why anodyne, soupy Nuits is a travesty – good Nuits is not merely meant to soothe, it is meant to challenge. Les Vaucrains is the slowest to mature, the most tannic and closed when young, but oh, so majestic when mature. Les St-Georges is the most complete wine, combining finesse with power, positively brambly and multidimensional in bouquet and taste. Les Porets is known for its pure Nuits *goût de terroir*, earthy, irony, wild, but generous and all-enveloping underneath. Les Cailles is more elegant, balanced and rich in texture, while Les Pruliers has strong Nuits character, softening with bottle age. Les Perrières and La Roncière (the proof that blackberries are not just fanciful!) may not have the colour of their neighbours, but make up for that with a touch more delicacy. On the other side of Nuits, there is wonderful flavour, if less breed. Aux Chaignots and Aux Boudots give lovely bottles, wines of body and character. There is less flesh but plenty of olfactory interest in La Richemone and Les Damodes, more subtly Vosne, less sturdily Nuits.

A Personal Selection of Nuits–St-Georges Producers

Domaine de l'Arlot
Premier Cru Clos des Forêts '89 with lots of earthy fruit, and an '89 white Nuits–St-Georges Premier Cru Clos de l'Arlot of beautiful, fresh nuttiness.

Domaine Robert Chevillon
Les Vaucrains and Les Cailles which usually match up to your expectations (if not your dreams) of Nuits, with strong black cherries and structure.

Domaine Faiveley
It is sometimes quite difficult to spot the difference between a Faiveley domain wine and one from their important *négoce* business, as the word 'Domaine' does not actually appear on the label. But Clos de la Maréchale, Premier Cru, is solely owned by the Faiveley family and is a cornerstone of their extensive estate. The wine is always powerful,

occasionally a touch too alcoholic, but loaded with Nuits character and earthy flavour.

Domaine Henri Gouges

A visit to the Gouges cellars is a liquid lesson in how this *appellation* should taste. Rich and fruity Les Pruliers, earthy, enveloping Clos des Porets, deep, tannic Les Vaucrains, and sublime Les St-Georges. There is also the strong and forceful white La Perrière, made from a white mutation of the Pinot Noir and not at all like Chardonnay.

Château Gris

Owned by a shipper, Lupé-Cholet, Château Gris is not a Grand Cru, as it says on the label (there are none in Nuits), but an enclave in the Premier Cru Les Crots. There are impressive bottles – recent vintages are marked by new wood in youth and promise well.

Domaine Jean Grivot

Linked to Domaine Jacqueline Jayer inasmuch as Etienne Grivot, the son of Jean, has been doing the winemaking for both since the '82 vintage. Marvellous Lavières (Vosne influenced) and Pruliers which is true Nuits, but I did find the '82 a bit heavy and sweet (extra chaptalization?).

Domaine Henri Jayer

Straight Nuits-St-Georges, unfiltered, with a stunning colour, power and lots of raw fruit; these wines need years.

Domaine Jacqueline Jayer

Straight Nuits-St-Georges of extraordinary quality, where the complexity, concentration and heady bouquet come from a vineyard with a goodly proportion of old vines – a fiftieth is uprooted each year, so there is perfect rotation.

Domaine Machard de Gramont

The wines are always stylish, going for flavour and elegance rather than massive body. The Hauts Pruliers is most successful.

Domaine Alain Michelot

Aux Chaignots which is good and earthy.

Domaine Moillard–Grivot

Clos de Thorey which has minerally Nuits character, vanillin and violets. The alcohol is fairly massive, but in the '83s that is expected – the wines need time.

Domaine Henri Remoriquet
Les Allots which is full of Nuits scent and flavour.
Domaine Daniel Rion
Fine bottles are made here: an earthy yet elegant Nuits-St-Georges Clos des Argillières, and especially the Hauts Pruliers, a strong and muscular wine with a marked minerally character when young, mellowing beautifully with age.

● ○ # Prémeaux

The fate of Prémeaux is inextricably linked with that of Nuits-St-Georges, and the vineyard area is broken down into the following proportions:

Nuits-St-Georges Premiers Crus	42·25	*hectares*
Nuits-St-Georges	11·79	*hectares*
Côte de Nuits-Villages	4·97	*hectares*

There are a large number of *clos* among the Premiers Crus (listed under Nuits-St-Georges). Differences in taste exist between the Premiers Crus, but too often these are difficult to detect, as the style seems to be 'solid *négociant*' rather than subtle and distinctive – these *clos* tend to be monopolies owned by the important *négociant* houses of Nuits. In principle, Clos des Argillières is often the most complete wine, combining structure with elegance – the vineyard is on rock with thin soil. This occurs again at the Clos Arlot, part of which is on a steep slope, whereas the Clos de la Maréchale is practically flat with deeper soil. Aux Corvées is on clay-limestone soil. There are many old vines in the area.

● ○ # Côte de Nuits-Villages

1990 production: Côte de Nuits-Villages ●   7,295 *hectolitres*
Côte de Nuits-Villages ○   125 *hectolitres*

The villages which make up this *appellation* are: Brochon, Comblanchien, Corgoloin, Fixin and Prémeaux (Prissey). Of these, only Fixin can choose to sell its wines either under the name of Fixin itself or Côte de Nuits-Villages. There has long been discussion and political manoeuvre as to whether Marsannay, Couchey and even Chenôve should have the right to the Côte de Nuits-Villages *appellation*, but so far promotion has been resisted. This is a pity, if only because this higher recognition would help to prevent the ever-spreading mushroom growth from Dijon of supermarkets, garages and all the other paraphernalia deemed necessary for comfortable modern living – Pessac in the Graves is under the same threat from the city of Bordeaux.

The wines can be quite blunt and tannic when young, but the graph of development is more rapid than with a better *appellation*, so at three to five years they are usually at their most appealing. The danger is that most Côte de Nuits-Villages is a blend of wines from varying sources, so you can end up with a very neutral brew.

For those interested in marble quarries, and their unsightly tips, they are spread out by the side of the road and up the Côte between Prémeaux and Ladoix. Comblanchien marble is a pink-beige colour. It was used to build the Paris Opéra, the Palais de Justice in Brussels and, more recently, Orly Airport.

● ○   Hautes Côtes de Nuits and Hautes Côtes de Beaune

1990 production:	Hautes Côtes de Beaune	*18,163 hectolitres*
	●	*16,590 hectolitres*
	○	*1,573 hectolitres*
	Hautes Côtes de Nuits	*21,329 hectolitres*
	●	*18,713 hectolitres*
	○	*2,616 hectolitres*

These are the villages which have the right to the Hautes Côtes de Beaune *appellation*: Baubigny, Bouze les Beaune, Cirey les Nolay,

Cormot, Echevronnne, Fussey, La Rochepot, Magny-les-Villers, Mavilly Mandelot, Meloisey, Nantoux, Nolay and Vauchignon. In Saône et Loire, the following villages are included: Change, Créot, Epertully, Paris l'Hôpital and part of Cheilly-les-Maranges, Dezize-les-Maranges and Sampigny-les-Maranges.

Much of this area is plateau. However, between Mavilly Mandelot and La Rochepot, the vineyards are on slopes at an altitude of 350–450 metres (1,170–1,470 feet). As a result, picking on the Hautes Côtes is about a week later than on the Côte d'Or. The geological debris favours vine growing and the slopes face east-south-east, which is very important at such heights. The plateau of Meloisey has brown limestone soil and is well sited for making wines of quality.

These are the villages which have the right to the Hautes Côtes de Nuits *appellation*: Arcénant, Bévy, Chaux, Chévannes, Collonges-les-Bévy, Curtil Vergy, L'Etang Vergy, Magny-les-Villers, Marey-les-Fussey, Messanges, Meuilley, Reule Vergy, Villars Fontaine, Villers-la-Faye.

Some of the best communes are on gentle slopes, sheltered from the west winds; examples are Villers-la-Faye and Magny-les-Villers. At Villers there is deep, brown limestone, which gives quality. It must be said that vineyards hovering round the 400 metre mark (1,300 feet) are at a disadvantage when it comes to consistent quality production, and they need the benefit of the best possible site to compensate for this.

The wines from these two areas have the right to the basic Bourgogne *appellation*; only after tasting can the Hautes Côtes label be awarded.

A Personal Selection of Hautes Côtes Producers

Les Caves des Hautes Côtes Groupement de Producteurs
The cooperative now vinifies about 25 percent of the total production, and the quality is very good. Recently I have been immensely impressed by their wines from the two Hautes Côtes, and consider them some of the best value in Burgundy.

Domaine François Charles

Lovely raspberryish Hautes Côtes de Beaune from Nantoux.

Maison Delaunay

Excellent wines from the family's vineyards and others in the Hautes Côtes de Nuits.

Domaine Guy Dufouleur

Vibrant, fruity Hautes Côtes de Nuits, reminiscent of loganberries.

Domaine Bernard Hudelot/Domaine de Montmain

Splendid Hautes Côtes de Nuits from Villars Fontaine, and good Chardonnay too.

Domaine Lucien Jacob

A leading figure in the Hautes Côtes, with much official clonal experimentation at his estate at Echevronne. He also finds time to make good Hautes Côtes de Beaune (and Savigny too).

Domaine Jean Joliot & Fils

Hautes Côtes de Beaune from Nantoux, with a scent of violets and the fruit and body to be delicious at four to five years old.

Château Mandelot

This is a most agreeable wine, vinified and distributed by Bouchard Père & Fils.

Domaine Naudin

Commendable Hautes Côtes de Nuits from Magny-les-Villers. Also very good Hautes Côtes de Beaune from Henri Naudin-Ferrand.

Domaine Michel Serveau

This grower in La Rochepot makes superb Hautes Côtes de Beaune, gloriously scented and fruity. Exemplary for the *appellation*.

Domaine Thevenot-le Brun & Fils

Hautes Côtes de Nuits Clos du Vignon which is attractive and very easy to drink.

● ○   Pernand-Vergelesses

1990 production:	**Grand Cru** ○	
	Corton-Charlemagne	*2,139 hectolitres*
	Pernand-Vergelesses	
	AOC Communale	
	& Premiers Crus ●	*3,739 hectolitres*
	Pernand-Vergelesses	
	AOC Communale	
	& Premiers Crus ○	*1,518 hectolitres*

Premiers Crus Ile des Hautes Vergelesses, Les Basses Vergelesses, Creux de la Net (part), Les Fichots, Caradeux (part).

This pretty village, in the shadow of the *montagne* of Corton, has rather a schizophrenic existence, sharing as it does the red Grand Cru Corton and the white Grand Cru Corton-Charlemagne with the villages of Aloxe-Corton and Ladoix-Serrigny. Pernand also shares with Aloxe-Corton the currently unused white Grand Cru *appellation* of Charlemagne. The Pernand-Vergelesses side of the great hill of Corton is better suited to producing great white wines than red. The soil here is less ferruginous, with a higher limestone content in the marl, and a fair idea of what should be planted where on the Corton hill can be obtained by the naked eye – where the soil is redder, it should be Pinot Noir, where it is more chalky white, the Chardonnay is unsurpassed. The 'nervy' character of Corton-Charlemagne is undoubtedly due to vine roots going down into the rock to a depth of 2 metres (7 feet) or more, with slight differences in the ultimate taste according to whether the soil is blue or white marl, the former a touch richer and more perfumed, the latter more dry and flinty. The best site is farther away from the village, facing south–south-west. Les Vergelesses comes from soil with about one-third clay in its content, leading to firmer red wines than those of lesser *crus*.

Corton-Charlemagne is probably the slowest to mature of all Burgundian white wines, and it is nearly always drunk too young. With bottle-age, its great bouquet, often slightly peppery in youth, turns to grilled almonds and cinnamon. There is a tautness about top Corton-Charlemagne which is not found in the richer, more unctuous Le Montrachet. White Pernand-Vergelesses is, naturally, much softer and should be drunk relatively young. Red Corton is, of course, a *vin de garde* to rival the Grands Crus of the Côte de Nuits, but red Pernand-Vergelesses at Premier Cru level is much softer, more seductive, with its bouquet of raspberries and violets, sometimes with a taste of quince jelly on the palate. Together with Savigny-lès-Beaune, these are the *prettiest* wines of the Côte de Baune. Straight *village* Pernand is more earthy and less charming, even harsh in some years, but usually good value. Pernand has long made a speciality of its Aligoté, planted on marly, well-sited slopes which give it a round, full taste.

A Personal Selection of Pernand-Vergelesses Producers

Domaine Besancenot-Mathouillet
Picked later than his Beaune wines of the domain (vines on the slopes need longer to attain ripeness), there is sometimes an earthiness in the taste, but a good deal of fruit too.

Domaine Bonneau du Martray
Lying at the very heart of Pernand-Vergelesses and Aloxe-Corton, and probably the original estate of the Emperor Charlemagne, this is a remarkable domain with fabulous Corton-Charlemagne. They even make stunning wine in medium-quality years.

Chanson Père & Fils
Excellent Les Basses Vergelesses, floral and redolent of violets.

Maurice Chapuis
Delicious Corton-Charlemagne, not as long-lived as some.

Maison Delaunay
The company makes particularly good selections from Les Basses Vergelesses.

Domaine P Dubreuil-Fontaine Père & Fils
The red Clos Berthet is perfumed and tempting at four to five years; the white is absolutely lovely at two to four years. A delicious pair.

Domaine Jacques Germain

François Germain makes superb white Pernand, all rich cinnamon and honey. Utterly delicious.

Domaine Michel Juillot

Michel Juillot's first vintage of Corton-Charlemagne – from vines *en fermage* – was in 1986. This is a beautifully scented, taut and concentrated wine of authority and length. Worth seeking out.

Domaine Laleure-Piot

This domain is really a white wine specialist, including very good Aligoté; but this should not denigrate the reds.

Domaine Louis Latour

Consistently fine Ile des Vergelesses, often violets and strawberries. Exemplary Corton-Charlemagne, built to last.

Domaine Michel Voarick

Quite big for Pernand-Vergelesses, with the taste often better than the bouquet – nice texture and flavour of cherries.

● ○   Ladoix-Serrigny

1990 production:	Ladoix-Serrigny AOC Communale & Premiers Crus ●	3,527 *hectolitres*
	Ladoix-Serrigny AOC Communale & Premiers Crus ○	495 *hectolitres*

Premiers Crus La Micaude, La Corvée, Le Clou d'Orge, Les Joyeuses, Bois Roussot, Basses Mourettes and Hautes Mourettes.

The *appellation* name is really that of two villages, of which Ladoix is more important viticulturally. With Pernand-Vergelesses, it marks the northern end of the Côte de Beaune. This is another of Burgundy's schizophrenic *appellations*, because much of its production can be classified as Grand and Premier Cru Aloxe-Corton, and it is rare to see Ladoix-Serrigny on a label. This wine is more often than not declassified into Côte de Beaune-Villages.

Brown limestone soils are suitable for the production of red wines, whereas white marl is better for the Chardonnay. Gréchons and Les Fautrières, facing east-south-east and high up on the slope, produce good white wines.

The best-placed *climats* of Ladoix provide wines of body and character, derived from microclimate and a favourable position on the slope. Perhaps they are the bridge between the two Côtes. The names to trust are those that make good Aloxe, but there are some terrible 'apologies' for fine Burgundy in this area – overdoses of alcohol seem rampant. The **Domaine Chevalier** makes honourable Ladoix, with the bouquet perhaps even better than the taste.

● ○   Aloxe-Corton

1990 production:	**Grand Cru**	
	Corton ●	*3,707 hectolitres*
	Corton ○	*57 hectolitres*
	Aloxe-Corton AOC Communale & Premiers Crus ●	*5,735 hectolitres*
	Aloxe-Corton AOC Communale & Premiers Crus ○	*30 hectolitres*

Premiers Crus (in the commune of Ladoix-Serrigny) Les Maréchaudes, La Toppe au Vert, La Coutière, Les Grandes Lolières, Les Petites Lolières, Basses Mourettes. (Premiers Crus in the commune of Aloxe-Corton) Les Valozières (part), Les Chaillots (part), Les Fournières, Les Maréchaudes (part), Les Paulands (part), Les Vercots, Les Guérets.

The small village of Aloxe-Corton nestles beneath the Massif du Corton, with the vines so close to the houses that you would not be surprised to see them creeping through the doorways. The village has a share in the two glittering Grands Crus of Corton and Corton-

Charlemagne, while the Premiers Crus and the straight *village* wine
spill over into Ladoix-Serrigny.

A further elaboration of the *appellation* edicts allows these
vineyards to use the distinguished label Corton: in Ladoix-Serrigny
– Les Vergennes (part), Le Rognet-Corton (part); in Aloxe-Corton
– Le Corton, Le Clos du Roi, Les Renardes, Les Bressandes, Les
Maréchaudes (part), Les Paulands (part), Les Chaumes, La Vigne au
Saint, Les Meix Lallemand, Les Meix (part), Les Combes (part), Le
Charlemagne (part), Les Pougets (part), Les Languettes (part), Les
Chaumes et la Voierosse, Les Fiétres, Les Perrières, Les Grèves; in
Pernand-Vergelesses – Le Charlemagne (part) (red wines only).

The parts of this great bluff reserved for making red Corton are
those where the soil is red and irony, while the white is made from
more calcareous marl. As the base is rock and the soil is poor and
thin, yields are not big. Corton-Bressandes is partly on an old
quarry, always a feature of very hard limestone. Corton-Charlemagne is produced on the top of the hill, where the soil is whiter,
with the Chardonnay planted right up to the Bois de Corton. Of
course, the subsoil has an origin of lava, as can be seen in *crus* such as
Clos du Roi or Les Perrières. In many of the Premiers Crus, such as
Les Maréchaudes, Les Valozières, Les Chaillots, Les Fournières and
Les Vercots the soil is somewhat ferruginous and deeper. The
straight Aloxe-Corton wines come from quite deep, red-brown
soil, with more sand in the subsoil due to an alluvial influence.

These three famous *appellations* are spread over the three
communes as the figures in the table opposite show.

Red Corton is the most powerful, often the most tannic of all the
Côte de Beaune red wines. It needs time for its bouquet to develop
and for a certain youthful hardness to soften. There is almost a
thickness to it, a texture of mouth-coating body and richness.
Corton Clos du Roi is very structured in youth, even quite severe,
but opens out majestically. Corton-Bressandes is rounder and
fatter, with enormous flattering flavour on the palate. Corton-
Renardes is meant to have a *côté animal*, which just might be auto-
suggestion, but there is a raw, gamey side to it, and always punchy
flavour, which is a feature of these top growths. Truffles, too, can be
detected in the top red wines from ripe years.

The Premiers Crus do not have this depth or richness, but some
have finesse and elegance. It is a mistake to 'make' them big when

	Hectares	Ares	Centiares
In Aloxe-Corton:			
Appellation Aloxe-Corton	111	82	
Appellation Aloxe-Corton 1er Cru	29	17	
Appellation Corton	109	64	
Appellation Corton-Charlemagne	45	68	
In Pernand-Vergelesses:			
Appellation Pernand-Vergelesses	136	74	61
Appellation Pernand-Vergelesses 1er Cru	56	51	09
AC Corton, Corton-Charlemagne & Charlemagne	17	25	89
In Ladoix-Serrigny:			
Appellation Ladoix-Serrigny	121		
Appellation Ladoix-Serrigny 1er Cru	14	38	
Appellation Aloxe-Corton 1er Cru	10	76	
Appellation Corton & Corton-Charlemagne	22	42	

that quality is not intrinsically theirs, but there should be a pleasant fullness in good years. After all, a Premier Cru such as Les Valozières is just a path's distance away from Corton-Bressandes. Straight Aloxe-Corton will obviously have less style, but can be a good, generous bottle.

The sheer, flinty glory of Corton-Charlemagne is extolled under Pernand-Vergelesses, and nothing can replace that heady, honeyed bouquet and molten taste. Perhaps there is volcanic richness in it. White Aloxe-Corton is a rarity; the Domaine Senard makes it from the Pinot Beurot (Pinot Gris or Tokay d'Alsace). Planted here, the wine is round, powerful and alcoholic, not at all like Chardonnay.

A Personal Selection of Aloxe-Corton Producers

Domaine Adrien Belland
Corton-Grèves, which seems to have a great future as the wines in extreme youth display such depth of fruit.

Domaine Bonneau du Martray
Often not very deep in colour, this Corton nevertheless shows lovely Pinot Noir character and lingering flavour.

Bouchard Père & Fils/Domaines du Château de Beaune
Majestic Le Corton which can last and last.
Domaine Hubert Bouzereau-Gruère
Corton-Bressandes with a smell of undergrowth and wet
foxes. Oaky vanilla too, and good structure.
Domaine Chandon de Briailles
Corton-Bressandes which can have glorious fruity depth,
but there is something 'hit and miss' with this domain.
Domaine P Dubreuil-Fontaine Père & Fils
Corton-Bressandes and Clos du Roi which do not impress
by their colour but most certainly do by their flavour.
Domaine Michel Gaunoux
Corton-Renardes which is usually very big, strapping wine
– some people think this is bliss, I think it is merely good.
Maison Louis Jadot
Corton-Pougets displays good, juicy fruit, sometimes with
a taste of strawberries. Corton-Bressandes is just as reliable.
Maison Louis Latour
Château Corton-Grancey is the jewel in the crown, and
there are some fine vintages, beautifully gamey and
flavoursome. Sometimes the Corton Clos de la Vigne au
Saint has more finesse and satiny sheen, and there are some
superb bottles. Aloxe-Corton Les Chaillots can taste of
plums.
Domaine Moillard-Grivot
The '83s are massive and would seem to promise well.
Have patience with the Clos du Roi. Corton-Charlemagne
with a nose of mayblossom and cardamom and a texture of
honey – it usually develops far more quickly than that of
Louis Latour.
Domaine Parent
Corton-Renardes with character and a kernel flavour to it.
Domaine Daniel Senard
The Corton Clos des Meix is probably the best wine. Some
successes here, but some disappointments.
Domaine Tollot-Beaut & Fils
Straight Aloxe-Corton which is a very good mouthful.

Château de Corton-André

● ○ Savigny-lès-Beaune

1990 production: Savigny-lès-Beaune
AOC Communale
& Premiers Crus ●   *13,961   hectolitres*
Savigny-lès-Beaune
AOC Communale
& Premiers Crus ○   *973   hectolitres*

Premiers Crus Aux Vergelesses, Bas Marconnets, Les Jarrons (formerly Les Hauts Jarrons and La Dominode), Basses Vergelesses, Les Lavières, Aux Gravains, Les Peuillets (part), Aux Guettes (part), Les Talmettes, Les Charnières, Aux Fourneaux (part), Aux Clous (part), Aux Serpentières (part), Les Narbantons, Les Hauts Marconnets, Les Hauts Jarrons, Redrescut (part), Les Rouvrettes (part), Petits Godeaux (part).

Technically, it should always be Savigny-lès-Beaune, with the accent, as *lès* comes from the Latin *latus*, presumably 'at the side' of Beaune. Savigny is a beautiful Burgundian village, to be glimpsed from the autoroute, but only to be savoured if visited at leisure. After Beaune and Pommard, Savigny produces more red wine than anywhere else on the Côte de Beaune, and although the wines do not have the staying power of the best examples of its rivals in size, there are some exquisite bottles of Savigny.

The village itself is at the entrance to the lovely valley of Fontaine-Froide. The vineyards can be neatly divided into two parts – those on the Pernand-Vergelesses side and those on the Beaune side. The former group forms a broad sweep under the charmingly named wooded summit of the Bois de Noël, facing due south, and including Aux Vergelesses, Les Lavières, Aux Gravains, Aux Serpentières and Aux Guettes. Here the soil is rough and gravelly, with irony oolite above. Below Les Lavières, it is straight *appellation* territory, with reddish-brown limestone, some clay and few pebbles – the drainage is thus less good, the wines a little blunter. On the opposite hillside, on the slopes of Mont Battois, the vineyards include Les Narbantons, Les Jarrons, Les Marconnets and Les Peuillets, facing east-north-east. Here the soil is more sandy and less pebbly, with deeper debris at the foot of the slopes.

The great mark of good Savigny is a heady perfume, a searing scent of violets, raspberries, flowers and red fruits. There is sometimes an enchanting lightness of touch in Savigny, an enticing quality that is particularly seductive when the wines are quite youthful. The wines of the Pernand side, Premiers Crus such as Les Lavières and Aux Guettes, should often be drunk young to see this unforgettable charm, while the Premiers Crus on the Beaune side, Les Narbantons, Bas Marconnets, Les Peuillets and La Dominode are more solid, they have a bit more 'stuffing' and that bouquet might take a few more years to reach its apogee. A great deal depends, as always, on the age of the vineyard. I remember drinking remarkable 20-year-old La Dominode from venerable vines. The rare whites can be charming and floral when drunk young – there is some Pinot Blanc here as well as Chardonnay. It must be nostalgia which causes some producers to retain the Pinot Blanc, as in Burgundy the Chardonnay certainly makes more interesting wine. The Pinot Blanc seems to be at its best in Alsace.

A Personal Selection of Savigny-lès-Beaune Producers

Domaine Simon Bize & Fils
Copybook wines which could provide a valuable lesson to some other producers. The son of the house, Patrick Bize, makes Les Vergelesses, Les Marconnets and Aux Guettes – the latter redolent of violets. These are true, frank, fruity wines – delicious at four to five years old.

Domaine Bruno Clair
Savigny-lès-Beaune La Dominode from a clayey soil, yielding a firm, concentrated, long-lasting wine.

Maison Delaunay
These reputed *commissionnaires en vins* make superb selections in Les Peuillets and Aux Guettes.

Domaine Pierre Guillemot
Outstanding examples of Savigny, including a white which is immensely flowery and enchantingly full of fresh fruit.

Domaine Jean–Marc Pavelot
Straight Savigny and Aux Guettes with real potential for quality.

Domaine Tollot-Beaut
Champ-Chevry with a rich, sweet, old-style Pinot nose, and lovely depth and length on the palate.

● ○   Chorey-lès-Beaune

1990 production: Chorey-lès-Beaune
AOC Communale ●   *6,174 hectolitres*
Chorey-lès-Beaune
AOC Communale ○   *42 hectolitres*

The vineyards of Chorey-lès-Beaune lie on each side of the Route Nationale, but more to the east on a plain of geological debris – the height is only 230 metres (755 feet) and the soil is predominantly alluvial. There are no Premiers Crus, but a few *climats* are recognized. Les Champs-Longs and Pièce du Chapitre are among the best, on sandy alluvial topsoil, strong in iron content and more pebbly on the slope. Les Beaumonts, Les Ratosses, Les Crais and Poirier-Malchaussée are also good sites. Logically, it would seem that Les Beaumonts and Les Ratosses are more Savigny in type, while Les Champs-Longs resembles an Aloxe-Corton from the plain, and Poirier-Malchaussée and Les Crais, on marl, have good structure. Drink relatively young, to enjoy their fruity charm.

The three domains which do honour to Chorey are: **Jacques Germain** of the Château de Chorey, **Tollot-Beaut** and **Tollot-Voarick**. The two brothers at the **Domaine Gay** also make good wine from old vines; less refined and more rustic than the more noted domains, but well worth buying. In fact, the overall value at Chorey is not to be denied. Much of the wine made at Chorey is sold as Côte de Beaune-Villages.

● ○ # Beaune

1990 production:	Beaune AOC Communale & Premiers Crus ●	*17,011*	*hectolitres*
	Beaune AOC Communale & Premiers Crus ○	*1,283*	*hectolitres*

Premiers Crus Les Marconnets, Les Fèves, Les Bressandes, Les Grèves, Les Teurons, Le Clos des Mouches, Champs Pimont, Clos du Roi (part), Au Coucherias (part), En l'Orme, En Genêt, Les Perrières, A l'Ecu, Les Cent Vignes, Les Toussaints, Sur les Grèves, Aux Cras, Le Clos de la Mousse, Les Chouacheux, Les Boucherottes, Les Vignes Franches, Les Aigrots, Pertuisots, Tiélandry or Clos Landry, Les Sizies, Les Avaux, Les Reversées, Le Bas des Teurons, Les Seurey, La Mignotte, Montée-Rouge (part), Les Montrevenots (part), Blanche Fleur (part), Les Epenottes (part), Clos de la Feguine.

To many, Beaune is the hub of Burgundy, and certainly it must feel so to the bevy of historic firms which make up *le négoce beaunois*. It is everything a provincial town should be – a historic and artistic centre, a vibrant market town and an active business community. Wine has made it international and even those who will never visit it utter its name with awe. And yet the remarkable ramparts seem to keep its essential spirit to itself. The summer streets may be crowded with cars bearing foreign numberplates, and for three days each November the Hospices de Beaune Auction is a magnet for both the wine trade and amateur wine-lovers; but for the rest of the year, Beaune is quiet, even sleepy, with everyone battened down in their homes by nightfall. People work hard in Beaune, and wine is a serious business. The Hospices Sale engenders a heady atmosphere of pushing and bustling, lights over the cobbled streets and cafés brimming, but a more typical Beaune scene is to see that same Auction Hall transformed into the Saturday morning market, full of fruit, vegetables, cheese and *charcuterie*.

After having visited the magnificent Hôtel-Dieu, and seen tapestries, flamboyantly tiled roofs and beautiful woodwork, just wander through the streets looking at the fine town houses and the handsome churches. By day you will see the intricate stonework, by night the most lovely buildings and churches are suffused with soft light. This is when Beaune is magical, with the air smoky and cold and your heels on the cobbles the loudest sound in the air. These cobbles hide endless arched cellars, where the liquid wealth of Beaune matures and breathes and the walls blacken with age and humidity.

When stones and architecture hold no more fascination for you, go out into the vineyards, which come right down to the perimeter of Beaune.

The slope of the Beaune vineyards is divided in two by the Route Nationale 470 (the Route de Bouze, which is amusing for English speakers). On the northern side of Beaune, near the border with Savigny, the Autoroute slashes through the top vineyard, Les Marconnets, but apparently the original plan was to route it through Le Montrachet so perhaps we should heave a sigh of relief. The vineyards go up to about 330 metres (1,080 feet) and the soil is basically limestone debris. There are the usual nuances between the *climats*, and even within the *climats* themselves: Le Clos des Mouches, for example, is planted with Chardonnay on the upper part, and Pinot Noir below where the soil is browner and heavier.

There is clay and less gravel in Les Boucherottes and Les Chouacheux, while Les Grèves, naturally, has gravel and faces south-east. Les Bressandes and Les Fèves are on marked slopes, while the thin soil of Les Marconnets, Les Fèves and Clos du Roi, and the fact that the roots have to dig deep, contribute to the wines' longevity.

As a generalization, the Premiers Crus on the northern side of the Montagne de Beaune are the wines which take the longest to mature, while the vineyards to the south of the Route de Bouze are more delicate and show their beauty a little sooner. For instance, in a series of Beaune wines, one might begin with a Clos de la Mousse, go on to Beaune Teurons, then Marconnets, and finally Grèves, which combines finesse with depth. Clos du Roi is usually more robust than Cent Vignes.

Finally, it is often said in a somewhat derogatory manner that the Beaune vineyards are nearly all owned by the Beaune *négociants*, who combine that exacting role with being very important domain proprietors. Personally, the exact social and commercial status of a vineyard owner has never concerned me over-much; it is the quality of the wine in the bottle that counts, and there are many superb Beaune Premiers Crus from these historic owners that have stood the test of time and given much pleasure. Unadorned *village* Beaune is usually straightforward and without complication, produced on deeper soil with more clay, more often susceptible to frost than the Premiers Crus. The whites have an earthy touch and seem best when quite young, when their fruit and flavour are at their apogee, and the reds, too, are sturdy and almost crunchy in youth – drink them at about five years old, and then go on to the Premiers Crus.

A Personal Selection of Beaune Producers

Domaine Robert & Michel Ampeau
Clos du Roi of structure and character.

Domaine Besancenot–Mathouillet
An amazing array of Premiers Crus, including Grèves of finesse, rich Cent-Vignes, robust Theurons, mouth-filling Clos du Roi.

Bouchard Père & Fils/Domaines du Château de Beaune

The largest owner of Beaune Premier Cru vineyards, there is a magnificent range of wines, culminating in their splendid Grèves Vigne de l'Enfant Jésus, a satiny beauty of power and longevity. An excellent introduction to Beaune would be their Beaune du Château, a non-vintage Premier Cru blend in both red and white.

Chanson Père & Fils

Recently I have liked young vintages of Bressandes, Clos du Roi and Grèves, which have all had style and fruit, but my experience of mature bottles has been a little less favourable.

Domaine Joseph Drouhin

Red and white Clos des Mouches of high quality. I have a particular weakness for the white, which is rich and musky, with flesh and a taste of hazelnuts – a wonderful mouthful. There is often more than a hint of cherries in the red wines of Drouhin.

Domaine Jacques Germain

François Germain makes wine of enormous finesse and perfume, from the Château de Chorey, Chorey-lès-Beaune, through to Cent-Vignes, Vignes-Franches and Les Teurons – highly recommended. Look out for the Premier Cru Domaine de Saux.

Domaine Louis Jadot

The Clos des Ursules, an enclave within Les Vignes Franches, is usually a very good, sturdy bottle of Beaune, but I have often found the firm's Theurons and Boucherottes even better.

Domaine Michel Lafarge

Grèves which takes time to develop, but is worth the wait.

Domaine Louis Latour

Vignes Franches which is robust and straightforward when young, developing more complexity and texture with bottle-age.

Domaine Chantal Lescure

Well-made Chouacheux, with character and impact.

Domaine Machard de Gramont

Truly beauteous Les Chouacheux, all raspberries and flavour and impeccable balance.

Domaine Moillard-Grivot
Beaune Les Grèves '83 with a bouquet of liquorice and a taste of cocoa.
Domaine Bernard Morey
Really top-class Les Grèves of robust nature and concentration.
Domaine Parent
Les Epenottes, sometimes 'jammy', but always honourable.
Domaine Tollot-Beaut
Grèves with a wonderful bouquet, the kind that revives memories of past great bottles. There is always body and concentration in these wines, sometimes a dash too much alcohol for sheer perfection, but the standard here is consistently high.

Hospices de Beaune

The Sale of the Hospices' wines is held on the third Sunday of November. It is far too early to give really definite pronouncements on taste, especially in the case of the white wines, which are always shown with a considerable amount of residual sugar, but the date remains immutable. Since the wines are sold for the benefit of the Hospices, in a welter of publicity, and the Burgundians do genuinely feel they are supporting their local charity, prices are artificially high and do not always reflect the real market situation. The Hospices Sale prices tend to increase regardless of the quality of a particular vintage; it therefore follows that is is better value to buy at the Hospices in a good year rather than in a mediocre one. Two recent exceptions to this were in 1986, when there was a 40 percent fall in the average price per *pièce* from 1985, and in 1990, when the fall was 25 percent from the 1989 prices. Whilst worldwide recession partly accounted for the softening of prices for the excellent '90s, in both years there was certainly both a reaction to, and a correction of, the overheated bids for the '85s and '89s.

The *cuvées* produced by the Hospices are named after its benefactors and are nearly all blends of several vineyards in one village. The current list is shown on page 134. There are now three wines from the Côte de Nuits: Mazis-Chambertin Madeleine Collignon, first auctioned in 1977, and two *cuvées* of Clos de la Roche, Georges Kritter and Cyrot-Chaudron, both auctioned for the first time in 1991.

The Sale itself is interminably long – unlike the snappy pace at which business is done at Christie's and Sotheby's in London. Many of the Beaune *négociants* are faithful buyers and often out of *politesse*, I feel, their foreign agents are mentioned as co-buyers.

Monsieur André Porcheret took over the direction of the Hospices wine in 1977, and there was an immense improvement in all aspects of the winemaking during his ten years in the post. M Bruley, who succeeded him in 1987, stayed only until September 1988, since when M Roger Coussy has been in charge. Twenty-two fulltime vignerons are employed in the vineyards, and both vine treatments and the amount of fertilizer put in the ground (dehydrated manure) are strictly controlled. No weedkillers are used and pruning is not over-generous. Wine made from vines under eight years of age is not sold at the Sale but labelled differently under the name Centre Hospitalier. Fermentation is in open wood *cuves*, with regular *pigeage* to keep the skins in contact with the juice, and with the fermentation temperature for each vat now controlled by computer. The wine is subsequently put into 100 percent new wood barrels and the press wine is usually added in its entirety.

So, at the level of the Hospices itself, everything that can possibly be done to achieve quality is set in motion, and the standard of winemaking at present is very high indeed. But, as always, the quality of your Hospices de Beaune wine will depend to a very large extent on the people responsible for its *élevage*, or maturing. They can make or mar a wine. The rule seems to be *always* to find out, in shop or restaurant, who did the *élevage*. Then follow the names you trust: if you do not normally like Maison X's style of wine, do not buy an Hospices wine matured by the same house, because it most certainly will have left its mark on it. All the *cuvées* are either Grand Cru or Premier Cru, with the exception of Pommard *cuvée* Cyrot-Chaudron and Meursault *cuvée* Loppin, which are *village* wines.

Red wines

Appellation	Benefactor's Name	Hectares*
Clos de la Roche	Cyrot-Chaudron	} 0·45 ha
Clos de la Roche	Georges Kritter	
Corton	Charlotte Dumay	3·50 ha
Corton	Docteur Peste	3·00 ha
Pernand-Vergelesses	Rameau-Lamarosse	0·60 ha
Savigny-lès-Beaune	Forneret	1·66 ha
Savigny-lès-Beaune	Fouquerand	1·13 ha
Savigny-lès-Beaune	Arthur Girard	1·18 ha
Beaune	Nicolas Rolin	2·70 ha
Beaune	Guigone de Salins	2·40 ha
Beaune	Clos des Avaux	2·00 ha
Beaune	Brunet	2·37 ha
Beaune	Maurice Drouhin	2·20 ha
Beaune	Hugues & Louis Bétault	2·30 ha
Beaune	Cyrot-Chaudron	n/a
Beaune	Rousseau-Deslandes	2·39 ha
Beaune	Dames Hospitalières	2·49 ha
Pommard	Dames de la Charité	1·59 ha
Pommard	Cyrot-Chaudron	n/a
Pommard	Billardet	1·89 ha
Volnay	Blondeau	1·73 ha
Volnay	Géneral Muteau	1·73 ha
Volnay-Santenots	Jehan de Massol	1·50 ha
Volnay-Santenots	Guavain	1·80 ha
Monthélie	Lebelin	0·88 ha
Auxey-Duresses	Boillot	0·75 ha
Mazis-Chambertin	Madeleine Collignon	1·50 ha

White wines

Corton-Charlemagne	François de Salins	0·25 ha
Corton-Vergennes	Paul Chanson	0·25 ha
Meursault-Genevrières	Baudot	1·41 ha
Meursault-Genevrières	Philippe le Bon	0·60 ha
Meursault-Charmes	de Bahèzre de Lanlay	0·90 ha
Meursault-Charmes	Albert Grivault	0·50 ha

Meursault	Jehan Humblot	0·70 ha
Meursault	Loppin	0·60 ha
Meursault	Goureau	0·86 ha
Bâtard-Montrachet	Dames de Flandres	0·30 ha

★ These figures are very approximate as the actual area of vines used for winemaking may vary considerably according to how and when the parcels are replanted. No wine from vines under eight years old is used in the Hospices de Beaune *cuvées*.

● # Pommard

1990 production: Pommard
AOC Communale
& Premiers Crus   *14,014 hectolitres*

Premiers Crus Les Rugiens Bas, Les Rugiens Hauts (part), Les Grands Epenots, Les Petits Epenots (part), Clos de la Commaraine, Clos Blanc, Les Arvelets, Les Charmots, En Largillière, Les Pézerolles, Les Boucherottes, Les Saussilles, Les Croix Noires, Les Chaponnières, Les Fremiers, Les Bertins, Les Jarolières, Les Poutures, Clos Micot, La Refène, Clos de Verger, La Platière (part), Les Chanlins Bas (part), Les Combes Dessus (part), La Chanière (part).

Pommard can be over-priced and over-alcoholic, but when the best *crus* are made by the most gifted winemakers, they are probably the most exciting wines of the Côte de Beaune. Unfortunately, an easily pronounceable name has given the *appellation* added impetus on some markets and many less scrupulous producers and *négociants* have taken advantage of this fact.

Leaving Beaune to the south, the seeker after Pommard practically falls into its vines. Many of them are somewhat hidden behind strong vineyard walls and there are a number of important *clos* (current law on the use of the word *clos* insists that the named vineyard must be completely surrounded by a wall, unless the *clos* has been known as such for more than one hundred years). With the exception of the Premiers Crus Clos Micot and Les Combes Dessus, all the vineyard between the two roads N74 and N73 is straight *appellation* Pommard. The greatest Premiers Crus, Les Epenots and Les Rugiens, are on either side of the village of Pommard, Les Epenots nearest Beaune and Les Rugiens nearest Volnay. Within Les Epenots, which faces south-south-east, there is the Clos des Epeneaux; also the Clos des Epenots and Le Clos de Citeaux. Les Arvelets, Les Petits Noizons (a *village* wine) and Les Charmots face south, while Les Rugiens Bas is beautifully sited facing south-south-east. The Premiers Crus are mostly mid-slope and the clay-limestone (about 30 percent limestone) is red in colour, becoming very pebbly and white at the top of the *appellation*. Les Rugiens Hauts slopes more and is on a rocky subsoil, while Les Rugiens Bas is on a subsoil of Argovian limestone covered with a thick layer of fine marly-calcareous debris. All this leads to good drainage and wines of excellent colour and structure, more tannic than most wines of the Côte de Beaune. The straight *appellation* Pommard between the two roads has far more clay and is less stony, except for Les Perrières and La Levrière, which are on pebbly debris.

If I had the joyous task of awarding two new Grands Crus to the Côte de Beaune, they would have to be Les Grands Epenots and Les Rugiens Bas. Both have the capacity to age with true grandeur, which is one of the prerequisites for Grand Cru status. Les Rugiens Bas benefits from a superb microclimate which often enables the grapes to attain great ripeness. Here you can feel the power and richness in the wine, with concentration and intense perfume of liquorice and violets, and a colour reminiscent of the glowing red of the earth. Les Epenots also has fine character and construction, often more fruity and less hard in youth than Les Rugiens.

A Personal Selection of Pommard Producers

Robert Ampeau
Straight Pommard of character and flavour.
Domaine Comte Armand
The Clos des Epeneaux, owned in its entirety by Comte Armand, is for those who say that present Burgundy is too light. This wine always takes years to open out, with

power, structure and great flavour.

Domaine Henri Boillot

Les Jarollières with an excellent scent and, in good years, powerful structure – wine with the ability to age.

Domaine de Courcel

Madame de Courcel makes exemplary Epenots, with depth of bouquet and taste, real class, and a flavour of pure red fruits.

Domaine Michel Gaunoux

Grands Epenots which is rich and spicy – the wines always seem to have the body to last, and there are many old bottles to prove it.

Domaine Bernard Glantenay

Even the straight Pommard at this domain is built to last.

Domaine Lejeune

Les Argillières with a deep bouquet of strawberries – the '83 has a tarry, tannic background which needs time to soften. Rugiens of good colour, power, always an excellent mouthful.

Domaine Machard de Gramont

Stylish, elegant Le Clos Blanc.

Domaine de Montille

Stupendous Rugiens, immensely long on the palate, and Pézerolles which is rich in glycerol and fruit. Both are made for keeping – if you can.

Domaine Parent

Elegant, fruity wines, with delicious Pinot Noir character and the flavour of the *appellation*, without perhaps the sheer richness of the very best.

Domaine Pothier-Rieusset

Excellent Epenots, Rugiens and Clos de Verger. The style is luscious fruit backed by firm tannin.

St-Romain

● ○

1990 production: St-Romain
                        AOC Communale ●   *1,969   hectolitres*
                        St-Romain
                        AOC Communale ○   *1,876   hectolitres*

There are no Premiers Crus. This is really a forgotten little village, on a steep slope, and formerly belonging to the Hautes Côtes rather than to the Côte de Beaune. With cliffs and rocks all around, little of the area is planted with vines. The basic soil is calcareous clay with some pebbles. Slightly more red than white wine is produced, although the white has a wider reputation. Certain sites are better suited to the Chardonnay, such as the marly Sous Roches and the chalky Les Jarrons, facing from south-east to west. La Combe Bazin has rather irony red soil at the foot of the slope (above it is always more limestone-marl), Les Poillanges on the opposite slope has roughly the same soil makeup, facing east like the pebbly Sous le Château. The best sites have good sun exposure, protection from wind and lack of humidity.

The red wines have a strong cherry flavour and a certain *goût de terroir*. The whites are fresh and fruity, developing quite quickly, best when they have a sprightly taste and attack.

A Personal Selection of St-Romain Producers

Domaine Alain Gras
Elegant white and good, non-filtered, strong red.
Domaine René Gras Boisson
Delicious red St-Romain, with a nose of crushed violets and a taste of violet creams and redcurrants.
Domaine René Thévenin-Monthélie & Fils
Very commendable white wine, with some style.

● Volnay

1990 production: Volnay
                        AOC Communale
                        & Premiers Crus   *9,900 hectolitres*

Premiers Crus Les Caillerets, Cailleret Dessus, En Champans, En Chevret, Frémiets, Bousse d'Or, La Barre or Clos de la Barre, Clos des Chênes (part), Les Angles, Pointes d'Angles, Les Mitans, En l'Ormeau, Taille Pied, En Verseuil, Carelle sous la Chapelle, Le Ronceret, Carelles Dessous (part), Robardelle (part), Les Lurets (part), Les Aussy (part), Les Brouillards (part), Clos des Ducs, Pitures Dessus, Chanlins (part), Les Santenots (red), Le Village (part).

Volnay has some of the most beautiful old Burgundian houses on the Côte, reassuringly solid with their deep roofs and sense of permanence. However, only about 400 people live here, and most of them seem to be called Rossignol! The village sits proudly above its vineyards which face east and south, with the Premiers Crus situated over a wide variety of soils. Les Santenots, of course, lies in the commune of Meursault, but the Pinot Noir does splendidly on the Bathonian limestone covered with reddish earth and a fair amount of pebbles. Les Caillerets also straddles the two communes, again with reddish soil, pebbly and beautifully sited, with the top part of both En Champans and Cailleret Dessus sitting firmly on a rocky base.

Above them, the Clos des Chênes is on Bathonian limestone, with poor, pebbly soil having difficulty clinging to the marked slope, but benefiting from a beautiful east-south-east position. Taille Pied, Bousse d'Or and the Clos des Ducs are right up against the village, but here the soils are white Argovian limestone.

Les Caillerets is probably the grandest of all Volnays, the most likely to reach a superb old age in ripe years. Although you are never looking for power in Volnay, but rather fragrance and elegance, there can be fine structure in a Caillerets. Clos des Chênes is sometimes more lean than Caillerets, with finesse and a certain tautness when young but, with Champans, ageing well. All can have the Volnay scent of violets and sometimes redcurrants. Taille

Pied will not have the flesh of Caillerets but will be delicate, while flowery Frémiets, in spite of being near Pommard, has the Volnay fragrance. The Clos de la Bousse d'Or has potential for ageing, as does the Clos des Ducs. Santenots can last in bottle exceptionally well, especially from Les Santenots du Milieu.

A Personal Selection of Volnay Producers

Domaine Marquis d'Angerville
These wines rarely have much colour or power in evidence, but Clos des Ducs and Champans from good years can age with elegance. In smaller years, the wines are sometimes swamped by oak. At their best ('85s for example), the essence of elegant Volnay.

Bouchard Père & Fils/Domaines du Château de Beaune
Superb Volnay Caillerets Ancienne Cuvée Carnot, with structure and fruit, and scented Frémiets; Clos de la Rougeotte with breed rather than power – just as this wine should be.

Domaine Bernard Glantenay
Beautifully structured wines, at least from ripe years – they need time.

Domaine Michel Lafarge
Clos des Chênes which is all satin and silk, showing the *charm* of Volnay, but with good depth of fruit.

Domaine des Comtes Lafon
Volnay Santenots du Milieu of concentration and breed, which develops outstandingly in bottle.

Domaine de Montille
Maître Hubert de Montille is almost a sorcerer among winemakers – the tastes he conjures out of the vine! Floral Taillepieds, Mitans (young vines) tasting of cloves and chocolate, and brilliant, complex, long-lasting Champans with its bouquet of roses. The wines of Maître de Montille are the living, breathing example that excessive alcohol is not necessary to make superlative Burgundy – he prefers 12·1 to 13 percent.

Domaine de la Pousse d'Or
Gérard Potel makes satiny wines, full of fruit and flavour, especially the Caillerets Dessus Clos des 60 Ouvrées and Clos de la Bousse d'Or. He even makes a success of less propitious years, with only the '82s perhaps not quite of the same high standard.

Domaine Régis Rossignol–Changarnier
Straight Volnay and Les Brouillards with lovely vibrant, vivid fruit; real breed and violets in the latter.

● ○ # Monthélie

1990 production:	Monthélie		
	AOC Communale		
	& Premiers Crus ●	*4,738*	*hectolitres*
	Monthélie		
	AOC Communale		
	& Premiers Crus ○	*210*	*hectolitres*

Premiers Crus Sur La Velle, Les Vignes Rondes, Le Meix Bataille, Les Riottes, La Taupine, Le Clos Gauthey, Le Château-Gaillard, Les Champs Fulliot, Le Cas Rougeot, Les Duresses (part).

Monthélie is really the forgotten little sister of Volnay, sharing many of this *appellation*'s characteristics but in more muted form. The span of life is shorter, and Monthélies are generally at their most delectable when relatively young. Sandwiched between Volnay and Meursault, Monthélie is another lovely Burgundian village, with old stone houses flanking the sloping streets. The vines, too, are on the slopes above Meursault, and it is only comparatively recently that the wines of Monthélie have had an identity completely their own. The *appellation* is virtually all red wines – white wines can be made, but they have a tendency to maderize easily, and the growers feel that this is best left to Meursault next door.

There are, in fact, two distinct viticultural areas at Monthélie: the Coteau de Volnay, above the village, where the Premiers Crus are found – the vineyards face south or south-east, on Bathonian limestone, with reddish earth and marl on the summit; and the Vallée d'Auxey-Duresses, at the foot of the village along the north-south valley, with the vines thus facing west and east, and white Argovian limestone soil.

Good Monthélie, like Volnay, can have a tempting, scented bouquet and a sheen on the texture. It should never be heavy-weight, but the best sites produce wines of good structure. It is generally considered that the wines from the Coteau de Volnay have more finesse than those from the Coteau de la Vallée d'Auxey, where the wines can be broader. The Premiers Crus certainly have character, and when they have the balance, they can age well too.

A Personal Selection of Monthélie Producers

Château de Monthélie
M Robert de Suremain sells his red Monthélie under the *château* name and over the years it has proved to be the best of the *appellation*.

Ropiteau Frères
There have been good Les Champs Fulliot from this domain and a Duresses had a delicate nose, but too much apparent alcohol on the palate.

● ○ # Blagny

1990 production:	Blagny		
	AOC Communale ●	*241*	*hectolitres*
	Blagny		
	AOC Communale ○		*negligible*

This little village, squeezed in between Puligny-Montrachet and Meursault, has always posed a problem for the legislators, but the essential fact is that the *appellation* is for red wine only, although wine of both colours is made. White wine from the *climats* of La Pièce sous le Bois, La Jeunelotte and Sous le Dos d'Ane can be called

Meursault Premier Cru, but red wine would be Blagny Premier Cru. White wine made from the *climats* of Sous le Puits, La Garenne, Hameau de Blagny and Le Trézin can be called Puligny-Montrachet, but the red must be Blagny.

Red Blagny has a very distinctive taste, slightly earthy, slightly gamey. It can really 'attack' the palate when young, but it is this very lack of neutrality which is so alluring. White wine from Blagny is usually very fruity, very accessible – good value in restaurants, as it shows that someone has had the courage to leave the better-known *climats* of Meursault and Puligny, and you thus pay for a delicious taste rather than an overworked name. As for recommended producers, they are those who make their wine well in the neighbouring two *appellations*.

● ○   Auxey-Duresses

1990 production:	Auxey-Duresses		
	AOC Communale		
	& Premiers Crus ●	*4,505*	*hectolitres*
	Auxey-Duresses		
	AOC Communale		
	& Premiers Crus ○	*1,691*	*hectolitres*

Premiers Crus Les Duresses, Bas des Duresses, Reugne, Les Grands-Champs, Climat du Val, known as Clos du Val (part), Les Ecusseaux (part), Les Bréterins.

Auxey-Duresses is tucked in behind Monthélie, in a fertile valley at the foot of Mont Melian, and surrounded by slopes covered with vines. The *appellation* produces about one-third white wine to two-thirds red, but the areas of their production are quite well divided, with the white coming from the Coteaux du Mont Melian, an extension of Meursault and Puligny, and the red from the Montagne du Bourdon, an extension of Monthélie and Volnay. Les Duresses, on the Montagne du Bourdon, sits on a very pebbly marly-calcareous base, with more soil at the foot of the slope than on the top. It faces east and south-east. La Chapelle is very similar to

Duresses, with a little more marl than calcareous matter. The Clos du Val is magnificently situated facing due south, very calcareous, with more marl and pebbles than Les Duresses and La Chapelle and very little soil on the upper slopes. The soil on the Montagne du Mont Melian is even thinner, far better suited to making white wine than red.

Les Duresses produces fruity wine with some finesse, with notes of raspberry and good colour. La Chapelle can have more body and take longer to develop, with Clos du Val more powerful still, both leaning towards cassis. White Auxey has a lovely biscuity flavour, but should be drunk relatively young – its development is quicker than that of a Meursault.

A Personal Selection of Auxey-Duresses Producers

Robert Ampeau
> Soft, warmly earthy red wine, fruitily charming when young.

Bouchard Père & Fils
> White Auxey of pedigree – gloriously biscuity when young.

Domaine Jean-Pierre Diconne
> Wood is very evident in both red and white wines, with Les Duresses therefore needing some time to emerge from the ageing. The white Auxey is lanolin-smooth and very rich – drink young when the pleasure is at its optimum.

Domaine Alain Gras
> Very reliable red. He also vinifies for René Gras, and there is a good, mild white Auxey under this label.

Charles Jobard
> Les Ecusseaux was certainly very tannic and alcoholic, but this could be the '83 style rather than the *appellation*. Bouquet of minty earth and redcurrants.

Domaine Leroy
> The headquarters of the Leroy empire, but they also own vineyards in Auxey. The wines are always big and long-lasting.

Domaine du Duc de Magenta
Fine white wine, and usually good red.
Domaine Michel Prunier
Good white which is full of character; and supple, flavoury
red Clos du Val with real class.

○ ● # Meursault

1990 production:	Meursault AOC Communale	
	& Premiers Crus ○	*19,685 hectolitres*
	Meursault AOC Communale	
	& Premiers Crus ●	*891 hectolitres*

Premiers Crus (red and white wines) Les Cras (part), Les Caillerets
(part), Les Charmes-Dessus, Les Charmes-Dessous, Les Perrières
Dessus (part), Aux Perrières, Les Perrières Dessous (part), Les
Chaumes des Perrières (part), Les Genevrières Dessus, Les Chaumes
de Narvaux (part), Le Poruzot Dessus, Les Poruzots Dessous, Les
Genevrières Dessous, Les Bouchères (part), Les Gouttes d'Or, Le
Poruzot (part). (White wines) Les Santenots Blancs, Les Plures
(part), Les Santenots du Milieu, La Jeunelotte, La Pièce sous le Bois
(part), Sous le Dos d'Ane (part), Sous Blagny (the last four in the
commune of Blagny).

When the Santenots are planted with Pinot Noir, the wines are
called Volnay-Santenots, but the two hectares which are planted to
Chardonnay are called Meursault-Santenots.
   Many people's image of the perfect white burgundy is based on
their tasting impressions of Meursault. It usually has an imposing
bouquet, slightly nutty with overtones of cinnamon, and strong,
persistent flavour. The best wines are also rich and fat with a long
finish, all of which adds up to happy memories. The 'village' itself is
large and prosperous, a real county town, dominated by a tall and
elegant church spire. Many of the Premiers Crus may produce both
red and white wines, but the vast majority have opted for white.

The first slope of Meursault at the Combe de St-Aubin is of Bathonian limestone, while calcareous marl and pure marl dominate the middle part of the vineyard area, and there is a good deal of debris on the upper part of the slope. On the Blagny-Meursault side, there is brown calcareous soil over Callovian limestone, as well as white Argovian marly limestone. The vineyard rises to 300 metres (984 feet), with its south-east facing position giving a microclimate that is very favourable to quality. There is no doubt that the worldwide demand for white wine has led to some planting of the Chardonnay on parcels which are better suited to making red wines, and these are probably the heavy Meursaults without finesse.

Les Perrières could be considered as the Meursault which has the most class and refinement, particularly from Les Perrières Dessus, where the vines frequently attain great ripeness, giving power, but the rock base of the site gives the distinguished nose. A tiny path separates Les Perrières from Les Genevrières, which also has its partisans. Elegant, scented, with the real bouquet of hazelnuts, Genevrières produces immensely pretty and seductive wines. Les Poruzots is solid with a flinty nose, with excellent keeping potential, while Les Gouttes d'Or, as the name suggests, has a lovely golden colour and great capacity for ageing – robust rather than delicate. The steep slope compensates for the less well-exposed site. Les Charmes is at its best from Les Charmes-Dessus (which includes the middle part of the slope), while Les Charmes-Dessous is on deeper soil, with lovely round, fruity qualities.

A Personal Selection of Meursault Producers

Robert Ampeau
> Superb Perrières and Charmes, which last beautifully in bottle. Also good Blagny La Pièce sous le Bois.

Domaine Jean-François Coche Dury
> Perrières of glorious lanolin texture and true breed. But all the wines are marked by the master's touch.

Maison Jean Germain/Domaine Darnat
> Extremely reliable wines, made by an experienced and careful winemaker. Clos Richemont from Domaine Darnat

now comes under this *négociant*'s selection.

Domaine Albert Grivault

Refined, subtle, flinty Perrières, and Clos des Perrières (from the very heart of the *climat*) that has a hazelnutty bouquet and a long, luscious flavour followed by a splendid *arôme de bouche*.

Domaine des Comtes Lafon

Superb Meursault, from Perrières to Clos de la Barre, beautifully constructed and ageing in bottle to perfection. No filtering here.

Maison Louis Latour

The firm makes splendid selections in straight Meursault, Meursault Château de Blagny and Genevrières.

Domaine du Duc de Magenta

Usually very good and stylish.

Domaine Joseph & Pierre Matrot

Oaky and structured wines, which can age – a '79 Perrières was excellent recently.

Domaine du Château de Meursault

Patriarche owns this beautiful property and the wines are excellent.

Domaine Michelot-Buisson

Terrific wines. Big, rich Charmes – everybody's idea of fine Meursault – and Genevrières to die for.

Domaine Jean Monnier & Fils

Wines of elegance and finesse, including delightful Genevrières.

Domaine Guy Roulot

Excellent wines continue to be made by Guy Roulot's son Jean-Marc, with velvety Charmes and fat Perrières. The Tessons makes the bridge between a straight *village* wine and the Premiers Crus.

● ○   # St-Aubin

1990 production: St-Aubin
                         AOC Communale
                         & Premiers Crus ●   *3,081 hectolitres*
                         St-Aubin
                         AOC Communale
                         & Premiers Crus ○   *2,739 hectolitres*

Premiers Crus The situation is extremely complicated, with 16 *climats* encompassing 29 *lieux-dits*. In practice, several *lieux-dits* are grouped together under the same Premier Cru, the most frequently used being: La Chatenière, En Remilly, Les Murgers des Dents de Chien, Les Champlots, Le Charmois, Le Village, Les Castets, Sur le Sentier du Clou, Les Cortons, Les Frionnes, Sous Roche Dumay, Les Perrières.

Perhaps this is one of the 'undiscovered' gems of Burgundy, since the growers here seem to be particularly conscientious and the wines uniformly good. Recent tastings have produced extremely few disappointments and many delectable bottles, at prices which are not as exorbitant as other parts of the Côte d'Or. St-Aubin is a tiny village behind Puligny-Montrachet and Meursault, near the hamlet of Gamay, with the vineyards facing in all directions from south-east to south-west. The soils vary, as there are really two distinct parts of St-Aubin: the vineyards below Gamay on the Roche du May, which is the end of the Côte d'Or slope; and those on the Montagne du Ban which runs westwards. Here, the steep slopes contain much limestone, affecting Premiers Crus such as Frionnes, Sentier du Clou and Castets, while the Roche du May, Champlots, La Chatenière, Sous Roche Dumay and Dents de Chien (where but Burgundy would you find such names?) are on marl covered by calcareous debris and brown clay and chalk.

It is not deleterious to St-Aubin to say that its wines are slightly lighter, fresher versions of grander *appellations*. The reds can resemble Chassagne-Montrachet, with less body, and the whites veer more towards Puligny than Meursault, with less intense perfume and fat. I have found that many of the reds have a taste of strawberries, and there are inevitable nuances between the Premiers

Crus – Sous Roche Dumay tends to have more body and tannin in youth, while the limestone of Les Castets gives finesse. The best whites often come from La Chatenière and Les Murgers des Dents de Chien. Here, the hazelnuts bouquet is very marked.

A Personal Selection of St-Aubin Producers

Domaine Jean-Claude Bachelet
Delicate whites, redolent of hazelnuts and mayblossom.

Domaine Raoul Clerget
This is the big name in St-Aubin and the Clerget family have done much for the *appellation*. The domain makes wonderful Frionnes Blanc, with fruit, balance and breed, while the white wines of Raoul Clerget, *négociant-éleveur*, are consistently fine. Their white Domaine du Pimont le Charmois is good, floral and oaky. The red wines tend to have lengthy barrel-ageing.

Domaine Marc Colin
White La Chatenière, aromatic; with a taste of rose petals.

Maison Louis Jadot
Has good, white St-Aubin.

Domaine Michel Lamanthe
I have liked the full, nutty white wine, but have been more dubious about a bitter taste in a red.

Hubert Lamy
Excellent red Castets, built to last, while the white Frionnes mixes acacia with oak in a very stylish way.

Domaine Aimé Langoureau
Gilles Bouton, the grandson, makes white En Remilly which is rich and oaky, in a rather broad style.

Domaine André Moingeon
Pretty red wine, for relatively young drinking.

Domaine Henri Prudhon & Fils/Gérard Prudhon
Les Frionnes with a clear strawberry Pinot bouquet, a gently earthy flavour and very nice aromatic persistence.

Domaine Roux Père & Fils
Meticulous winemaking produces lovely whites of finesse, especially La Chatenière, and cherryish reds.

○ ● Puligny-Montrachet

1990 production:	**Grands Crus** ○		
	Le Montrachet	*522*	*hectolitres*
	Bâtard-Montrachet	*472*	*hectolitres*
	Bienvenues-Bâtard- Montrachet	*186*	*hectolitres*
	Chevalier- Montrachet	*221*	*hectolitres*

	Puligny-Montrachet
	  AOC Communale
	  & Premiers Crus ○
		11,445	*hectolitres*

	Puligny-Montrachet
	  AOC Communale
	  & Premiers Crus ●
		179	*hectolitres*

Premiers Crus Le Cailleret, Les Combettes, Les Pucelles, Les Folatières (part), Clavoillon, Le Champ Canet, Les Chalumeaux (part), Les Referts, Sous le Puits, La Garenne, Hameau de Blagny.

An innocent visitor to Puligny-Montrachet would never believe that it is the centre of what many would call the greatest dry white wines of the world. There are days when even the proverbial dog does not bark to break the silence. It is another of those slightly schizophrenic communes in Burgundy, rivalling Aloxe-Corton and Pernand-Vergelesses, because some of its most famous Grands Crus are shared with the neighbouring village of Chassagne-Montrachet. Chevalier-Montrachet and Bienvenues-Bâtard-Montrachet are entirely within the boundaries of Puligny-Montrachet, but Le Montrachet and Bâtard-Montrachet share their favours with Chassagne-Montrachet, whereas Les Criots lies entirely within Chassagne-Montrachet.

These fabled Grands Crus are the result of perfect microclimates, so sheltered and positioned on the slopes that they frequently give very ripe grapes, whereas elsewhere the sugar levels might be only adequate. Le Montrachet lies on a base of hard Bathonian limestone covered by debris, with an iron-oxide content. Chevalier-Montrachet is on Bajocian marly limestone, and Bâtard-Montrachet is composed of brown limestone rich in gravel. Bienvenues-Bâtard-Montrachet is virtually an enclave within Bâtard-Montrachet, with the same soil and facing east-south-east. Chevalier-Montrachet has a more marked slope, situated above Le Montrachet. The lower part of Le Montrachet has slightly deeper soil.

The sheer imposing glamour of the Grands Crus should not cause us to forget the Premiers Crus, which are of remarkable beauty at Puligny-Montrachet. Les Combettes is on pure rock with very thin soil, except where there are faults in the rock which allow the depth of the soil to jump from a matter of centimetres to metres. Les Referts and Clavoillon have very similar soil, while Les Folatières is on a more marked slope, with white limestone debris near the top; there is always the risk of erosion here. Le Cailleret shares many characteristics with Le Montrachet, but it is more pebbly and the orientation is not quite as good as for the Grand Cru. The Premiers Crus are divided from the *village* wines by the Sentier de Couches, which continues into Chassagne and Santenay.

In Puligny, the cellars cannot be built underground, as is usually the case in Burgundy, because of the relatively high water table.

So, what is all the fuss about? Why are Le Montrachet and its satellites 'the best'? Without doubt, if you drink any of these wines too young, particularly Le Montrachet, you will ask yourself this very question. The bouquet, particularly, takes time to develop, and it is really a vinous crime to drink Le Montrachet at under ten years of age. The colour begins as greenish yellow and deepens to a splendid gold in bottle, while with the years the taste gains in depth and complexity. Honey, almonds, hawthorn and great textured richness are all found in Le Montrachet, provided the wine is served at no less than $13°C$ (about $55°F$), which is perfect cellar temperature, and not refrigerator frozen.

There are those who would put Chevalier-Montrachet next in the hierarchy, followed by Bâtard, Bienvenues and Criots. Certainly I have had stupendous Chevalier, sometimes even surpassing Le Montrachet, for the hand of the winemaker counts just as much in this hallowed ground as anywhere else in Burgundy. The first two wines, particularly, need nearly as long to develop as Le Montrachet, and all are rich and mouth-filling. White Burgundy of this rank is almost a food as well as a wine, it is so multidimensional and nutritious, powerful and fleshy.

Among the Premiers Crus, Les Pucelles usually develops more slowly than Les Combettes, which can be soft in some years, less *nerveux* than other Premiers Crus. It has a certain hazelnuts quality which makes one think of neighbouring Meursault and is broader in taste than Clavoillon and Les Folatières, which both show great finesse. Le Cailleret has a good deal of body, but Le Champ Canet and Les Chalumeaux are lighter and ready for drinking earlier.

A Personal Selection of Puligny-Montrachet Producers

Robert Ampeau
Les Combettes of great beauty and ability to age.

Domaine Blain-Gagnard
See Chassagne-Montrachet.

Bouchard Père & Fils
Important owners in Le Montrachet (domain wines are always sold under the Domaines du Château de Beaune label), they make long-lasting, rich wine, full of subtle flavour. There is also fine Chevalier-Montrachet within the domain, with the 1983 astoundingly good, the nearest thing to liquid honey that I have ever seen.

Domaine Louis Carillon
Luscious, honeyed Bienvenues-Bâtard-Montrachet; not absolutely top class, but very good.

Maison Joseph Drouhin
This Folatières is not a domain wine, but it is always delicate and acacia-soft.

Maison Louis Jadot
Chevalier-Montrachet Les Demoiselles is shared with Louis Latour, and I always like the non-domain Les Referts.

Domaine Marquis de Laguiche (*Joseph Drouhin*)
The must is sent into Beaune for Drouhin to do the vinifying, *élevage*, bottling and selling. Le Montrachet of enormous charm and fruit, balanced and luscious.

Maison Louis Latour
Chevalier-Montrachet Les Demoiselles is positively exotic, rich, oaky and a great keeper. Splendid non-domain Les

Folatières and Les Referts, all almonds and mayblossom.

Domaine Leflaive

Quite simply, this domain makes some of the best white wines in the whole of Burgundy, ergo, the whole of the world. There are few things more pleasant in life than trying to decide with M Vincent Leflaive if his Bienvenues, his Bâtard or his unbelievable Chevalier is reminiscent of hawthorn, blackthorn or mayblossom. At the last attempt, I detected lavender honey in the Chevalier. Then there is floral Les Pucelles, rich Les Combettes, greengages on young Clavoillon and limetree blossom on the straight Puligny. There is always undeniable quality and breed.

Domaine Joseph & Pierre Matrot

Les Chalumeaux with lovely fruit marrying with the oak, sometimes needing bottle-age to 'fatten'.

Domaine Jean-Pierre Monnot

Les Folatières with a smoky, mayblossom nose and smooth breed, generally sold to Louis Latour.

Domaine Pierre Morey

See Chassagne-Montrachet.

Michel Niellon

See Chassagne-Montrachet.

Domaine Paul Pernot

Beautifully crafted Les Folatières with a creamy richness in good vintages, always long and elegant.

Domaine André Ramonet

See Chassagne-Montrachet.

Domaine de la Romanée-Conti

Le Montrachet of great style, simply crying out for bottle-age in order to show its voluptuous paces.

Domaine Etienne Sauzet

Glorious Les Combettes, with a bouquet of woodsmoke and greengages, backed up by oak.

Société Civile du Domaine Thénard

Le Montrachet from this domain is marketed by the firm of Remoissenet and the wine is usually very fine and stylish.

Henri de Villamont

This *négociant* is responsible for some lovely stylish Pucelles, with a smoky nose and oak on the palate.

● ○　Chassagne–Montrachet

1990 production:	**Grand Cru** ○		
	Criots–Bâtard–		
	Montrachet	*71*	*hectolitres*
	Chassagne-Montrachet		
	AOC Communale		
	& Premiers Crus ●	*6,695*	*hectolitres*
	Chassagne-Montrachet		
	AOC Communale		
	& Premiers Crus ○	*8,033*	*hectolitres*

Premiers Crus (red wines) Clos St-Jean (part), Morgeot (part), Morgeot known as Abbaye de Morgeot (part), La Boudriotte (part), La Maltroie (part), Les Chenevottes, Les Champs Gain (part), Les Grandes Ruchottes, La Romanée, Les Brussonnes (part), Les Vergers, Les Macherelles, En Cailleret (part). (White wines) Morgeot (part), Morgeot known as Abbaye de Morgeot (part), La Boudriotte, La Maltroie, Clos St-Jean, Les Chenevottes, Les Champs Gains, Grandes Ruchottes, La Romanée, Les Brussonnes, Les Vergers, Les Macherelles, Chassagne or En Cailleret.

Many of the best wines of Chassagne are made by members of three families – the Gagnards, the Delagranges and the Moreys. It is the second-to-last of the important villages on the Côte de Beaune, with only Santenay to follow. Naturally, the white wines are world famous, but the reds represent very good value and are frequently forgotten in the rush to get a more fashionable name. If the Grands Crus are white, the finest Premier Cru wines are red. The Clos St-Jean, surrounded by walls, possesses very gravelly soil, while Les Vergers, Les Macherelles and Les Chenevottes have red soil, clay with little gravel. Morgeot, the lower part of La Boudriotte, Les Champs Gain and Les Petits Clos are on white marl above and red gravelly earth lower down. The basic subsoil is oolitic limestone, grey, beige and pink and, when it is polished, it looks like marble and makes beautiful flagstones and fireplaces in the local houses. There is still a quarry above Clos St-Jean. Truffles apparently grow on a base of Bathonian limestone debris, on the edge of the vineyards and on uncultivated land, although I have not seen (or eaten) any evidence of this.

There are those who make the distinction between the Puligny part of Montrachet, facing south-east, and the Chassagne part which faces more due south, following the turn of the slope. The Puligny section is meant to have the edge in terms of finesse and sheer distinction, but to my knowledge this has never been proved at some meticulously organized tasting. As always, the hand of man probably makes the difference between fine and divine.

The one Grand Cru lying entirely in Chassagne, tiny Les Criots, has all the body and structure of its fellows. Among the white Premiers Crus, Les Ruchottes, Morgeot, Caillerets, Vignes Blanches and Les Champs Gain tend to have more body, while Les Vergers, Les Macherelles, Les Chenevottes and Les Chaumées are very fragrant and floral. La Boudriotte and Le Morgeot are the two most powerful reds, built for lasting in ripe years, reputed to have a taste of kirsch, and certainly the ground for the analogy with cherries is very detectable. Clos St-Jean often has softer fruit and matures a little earlier – prunes, peaches and violets can all be seen in these wines, while some are earthy in youth.

A Personal Selection of Chassagne-Montrachet Producers

Adrien Belland
Red Morgeot Clos Charreau with a raw, fruity nose redolent of strawberries – young wines only seen, but they should develop prettily.

Domaine Blain-Gagnard
Connected with Delagrange-Bachelet, this is a grandson making honeyed Bâtard, needing time for its full potential to emerge, and white Morgeot of full, robust flavour – both show oak when young.

Société Michel Colin-Deléger
White Les Chaumées '89 (classed as Premier Cru, but one of the *lieux-dits* which usually disappears inside a better-known name) with a glorious honeyed nose – alluring, heavenly. Real '*race*' – *et finesse*.

Domaine Georges Deléger

White Morgeot which is worth finding and, usually, drinking relatively early.

Domaine Fontaine-Gagnard/Domaine Gagnard-Delagrange

White Chassagne-Montrachets which are impressive: oaky, with a bouquet of acacia, mayblossom and woodsmoke leading to a smooth, firm taste. The young red is a mixture of loganberries and wood which promises well.

Domaine Jean-Noël Gagnard

The Bâtard-Montrachet of this brilliant winemaker opened my senses to white Burgundy, many years ago, and for that I shall always be grateful. He is still making stunning wine, rich, explosive of taste and beautiful enough to silence conversation. There is also white Les Caillerets, Morgeot and straight Chassagne, as well as a range of reds – I recommend that you try his Morgeot.

Domaine Bernard Morey

Red Chassagne which has a lovely frank taste of crunchy strawberries. White Les Caillerets often takes a few years to open out, while Les Baudines softens sooner. There is also white Les Embrazées at this domain.

Domaine Pierre Morey

Incredibly good Bâtard-Montrachet, tight at first, then full, rich and toasty.

Michel Niellon

An exemplary array of wines, from Bâtard and Chevalier down to straight Chassagne, all full, fat and strong on aromas and flavour.

Domaine André Ramonet

It is thanks to that great American wine-lover, Bipin Desai, that I tasted the most complete range of Ramonet wines ever shown. There are great whites, even in less fashionable years, ie the exotic '74 Bâtard. The Bâtard '69, '76, '79 and '87 are classics. Le Montrachet '78 and '85 have to be touchstones of the genre, but occasionally I have been shown Ramonet Montrachets which do not bear the stamp of the Grand Cru – mysterious and worrying. Les Ruchottes can be a 'bargain' – the '83 and '86 are amazing.

So are the Bienvenues '82, '83 and '86. I wish I had some Montrachet '88 to lay down, not to mention the Caillerets '89. This is a remarkable family which has created a legend – may they always honour it.

● ○ # Santenay

1990 production:

Santenay AOC Communale & Premiers Crus ●	*13,829*	*hectolitres*
Santenay AOC Communale & Premiers Crus ○	*847*	*hectolitres*

Premiers Crus Les Gravières, Le Clos de Tavannes, La Comme, Beauregard, Passetemps, Beaurepaire, La Maladière, Le Petit Clos Rousseau (part), Le Clos des Mouches, Le Clos Faubard, Le Grand Clos Rousseau.

Coming from the south, this is where the Côte de Beaune begins. Wits say that this is where water and wine meet, since Santenay is also a thermal resort. It is certainly a suitable port of call for those with digestive, liver or gout problems. And where there is a *Station Thermale*, there is always a Casino... The soil is somewhat varied, with the Premiers Crus of La Comme and Les Gravières, on the northern slope of Santenay, having a topsoil of gravel over marly-limestone. Whereas Les Gravières is nearly flat, La Comme and the very pebbly Beauregard are on the side of the slope. The *appellation* is essentially red, but within Les Gravières there is a plot producing white wine, including the very good Clos des Gravières. On the south side of Santenay, the soils are either brown limestone or deep in character, and the wines are inevitably more earthy here.

The red wines of Santenay are often marked by a *goût de terroir* and can be quite tannic and hard in youth with a marked earthy quality. Les Gravières has the greatest finesse, while La Comme is more robust. La Maladière can be elegant and supple and ready for drinking sooner. Violets, chestnuts, strawberries and almonds have all been found on the nose, while the whites can have a youthful bouquet of hazelnuts and ferns.

A Personal Selection of Santenay Producers

Adrien Belland
Good Santenay and even better, robust Santenay Comme.

Domaine Hubert Bouzereau-Gruère
Exemplary Santenay – gamey, 'wet dogs', crushed strawberries.

Château de la Charrière/Jean Girardin
Les Gravières is the top Girardin wine, with very good keeping potential. Straight Santenay too, and from Jacques Girardin.

Domaine Guy Dufouleur
The Clos Genêts of this domain has very good, earthy Santenay character, full but fruity and frank, not over-alcoholic and soupy.

Domaine Lequin-Roussot
A sizeable domain, with a good spread of Premiers Crus. Wines made to last and full of character. There is also a Santenay Blanc. René and Louis Lequin run the domain.

Mestre Père & Fils
Earthy and fruity Santenay Clos Faubard. A large domain, important in the Premiers Crus. Less than half the wine made is domain-bottled.

Domaine Bernard Morey
Superb Grand-Clos-Rousseau, with new wood and sheer finesse.

Domaine de la Pousse d'Or
Clos de Tavannes and Les Gravières which are often the best wines of the *appellation*. The only vintage which seemed not quite up to standard was the '82.

Domaine Prieur-Brunet
Particularly attractive Santenay-Maladière, with just a touch of new wood in the flavour.

Domaine Roux Père & Fils
Santenay made with a St-Aubin hand, and very fruity too!

Domaine de l'Abbaye de Santenay/Louis Clair
The Premier Cru Les Gravières has very good *appellation* character and the domain maintains a high standard.
Domaine St-Michel
A very important domain in the village, with Pierre Maufoux and Michel Gutrin running it jointly, but with the house of Maufoux doing the selling. Maufoux wines are marked with wood. They are strong in alcohol and meant for ageing.

● ○ # Maranges

1990 production: Maranges
                       AOC Communale
                       & Premiers Crus ●   *8,139 hectolitres*
                       Maranges
                       AOC Communale
                       & Premiers Crus ○   *54 hectolitres*

Premiers Crus Le Clos des Rois, Les Clos Roussots, La Fussière, Le Clos de la Boutière, La Crois aux Moines, Le Clos des Loyères.

The Maranges *appellation* was officially recognised on May 23rd 1989. It brings together under one name the wines of Cheilly-les-Maranges, Dezize-les-Maranges and Sampigny-les-Maranges. The *appellation* is immediately to the west of Santenay; indeed it is not officially in the Côte d'Or, but just over the border in Saône et Loire. The vineyards face south and south-east, on well-protected hillsides, and the soil contains a high proportion of Liassic clay. Hence the wines are quite tough and powerful – well-suited to ageing, indeed needing time to mellow.

● ○   Côte de Beaune

1990 production:	Côte de Beaune	
	AOC Communale ●	*532 hectolitres*
	Côte de Beaune	
	AOC Communale ○	*135 hectolitres*

This is really a redundant *appellation*. It covers the area of Beaune itself, as well as the *lieux-dits*: Les Topes-Bizot, Les Pierres Blanches, Les Mondes Rondes, Les Monnières, and La Grande Châtelaine, which is owned by the *négociant* Louis Max.

Worth finding is a white Côte de Beaune from the **Lycée Agricole et Viticole** at Beaune, which owns 4·58 hectares of vineyards and rents another 19·1 hectares, covering a range of *appellations*.

●   Côte de Beaune-Villages

| **1990 production:** | Côte de Beaune- | |
| | Villages | *1,696 hectolitres* |

This *appellation* covers the following 16 villages: Auxey-Duresses, Blagny, Chassagne-Montrachet, Cheilly-les-Maranges, Chorey-lès-Beaune, Dezize-les-Maranges, Ladoix, Meursault, Monthélie, Pernand-Vergelesses, Puligny-Montrachet, St-Aubin, St-Romain, Sampigny-les-Maranges, Santenay, Savigny-lès-Beaune.

All these villages can sell their wine under their own name but, especially in the case of the lesser-known villages or in communes where the white wines are paramount, it is more advantageous to use the Côte de Beaune-Villages label. This is, in fact, an *appellation* mostly sold by the *négociants*, who can make a more satisfactory wine by inter-village blending. There is another option, rarely seen, when the producer puts on the label the name of the village *appellation* followed by the term Côte de Beaune in letters of the same size. The wines can be quite structured and tannic, needing a few years in bottle to soften.

● ○ Côte Chalonnaise

The region known as the Côte Chalonnaise stretches from the valley of the Dheune near Chagny in the north to St-Gengoux-le-National, south-west of Châlon-sur-Saône, in the south. Vines cluster on propitious slopes, but it is by no means an uninterrupted viticultural landscape. The basic soil types are limestone or calcareous clay, although variations between the villages and *appellations* are based more on subtleties of microclimate than of soil. However, the Chardonnay should ideally be planted where there is high limestone content, and the Pinot Noir where there is more clay, as this helps provide stronger colour. Often the calcareous matter has a tendency to fall to the foot of the slopes. The Pinot Noir is the most important grape variety on the Côte Chalonnaise, with 67 percent of the vineyard area, while the Gamay covers 13·5 percent, the Chardonnay 10 percent and the Aligoté 9·5 percent. The best vineyard sites face east, south-east or south, but they can be planted up to a height of 350 metres (1,150 feet), which means later picking than on the Côte d'Or. This, coupled with the fact that it can be slightly cooler here in the summer months than around Dijon, means that in less than perfect years ripeness can be a problem. But when fate is kind, the wines of the Côte Chalonnaise are not just mini-replicas of the Côte d'Or – they have real regional character and a great deal to say for themselves. Given the current price of many wines from the Côte d'Or, they also represent excellent value for money Burgundy.

● ○ Bouzeron

The Aligoté wine produced in this village close to Chagny and Rully had long been appreciated as something exceptional, and in 1979 the *appellation* Bourgogne Aligoté de Bouzeron was created. The wines are often richer, spicier and fuller than elsewhere and make a very worthwhile bottle for those who can be lured away to something less usual. Bouchard Père & Fils own about two-thirds of the vineyard area at Bouzeron and so this wine is quite a speciality of theirs. Other very good domains for Aligoté de Bouzeron are those of Aubert and Pamela de Villaine and the Clos de la Fortune of Chanzy Frères. Delorme, also, are known for their particularly well-made Aligoté.

The Principal Bouzeron Producers

Chanzy Frères/Domaine de l'Hermitage

Bouzeron, 71150 Chagny. 1er Cru: Mercurey Clos du Roy (red and white). Rully (red and white); Mercurey Carabys; Bourgogne Aligoté de Bouzeron: Clos de la Fortune, Les Clous; Bourgogne Clos de la Fortune (red and white).

A range of red and white wines from the Côte Chalonnaise (Mercurey and Rully), but the Bourgogne Aligoté is their best wine, and their basic Bourgogne Clos de la Fortune (red and white) is good.

A & P de Villaine

Bouzeron, 71150 Chagny. 18 ha (2 ha *en métayage*). Rully (white), Bourgogne Aligoté de Bouzeron, Bourgogne Côte Chalonnaise (red and white).

A very well run property, making wines that are an excellent introduction to the tastes of Burgundy. The Aligoté and the Rosé de Pinot Noir are given a very light pressing and are vinified at 21°C maximum in concrete vats but, above all, in large oak *foudres*. The Chardonnay is partly vinified in oak vats and partly in oak barrels. The red wines are vinified in wooden *cuves*, with frequent *pigeages*, and *élevage* in barrels. In years when more concentration is desired, some juice is drawn off to get a better ratio of matter to fermenting must. Prospects look most exciting for the 1990s, with some intelligent experimental wine-making. The '90 Aligoté de Bouzeron is a tiny yield marvel, rich and guava-like.

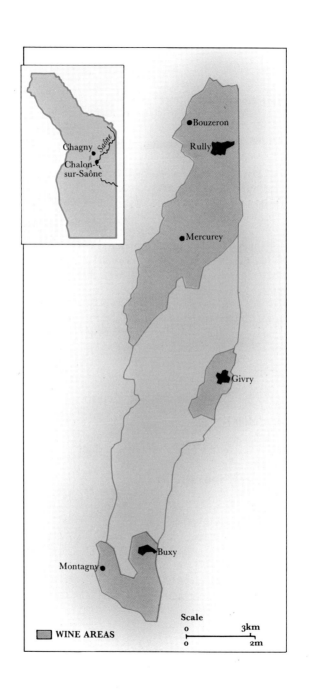

Chagny

Saône

Chalon-
sur-Saône

Bouzeron

Rully

Mercurey

Givry

Buxy

Montagny

Scale

0   3km

0   2m

WINE AREAS

Rully

● ○

1990 production: Rully
              & Premiers Crus ●   *5,462 hectolitres*
              Rully
              & Premiers Crus ○   *7,707 hectolitres*

Premiers Crus Margotey, Grésigny, Vauvry, Mont-Palais, Meix-Caillet, Les Pierres, La Bressande, Champ-Clou, La Renarde, Pillot, Cloux, Raclot, Raboursay, Ecloseaux, Marissou, La Fosse, Chapitre, Préau, Moulesne.

The white wines of Rully are particularly known for their finesse and straw-like quality, often with a taste which is half floral, half the contents of the spice shelf, perhaps with a preponderance of cinnamon.

The reds are pure Pinot, never very dark in colour, sometimes violetty, sometimes more raspberries, with a nicely balanced kernel of flavour to them – the results are so much better in Rully when the vines have a bit of age.

The Principal Rully Producers

Domaine Belleville
71150 Rully.
      White wine with a lovely nose, but a slightly more vulgar finish.

Domaine Jean-Claude Brelière
71150 Rully.
      Good reputation.

Domaine Michel Briday
Grande Rue, 71150 Rully. 1ers Crus: Rully: La Bergerie, Champ-Clou, Grésigny, La Pucelle; Mercurey. Rully: Les Chailloux, Vieilles Vignes; Mercurey; Bourgogne Rouge.
      Good white Rullys, without being top notch; aged in 25 percent new wood.

Emile Chandesais
SCEA Champs Perdrix, St-Nicolas, 71150 Fontaines. 11 ha. Rully

Les St-Jacques, Bourgogne Côte Chalonnaise (red and white). An important *négociant* based in the Côte Chalonnaise. Whilst most of the wines are just good – no more – the firm always buys at the Hospices de Beaune and I have been impressed by some of their *élevages*, which are usually silky and give evidence of new wood. I have also liked their Passe-Tout-Grains, but not their Rully wines. The domain wines receive careful vinification, the reds in stainless steel vats, with total destalking and maturing in oak barrels, some of which are new. The whites are fermented in new oak barrels. Domains whose wines they distribute include the Château de Néty (Beaujolais-Villages), Domaine Hermitage (Rully Rouge and Blanc, Mercurey and Bourgogne), and Domaine Gouffier (Bourgogne, Mercurey and Bourgogne Aligoté).

Domaine Pierre Cogny
Bouzeron, 71150 Chagny.
Good red and white Rully, slightly rustic.

Domaine Jean Coulon
71150 Rully.
Rully Blanc Grésigny of real interest.

André Delorme
Rully, 71150 Chagny. 66 ha, two-thirds owned by J-F Delorme, the rest by members of his family. 1ers Crus: Rully: Grésigny, Les Cloux, La Fosse, Marissou; Givry Clos du Cellier aux Moines. Rully: La Bergerie, Chaponnière, La Chaume, La Martelle, Monthelon, Montmorin, Les Thivaux, Varot; Mercurey: Les Chenaults, Les Clos, Les Crêts, Les Lamberots, Les Monthelons, Les Murgers, Les Velles, Ropiton; Montagny l'Epaule; La Rochepot; Bourgogne Aligoté de Bouzeron. (Pinot Noir and Chardonnay for making Crémant de Bourgogne.)

Jean-François Delorme has done much for the renaissance of the Côte Chalonnaise and has greatly extended his vineyard holdings of the Domaine de la Renarde (qv). As the vines age, the quality visibly improves. The white grapes are pressed very slowly, to avoid any bitterness, and then go through a *débourbage*, or clarifying of the must, at low temperature to concentrate the aromas. The reds are partially destalked, with the aim of achieving finesse and fruit. Rully Varot, principally planted to Chardonnay, is an 18 hectare parcel and the wines have a seductive cinnamon quality. The *négociant* business of Delorme-Meulien/André Delorme makes very good selections, especially a Bourgogne Rouge La Croix-Lieux, and the house is renowned for its Crémant sparkling wines.

Harvesting the grapes by hand at Rully

Domaine Dureuil-Janthial
71150 Rully.
> No destalking and long fermentation for the reds; the whites are made from very old vines. Both are aged in up to 20 percent new wood, the whites for six to nine months, the reds considerably longer. Solidity rather than subtlety.

Domaine Duvernay
71150 Rully.
> Good, straightforward white wines.

Domaine de la Folie
71150 Chagny. 16 ha (2 ha *en métayage*). 1ers Crus: Rully: Clos du Chaigne, Clos St-Jacques. Rully: red, white, Clos Roch (white),

Clos de Bellecroix (red), En Chaponnière, Passe-Tout-Grain. A well-run domain, with both red and white wines. Xavier Noël-Bouton believes in long vattings at low temperature in order to make wines which will keep, but I have always found these wines extremely pleasant when comparatively young. Sales are to French restaurants, direct to private clients and to the export markets. The red Clos de Bellecroix can be both fruity and gamey. The white Clos St-Jacques has elegance and charm.

Paul & Henri Jacqueson

71150 Rully. 7·3 ha. 1ers Crus: Rully: La Bressande, Clouds, Grésigny, Marissou-St-Jacques, Mont-Palais, La Pucelle, Rabourcé, Vauvry; Mercurey Naugues. Rully Les Chaponnières, Mercurey, Bourgogne Aligoté, Bourgogne Passe-Tout-Grains.

A small, meticulously-run domain, created by Henri Jacqueson and now run by him and his son Paul. The family is of Welsh origin as, in the 15th century, the personal guard of Marguerite de Bourgogne was Welsh, and the Jacquesons descended from this line. Exports account for 65 percent of sales, with private customers also an important element. The predominantly red wines are made with grapes which have not been destalked, with treading morning and evening to keep the skins in contact with the juice – the vinification lasts 15–22 days and the wines are intended for keeping. The whole white grapes are pressed immediately in horizontal presses (for two hours), then the juice clarifies naturally in tanks for eight to ten hours before fermentation at a cold temperature. *Elevage* is in oak barrels, 30 percent new each year, and bottling at the end of September. Very attractive wines.

Domaine Ninot-Cellier-Meix-Guillaume

71150 Rully.

Good white Rully Grésigny and red Mercurey.

Domaine du Prieuré (Armand Monassier)

Rully, 71150 Chagny.

Armand Monassier has made strawberryish Sous Mont-Palais, but recently the quality here has been a bit patchy.

Domaine de la Renarde

Rue de la République, 71150 Rully. 35 ha (32 ha *en métayage*).

Jean-François Delorme has built up a very important
domain at Rully owning, amongst other things, all of the
18-hectare Varot vineyard which produces elegant white
wine with a scent of newly mown grass. What is unusual in
Burgundy is to have 18 hectares in one parcel, rather than
in scattered plots. The red Rully has greatly improved as
the vines have aged and now both raspberries and
strawberries spring to mind when tasting. The range of
Delorme wines generally represents a very good *rapport
qualité-prix*.

Château de Rully
71150 Rully.
    Red Rully which is fairly chewy, needing time in bottle;
exceptionally good, lightly-oaked, elegant, buttery white
with considerable finesse for the AC. *See also* Antonin
Rodet, Mercurey.

Domaine de Rully St-Michel
Rue du Château, 71150 Rully. 10 ha. 1ers Crus: Rully: Les Cloux,
Raclot, Rabourcé (white); Champs Clouds, Les Cloux (red). Rully
Clos de Pellerey (red).
    Softly fruity reds and very classy white Rullys – the
Rabourcé is outstanding.

● ○   # Mercurey

1990 production: Mercurey
                & Premiers Crus ●   *26,018 hectolitres*
            Mercurey
                & Premiers Crus ○   *2,577 hectolitres*

Premiers Crus Clos-du-Roi, Clos-Voyen or Les Voyens, Clos-
Marcilly, Clos-des-Fourneaux, Clos-des-Montaigus.

Mercurey produces wines which are almost exclusively red and
they are the biggest, most structured wines of the Côte Chalonnaise. They can be solid and quite earthy, and certainly they last
longer than the red wines of the other *appellations*. Sometimes there

is more than a hint of *terroir* in the taste, derived from the marl and limestone soil which predominates here. At their best, the wines are robust and frank, with an attractive 'wet earth' bouquet; at their worst, they are dry and rustic.

The Principal Mercurey Producers

Domaine du Château de Chamilly
Chamilly, 71510 St-Leger-sur-Dheune.
 Louis Desfontaine makes wines with very good *appellation* character. They have body, bouquet and balance, and a good deal of earthy fruit.

Domaine du Château de Chamirey/Domaine du Marquis de Jouennes d'Herville
71640 Mercurey. 35 ha. Mercurey (red) 25 ha, Mercurey (white) 10 ha.
 The Château de Chamirey red and white wines are now both made and distributed by the *négociant* firm of Antonin Rodet. The grapes are mechanically harvested and both wines are vinified in stainless steel before being aged for nine to twelve months, one-third in new wood, one-third in old wood and one-third remaining in vat. Increasingly good quality; especially the white which is particularly successful and has given me much pleasure. It is supple, elegantly textured, ripe and flowery, with hints of mayblossom; while the red is firm with a chewy, cherry fruit and distinct earthiness of flavour – a wine which needs time to mellow. The Marquis de Jouennes d'Herville, son-in-law of Antonin Rodet, owns the domain and is head of the *négociant* firm. The wines are seen widely around the world.

Domaine Jeannin-Naltet Père & Fils
71640 Mercurey.
 Ripe and earthy Premier Cru Clos des Grands Voyens, a *monopole*.

Domaine Michel Juillot
71640 Mercurey. 30 ha. Grands Crus: Corton-Charlemagne, Corton-Perrières. 1ᵉʳˢ Crus: Mercurey: Clos des Barraults, Clos

Tonnerre, Les Champs Martins (red and white), Les Combins. Aloxe-Corton Les Caillettes, Bourgogne Côte Chalonnaise (red and white), Mercurey (red and white).

There is a wealth of experience behind the skills of Michel Juillot – his family have been vignerons since 1404, and his grandfather became a master grafter of vines at national level, something much needed following phylloxera. Vinification is in open *cuves*, after total destalking. There is always one-third new wood in the cellars, and no barrel is more than three years old. Bottling is carried out after 18–24 months of *élevage*. There is often a scent of ripe, wild fruits in the reds. White Mercurey with a *goût de terroir* and a touch of liquorice and new oak. The reds are excellent, benefiting from about one-third new barrels in the cellar, scented, fruity and well made. The Clos des Barraults is usually a more complete and more tannic wine than the Champs Martins, taking longer to mature (five to eight years). Both red Mercureys are delicious burgundies, of exceptional quality in '90. M Juillot also makes very fine Corton-Charlemagne.

Domaine Marceau

71640 Mercurey.

Another well-regarded domain.

Jean Maréchal

71640 Mercurey.

Very good quality 'typical' Mercureys. Both red and white are aged in 20 percent new wood.

Domaine du Meix-Foulot

Clos du Château de Montaigü, 71640 Mercurey. 16·5 ha. 1ers Crus: Mercurey: Clos du Château de Montaigü, Les Biots, Les Veleys. Mercurey (red and white), Bourgogne Aligoté.

A family domain planted around the ruins of the medieval Château de Montaigü, and making good to very good wine. The grapes are destalked, and vatting lasts from eight to ten days, with treading. The wines are left in vats for six months, with no heating of the cellars, so that the malolactic fermentation can take its own time. Ageing is in oak barrels, where the wines stay for six months to a year, depending on the character of the vintage and the *cuvée* –

thus, some wines are bottled just before the following harvest, but more often between March and June of the next year, which gives a total ageing of 18 months. The wines are often not filtered. Both the red, and the small amount of white wine, can keep well. If you are passing through Mercurey and decide that you want to visit the domain, it is as well to ask for careful directions, as it is somewhat hidden, isolated amid the vine-covered slopes.

Domaine de la Monette
71640 Mercurey. 9 ha.

Paul-Jean Granger makes mainly red Mercurey and just a little white. The red is aged in 20 percent new oak for 18 months, and both the straight Mercurey and the Premier Cru are delicious examples of the *appellation*.

Domaine du Prieuré (Armand Monassier)
Rully, 71150 Chagny. 9 ha. 1ers Crus: Rully: Rouge Mont Palais, Préau; Rully Blanc Mont Palais, Grésigny. Rully (red and white), Mercurey (red), Crémant de Bourgogne.

Clos de la Vigne de Devant with creditable fruit.

Domaine Maurice Protheau & Fils/Domaine François Protheau & Fils
Le Clos l'Evêque, 71640 Mercurey. 38 ha (55 ha *en métayage*). 1ers Crus: Rully Les Grésigny; Mercurey Clos l'Evêque, Les Vellées. Rully (white), Rully La Chatalienne; Mercurey: red, Clos des Corvées, La Fauconnière, Les Ormeaux; Bourgogne Vigne de Champrenard.

An important Côte Chalonnaise domain, with the wines distributed by the *négociant* François Protheau & Fils. The Protheau family have been growers in Mercurey since 1720, but created a new vineyard in Rully in 1976. The red grapes are completely destalked, vatted for eight to ten days and aged in oak barrels for 12–14 months. Clos l'Evêque and Clos des Corvées are treated to new oak. The reds tend to be tannic and slow-maturing. The white Mercurey attains richness with age. Switzerland is the leading client.

Antonin Rodet
71640 Mercurey. Domaine du Château de Chamirey 32 ha, Domaine du Château de Rully 36 ha, Château de Mercey/Domaine Rodet 65 ha.

Both this important *négociant* firm and the Château de Chamirey belong to the de Jouennes family, with a son-in-law, Bertrand Devillard, now running the company with great dynamism. Considerable expansion has taken place here since the mid-1980s. In 1986 Rodet started to make and distribute the wines of the Château de Rully (including Domaine Monassier); in 1988 they acquired a 10 percent stake in Domaine Jacques Prieur (qv) half of whose production they also sell, and in 1989 they purchased the Chateau de Mercey at Cheilly-les-Maranges. They vinify most of their white wines from must bought from Meursault, Puligny, Chassagne and Chablis, and the recent white wines certainly show the great progress made both in selection and in methods of *élevage*. (The white Château de Rully and Château de Chamirey are particularly good value.) Antonin Rodet exports 55 percent of its production to most parts of the world and is certainly one of the most improved Burgundy houses of the last few years.

Domaine Fabian & Louis Saier
71640 Mercurey. 25 ha. 1er Cru: Mercurey Les Champs Martins. Mercurey (red and white), Bourgogne Rouge, Bourgogne Passe-Tout-Grains.

Les Champs Martins which can be lovely young drinking, but quality here is patchy.

Domaine de Suremain
71640 Mercurey.

This domain used to be a reliable source of Mercurey with scent and regional character: a cherry-fruited straight Mercurey and a bigger, firmer Clos-Voyen. At the moment, whilst there are some good wines, quality is patchy and others are distinctly rustic.

Givry

● ○

1990 production:	Givry ●	*7,772*	*hectolitres*
	Givry ○	*1,132*	*hectolitres*

There are no official Premiers Crus, but the following vineyards appear on labels: La Barande, Bois-Chevaux, Cellier aux Moines, Clos St-Paul. Clos St-Pierre, Clos Salomon, and Champ Poureau for white wine.

Known, somewhat strangely, on some labels as the 'preferred wine of King Henri IV', when it was thought he was more closely associated with Jurançon in the Pyrenean foothills of south-west France, Givry can have a lovely fragrance and a delicious, lingering Pinot Noir charm. The wines do not have the body of Mercurey; they boast a more delicate flavour. But if, as it is rumoured, the King's mistress did in fact have a vineyard at Givry, that is all as it should be.

The Principal Givry Producers

Domaine Jean Chofflet
71640 Givry.

> Smoky Pinot fruit on nose, with a touch of violets. Earthy, raw truffles flavour – very frank Pinot without having the style of the classiest Givry.

Michel Derain
St-Désert, 71390 Buxy.

> Good white Givry and traditionally vinified reds.

Propriété Desvignes
Poncey, 71640 Givry.

> Correct red Givry.

Domaine du Gardin
16 rue de Clos Salomon, 71640 Givry. 6·8 ha.

> This historic estate produces Clos Salomon of subtlety, charm and fruit.

Domaine Joblot
71640 Givry.

> Vincent and Jean-Marc Joblot take their vineyards and their

winemaking very seriously. They make 80 percent red and 20 percent white, using 40–80 percent new wood in which to age the wines. It is a tribute to the quality of the grapes and vinification that they do not taste too oaky. Well-balanced wines, harmonious and true-to-type with an impressively rich and elegant red Clos de la Servoisine.

Domaine Thierry Lespinasse

71390 Rosey.

Gently earthy, savoury red Givry en Choué, and a fresh and delicate white. Lovely wines which need a little bottle-age. M Lespinasse matures his wines in one-third new oak, the red for 12–18 months, the white for eight months. He also makes a delicious Crémant de Bourgogne.

Domaine Gérard Mouton

Poncey, 71640 Givry.

Very good oak-aged (25 percent) red and white Givry.

Domaine Ragot

Poncey, 71640 Givry.

The white Givry has been very good in the past, rich and nutty, but quality has been less consistent recently.

Domaine de la Renarde

Rue de la République, 71150 Rully.

Red Clos du Cellier aux Moines which can have a fascinating nose of toasted bread; at other times it smells of all the herbs of Provence. The taste is always very Pinot and long-lingering.

Société Civile du Domaine Thénard

7 rue de l'Hôtel de Ville, 71640 Givry. 23·8 ha. Grands Crus: Grands Echézeaux; Corton Clos du Roi; Montrachet. 1ers Crus: Pernand-Vergelesses Ile des Vergelesses; Chassagne-Montrachet Clos St-Jean; Givry Cellier aux Moines, Givry Clos St-Pierre, Givry Les Bois Chevaux. Givry (red and white).

Best known for its substantial holding of Le Montrachet, but the more modest Givrys are good too, especially the Clos St-Pierre. The wines are distributed by the Beaune *négociant* Remoissenet.

○   # Montagny

1990 production: Montagny   *9,558 hectolitres*

All the vineyards in the area have the right to the *appellation* Premier
Cru, provided that the wines reach 11·5 percent alcohol before
chaptalization.

The vineyards of the *appellation* Montagny are spread over the
villages of Montagny itself, Buxy, St-Vallerin and Jully-les-Buxy.
The wine was meant to be that preferred by the monks of Cluny, as
opposed to royalty. It is also said that it keeps the mouth fresh and
the head clear. Be that as it may, cool, white Montagny is absolutely
delicious. It is a mite fuller and fatter, sometimes broader, than
white Rully, which can have more breed and elegance. There is
more almondy honey in Montagny, and more straw and cinnamon
in Rully. It is interesting to note that there is Kimmeridgian
limestone at Buxy.

The Principal Montagny Producers

Cave Coopérative de Buxy
71390 Buxy.
>   This large cooperative is the source of supply for many
>   people, both in the French and the British trade. Naturally,
>   there is variation amongst the *cuves*, but the best are most
>   worthy of the name of Montagny. The cooperative also
>   makes red and white Bourgogne, Passe-Tout-Grains and
>   Aligoté, generic *appellations* commonly produced on the
>   Côte Chalonnaise.

Château de Davenay (*Moillard*)
72840 Montagny.
>   The proprietors are the Héritiers Gilardoni. Full, nutty,
>   even spicy wine; good, without being imbued with breed.

Maison Delaunay
L'Etang-Vergy, 21220 Gevrey-Chambertin.
>   This house produces very fine Montagny selections.

Domaine Lucien Denizot
Bissey-sous-Cruchaud, 71390 Buxy.

Frank, fruity Bourgogne Rouge, redolent of cherries and cassis. One was *Chante-Flûté*, which is the Côte Chalonnaise version of *Tasteviné*. (A jury selects a high quality wine which is then given a numbered label, bearing the name of the producer, the vintage and the words *Chante-Flûté*).

Domaine Michel Goubard

Basseville, 71390 St-Désert. 18 ha. Bourgogne Côte Chalonnaise, Bourgogne Blanc and Aligoté, Bourgogne Passe-Tout-Grains.

The Goubards have been on the Côte Chalonnaise since 1600. Two-thirds of the vineyards they now have are on marked slopes, beautifully facing south-east for maximum sun exposure. The Bourgogne Rouge is fruity and charming, made by a semi-carbonic maceration method and meant for relatively young drinking. Half the production is sold direct, while half is exported. Good value Burgundy for those who like to buy their wine and drink it right away.

Maison Louis Latour

18 rue des Tonneliers, 21204 Beaune.

This famed Beaune shipper always makes superb selections of Montagny.

Domaine Bernard Michel

St-Vallerin, 71390 Buxy.

Graceful Les Coères with a slight earthiness in its flavour.

Château de la Saule/Domaine Roy-Thévenin

Montagny-les-Buxy, 71390 Buxy. 13 ha. Montagny, Bourgogne Aligoté, Bourgogne Passe-Tout-Grains.

This is a very reliable domain, with labels under the names of both Alain and Marcel Roy-Thévenin. The grapes for the Montagny are pressed rapidly and then the clarified must ferments in *foudres* (wooden vats), enamel-lined tanks, and a part in oak barrels. The wines are then racked in March/April for an early bottling. The result is fresh and youthful, and always in balance. The Aligoté is very worthy too. The wines are now nicely spread in France and on the export markets.

Domaine Jean Vachet

St-Vallerin, 71390 Buxy.

Broad, polished Les Coères; whites better than reds.

● ○ ◑ The Mâconnais

Geologists love the Mâconnais, because there are some fascinating cliff formations in the southern part, and visitors love it no less for the pretty green countryside and the wealth of Romanesque churches. If you can tear yourself away from the fruit and nut trees, the small brown goats and the white cattle dappling the hillsides, the wines are very rewarding as well.

The whole district covers about 50 kilometres (31 miles) from north to south but is only 15 kilometres (9 miles) wide. The area is determined to the east and west by the two valleys of the Saône and

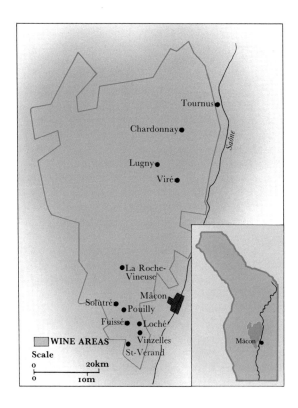

the Grosne, but the line of hills runs from north-north-east to south-south-west. The site and altitude of the vineyard is critical to ultimate quality, because although the summers can be very hot in the Mâconnais, the winters are cold, with frost a danger until the four days (May 12–15) of the Ice Saints are past.

There are two main soil types: low-acid, calcareous soil for the Chardonnay, an excellent combination for making fine white wine; and more acid, clay, sand or siliceous soil for white wines destined for very young drinking and for the Gamay for Mâcon Rouge. The most impressive slopes, magnificently exposed to the sun (hence the frequent high natural alcohol levels), are in the southern part of the region, the hills of Pouilly, Solutré and Vergisson, Indeed, the last two are really cliffs, formed by the same Jurassic strata found in the Côte d'Or, but in rather more dramatic shape. The Chardonnay dominates in the Mâconnais, covering 67 percent of the vineyard area, with the Gamay occupying 25 percent, the Pinot Noir 7·5 percent and 0·5 percent planted to Aligoté. The grape variety proportions reflect the fact that it is far easier to sell white Mâcon than red. In the Mâconnais, there are 3,775 hectares of AC vineyard under vine.

Most Mâcon Blanc is made without seeing any wood – it is kept in vat and bottled young. Of course, there are individual growers who bottle their wines, especially in Pouilly-Fuissé, and here there are hogsheads and even wooden vats in the cellars, but as the cooperatives handle about 85 percent of the white wine, logistics demand modern methods. About 20 percent less red wine goes through the cooperatives, but that is still a significant quantity. Much Mâcon Rouge is made by the *macération carbonique* method (for a description of this, see the section on Beaujolais), which is an attractive way of treating the Gamay if the wine is not intended for keeping. The Pinot Noir can be made into Bourgogne Rouge or be included in Passe-Tout-Grains, and it is sometimes vinified by a semi-*macération carbonique* process, which means that the wine should be drunk young.

I somehow feel that the Mâconnais is the proverbial 'gateway to the south' – the grey north gives way to the ochre Midi. The houses are covered with warm-coloured, curvy tiles, reminiscent of Provence, and they have verandahs running the length of them, indicating sunny days. That might be difficult to believe in the grip of a glacial winter, but the summer gives you a vision of France in all its rural splendour.

Mâcon

1990 production: Mâcon   *167,972 hectolitres*

Here the *appellation* is Mâcon-Villages or Mâcon with one of 43 village names. This might sound baffling, but in practice the following villages are most often seen: Lugny, Viré, Prissé, Clessé, Vinzelles, La Roche-Vineuse and Chardonnay, which may or may not have given its name to the grape variety.

On the whole, these wines are at their best at one to two years old, when all their fruit and blossomy scents are at their most tantalizing. The two enemies of good Mâcon Blanc are lack of freshness and a certain vulgarity, usually brought about by a rustic approach to winemaking. A charming characteristic is a smoky muskiness, coming from the Chardonnay clone used in the area.

The Principal Mâcon Producers

Bénas Frères
Serrières, 71960 Pierreclos.
   Some muskiness on the nose, broad and fat on the palate.
Domaine André Bonhomme
14500 Viré.
   Exemplary Mâcon-Viré year in, year out; vivid wines of
   delicious texture and length which spend up to six months
   in 25 percent new oak.
Cave Coopérative de Clessé
71260 Clessé.
   Light, straightforward whites and reds; the supple Blanc de
   Blancs *méthode champenoise* is probably the best of the range.
Cave Coopérative d'Igé
71960 Igé.
   Because of the suitability of the local soils for red grapes,

this cooperative produces more red than white wine. Amongst the whites there is a deliciously full and round Mâcon-Igé, Château London from a particularly well exposed *lieu-dit*, and a classy St-Véran. The red Mâcons are sturdy without being coarse, and the two Pinot Noirs are very successful for the level: a vividly fruity basic Bourgogne Pinot Noir, and a more substantial *fût de chêne cuvée* where the oak is well integrated and not overdone.

Cave Coopérative de Lugny
71260 Lugny.

One of the few local cooperatives that, sensibly, does not attempt an 'oaked' *cuvée*. Its range of whites is very well made, with noticeably pure apple-and-melon Chardonnay flavours. Particularly good are the Mâcon-Lugny Les Charmes, which is elegant and smoky with good acidity, and their supple, fruity Mâcon St-Gengoux. The red Mâcons are better value than the Bourgogne Pinot Noirs. Well worth a visit, as they have an attractive reception area and good tasting facilities.

Cave Coopérative de Viré
14500 Viré.

Reliable wines right across the range: fresh, lemony Mâcon-Viré, consistently good Crémant de Bourgogne from pure Chardonnay, and two nicely balanced 'oaked' *cuvées* of Mâcon-Viré and Bourgogne Rouge which are successful because only 20 percent new wood is used and the flavour of the wines is enhanced, not masked.

Jean-Noël Chaland
71260 Viré.

Lanolin-smooth Mâcon-Viré; a good bottle.

Domaine des Chazelles
14500 Viré.

A very small domain producing a particularly opulent Mâcon-Villages of much higher quality than its modest *appellation* would suggest.

Domaine de Chervin
Burgy, 71260 Lugny.

Mâcon-Burgy made by Albert Goyard of the Domaine de Roally (qv) family. Delicate, pretty wines of finesse.

Domaine de la Condemine

71260 Péronne.

Véronique and Pierre Janny make good, nutty Mâcon-Villages, when they do not use too much sulphur dioxide.

Coron Père & Fils

21205 Beaune. 8·61 ha. Mâcon-Villages: Château de Loché, Le Clos du Château; Pouilly-Fuissé Château de Loché; Pouilly-Loché Château de Loché; Pouilly-Vinzelles Château de Loché.

Coron produces both domain and *négociant* wines under the same name. I am afraid I am not keen on them, though, to be fair, I have not seen a domain wine recently.

Domaine Jacques Depagneux

69400 Villefranche-sur-Saône.

A good, and reliable, range of Beaujolais *crus*, Beaujolais-Villages and Mâcon-Viré.

Domaine des Gandines

71260 Clessé.

Unoaked Mâcon-Clessé, lemon-fresh and delicious young, but keeps well too.

Emilian Gillet

Quintaine, 71260 Clessé.

Good, fruity Mâcon-Clessé and Mâcon-Viré.

Domaine des Granges

71570 Chaintré.

Jean-François Cognard makes good Mâcon-Chaintré and a prizewinning Beaujolais Blanc.

Château de la Greffière

La Roche-Vineuse, 71960 Pierreclos.

Messieurs Greuzard make broad, perfumed Mâcon-Villages (though the '90 La Roche-Vineuse was tired by the time it was a year old). There is also a lovely Bourgogne Rouge Pinot Noir.

Domaine Adrien Guichard

Montbellet, 71260 Lugny.

Mâcon-Villages which is always tempting.

Domaine Guillemot-Michel

71260 Clessé.

Mâcon-Clessé Quintaine that is light, flowery and stylish. Quintessential Quintaine!

Domaine Henri Lafarge

71250 Bray.

Wonderful floral, acacia nose; great elegance and balance.

Domaine Pierre Mahuet

La Roche-Vineuse, 71960 Pierreclos.

Mâcon-La Roche-Vineuse with a nose of almonds – excellent fresh wine.

Domaine Manciat-Poncet

71850 Charnay-lès-Mâcon.

Very perfumed, full, immensely seductive Mâcon-Charnay; excellent Pouilly-Fuissé. The latter's Vieilles Vignes is the only 'oaked' wine: six months in 50 percent new wood.

Domaine René Michel

71260 Clessé.

Concentrated Mâcon-Clessé with a nice nuttiness.

Château de Mirande

71260 Lugny.

Baron Patrice de l'Epine makes elegant, delicious Mâcon-Villages, with a lovely nose of acacia and mayblossom.

Domaine du Prieuré

71260 Lugny.

Very well made Mâcon-Villages.

Domaine de Roally

14500 Viré.

Henri Goyard makes Mâcon-Viré (and fights the dominance of the coop!) and succeeds admirably. Wonderful acacia nose, hazelnuts, excellent fresh wine. On the neck label he says *Raisin Cueilli à la Main* – the grapes were picked by hand.

Domaine Talmard

71700 Uchizy.

Of Paul and Philibert Talmard's 31 hectares of vines, 29 hectares are planted with Chardonnay, from which they make a deliciously clean and flavoursome Mâcon-Uchizy.

Jean Thévenet/Domaine de la Bon Gran

Quintaine, 71260 Clessé. 7·5 ha.

Very good Mâcon-Clessé from low yields and slow fermentation. In a hot year the Domaine de la Bon Gran *Cuvée Tradition* weighs in at 14·5 percent, with super-ripe apple and peach flavours and enormous concentration. Occasionally Jean Thévenet even makes a Sauternes-style Mâcon-Clessé from botrytized Chardonnay grapes, such as the luscious '83.

Domaine de Thurissey/Les Vieux Ceps
Thurissey, 71260 Montbellet.
Robert Bridon makes scented wines with a big, broad taste.

Trenel & Fils
71850 Charnay-lès-Mâcon
Négociants producing a consistently good range of Mâconnais, Beaujolais and Beaujolais *cru* wines.

Société Coopérative des Viticulteurs de Saône et Loire
Nutty wines, full and fat.

Other excellent wines: Mâcon-Lugny Les Genièvres of Louis Latour, Mâcon-Viré of Piat, Mâcon-Prissé of Georges Duboeuf, Mâcon-Viré of Louis Jadot, Mâcon-Viré, Château de Viré, owned by Hubert Desbois but distributed by Prosper Maufoux, and Mâcon-Villages Laforêt of Joseph Drouhin.

Mâcon Supérieur Rouge	1990 production:	*56,450*	*hectolitres*
Mâcon Supérieur Blanc	1990 production:	*6,270*	*hectolitres*
Mâcon Rouge and Rosé	1990 production:	*2,357*	*hectolitres*
Mâcon Blanc	1990 production:	*1,015*	*hectolitres*

White Mâcon, made from Pinot Blanc or Chardonnay, can also be called Pinot-Chardonnay-Mâcon which, in these days of greater accuracy with regard to grape varieties, is slightly old-fashioned.

There is also a small amount of red wine labelled as Mâcon, plus the village name, then *Villages*. The *Supérieur* denotes one per cent more alcohol for both the red and white wines, ie the minimum level of alcohol before chaptalization for Mâcon Supérieur Rouge is ten percent and for Mâcon Supérieur Blanc, 11 percent. The white wines of this category can be 'declassified' into Bourgogne, providing a valuable source of supply for many a merchant.

I have to say that most Mâcon Rosé wines which have come my

way have been very unappealing, with the exception of one from the Maison Mâconnaise des Vins (Société Coopérative des Viticulteurs de Saône et Loire).

Good Mâcon Rouge or Mâcon Rouge Supérieur has come from: Cave Coopérative de Prissé, Jean-Claude Thévenet, Cave Coopérative de Lugny, the Domaine des Provenchères of Maurice Gonon, Henri Lafarge, and Mâcon-Serrières from Bénas Frères (this is a different variety of soil and the wine is not Beaujolais in type; it is traditional, needing time, becoming more 'Pinot Noir' in character with age).

The Cooperatives generally maintain a high standard although, as always, the art is in selection. They are: Aze, Bissey-sous-Cruchaud, Buxy, Chaintré, Chardonnay, Charnay-lès-Mâcon, Genouilly, Igé, Lugny, Mancey, Prissé, Sennece-lès-Mâcon, Sologny, Verzé, 'La Vigne Blanche' at Clessé, Vinzelles, Viré.

○ # Pouilly-Fuissé

1990 production: Pouilly-Fuissé   *43,080 hectolitres*

There are no Premiers Crus, but sometimes a vineyard name is added to the wine label, particularly when a site has become known, over the years, for producing fine wine. The villages which produce Pouilly-Fuissé are Pouilly, Fuissé, Solutré, Vergisson and Chaintré. There are nuances in taste between the villages, with Pouilly making a bid for top position and Solutré for the wines with more body, but probably the hand of the winemaker, and maybe the age of the vines, is of more importance.

The actual rock of Solutré is somewhat menacing, especially when you know that at its feet lies nearly a hectare of the bones of wild horses driven over the cliff by 'Solutréen' Man 15,000–12,000 BC. It is quite a surprise to see the escapades of this creature so well documented on the other side of France, in the Museum of Prehistory at Les Eyzies in the Dordogne. But the wine of Solutré singularly lacks menace. It is a rich, full, even earthy Chardonnay, not infrequently attaining 13–14 percent alcohol naturally. There is not the steeliness and 'nerve' of Chablis, nor the finesse or breed of, say, Puligny-Montrachet, but there is plenty of flavour.

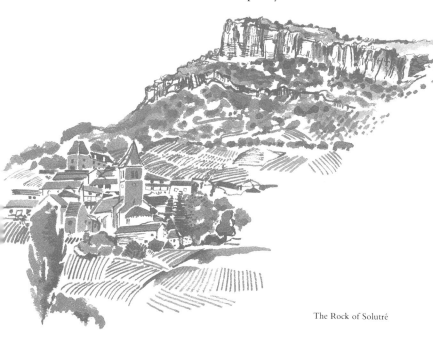

The Rock of Solutré

The Principal Pouilly-Fuissé Producers

Domaine de l'Arillière
71960 Fuissé.
> Stylish and fruity, rather than rich and full. *See also* Société Civile du Château de Fuissé.

Maison Auvigue
Le Moulin du Pont, 71850 Charnay-lès-Mâcon. 5·5 ha. Pouilly-Fuissé: Les Bouthières, Les Chailloux, La Frairie.
> Pouilly-Fuissé that is always good when found in top French restaurants. The best *cuvées* spend four months in new wood.

Daniel Barraud
Vergisson, 71960 Pierreclos.
Good St-Véran; rich, oaky Pouilly-Fuissé Vieilles Vignes.

Château de Beauregard
Fuissé, 71960 Pierreclos. 35 ha. Pouilly-Fuissé, St-Véran, Moulin-à-Vent, Fleurie, Mâcon-Villages, Beaujolais-Villages.
Good wines, with the St-Véran usually better value – but that is often the case except for the most exciting Pouilly-Fuissés. Ageing in up to one-third new oak.

Domaine Bressand
71960 Fuissé.
Well-made wines.

Domaine Roger Cordier
71960 Fuissé.
Finesse and complexity on the nose, taste good but not quite as exciting as the bouquet. However, 'on the up', with evidence of wood ageing.

Domaine Corsin
71960 Fuissé. 9·7 ha. Pouilly-Fuissé, St-Véran, Mâcon-Villages (white), Mâcon Supérieur (red).
Very reliable, down-the-line Pouilly-Fuissé and St-Véran.

Domaine Louis Curveux
71960 Fuissé. 6 ha. Pouilly-Fuissé, Mâcon-Fuissé, Mâcon-Chaintré.
Wines of excellent fruity character and dimension. Mâcon wines vinified and aged in stainless steel only; Pouilly-Fuissé sees a small proportion of new wood.

Roger Duboeuf
Chaintré, 71750 La Chapelle-de-Guinchay.
Small producer making a good Pouilly-Fuissé Les Plessis, oak-aged with a small proportion of new wood.

Domaine Jeanne Ferret
Fuissé, 71960 Pierreclos.
Outstanding Pouilly-Fuissé from old vines, low yields and modest use of new wood.

Domaine Michel Forest
71960 Vergisson.
Terrific winemaking with a gloriously fruity and succulent Les Crays and a very elegant but more austere La Roche. Excellent examples of the genre.

Société Civile du Château de Fuissé

71960, Fuissé. 25 ha. Pouilly-Fuissé, St-Véran, Mâcon-Villages.
Jean-Jacques Vincent vinifies and ages his various *cuvées*
according to the age of the vines and their vineyard
location. The St-Véran, Pouilly-Fuissé Première Cuvée and
Domaine de l'Arillière are vinified principally in tank and
bottled early; the Château Fuissé is aged in 20 percent new
oak, and the Château Fuissé Vieilles Vignes is a selection of
cuvées from vines with an age of 30 years and more. The
Château Fuissé wines have attained record price levels, but
they are an experience in intense flavour. The apogee is
attained with the Vieilles Vignes in a really ripe year –
positively mindblowing. And these wines are keepers. Jean-
Jacques Vincent is, in my opinion, one of the most brilliant
makers of white Burgundy. His Pouilly-Fuissé Vieilles
Vignes easily rivals the best from the Côte d'Or. Much
research has been carried out on different types of oak, and
the sheer dimension of his '90s almost defies description.

Domaine Guffens-Heynen

79160 Vergisson. 3 ha (1 ha *en métayage*). Pouilly-Fuissé (various
lieux-dits), Mâcon-Pierreclos (white), Mâcon-Pierreclos (red).
Belgian Jean-Marie Guffens owns and runs this remarkable
little property, in addition to the *négociant* Verget (qv)
which he founded in 1990. The domain white wines are
refined examples of their *appellations*; the product of old
vines, very low yields and meticulous winemaking. Subtle
Pouilly-Fuissés which age well for six to eight years; very
good white Mâcon-Pierreclos which is best at three to four
years. The whites ferment and age in one-third new oak.
The red Mâcon-Pierreclos, pure Gamay, spends eight to
nine months in 50 percent new wood. It has extract and
tannin – yes; but charm and drinking appeal? No.

Domaine Roger Luquet

71960 Fuissé.
Pouilly-Fuissé en Chatenet with fruit, elegance and style.

Domaine Gilles Noblet

71960 Fuissé.
Excellent, ample Pouilly-Fuissé.

Domaine Jean-Paul Paquet
71960 Fuissé.
Full and broad with some complexity of bouquet.
Domaine Roger Saumaize
Vers-la-Croix, 71960 Vergisson. 2 ha (5 ha *en métayage*).
Light and lively unoaked Mâcon-Villages and Pouilly-Fuissé Vignes Blanches; more 'serious' Pouilly-Fuissé Clos de la Roche and Ronchevats which spend some time in new wood and benefit from bottle-age. Very well made wines, worth looking out for.

Pouilly-Vinzelles and Pouilly-Loché

1990 production: Pouilly-Vinzelles and
                         Pouilly-Loché   *4,349 hectolitres*

These two 'satellite' *appellations* would make a good alternative to the expensive Pouilly-Fuissé if the quantity produced were more significant. They can be slightly more earthy than the very best Pouilly-Fuissé, but the best wines have both definition and character and they make interesting bottles.

The Principal Pouilly-Vinzelles and Pouilly-Loché Producers

Domaine Jean Mathias
71570 Chaintré.
Fine, fruity Pouilly-Vinzelles.

Excellent selections of Pouilly-Vinzelles are made by Georges Duboeuf and Maison Delaunay.

○
St-Véran

1990 production: St-Véran   *28,877 hectolitres*

An *appellation* created in 1971, this virtually replaced Beaujolais Blanc (Louis Jadot is one of the few houses that still makes a speciality of this). Confusingly, the village of St-Vérand is within the *appellation* St-Véran, as are Chânes, Chasselas, Davayé, Leynes, Prissé, St-Amour and part of Solutré.

Although maturing slightly more quickly than Pouilly-Fuissé, the wines are nearly always better at two years than one, showing more interest and complexity.

The Principal St-Véran Producers

Cave Coopérative de Prissé
Prissé, 71960 Pierreclos.
> The white wines are light but well made, though the St-Véran *élevé en fût de chêne* makes little sense as the wood quite obliterates the essential fruit flavours. Their Mâcon Rouge is a good, savoury Gamay and they make an appealing unoaked Bourgogne Pinot Noir.

Château de Coreaux
Leynes, 71570 La Chapelle-de-Guinchay.
> Full, pure and fruity.

Domaine André Depardon
Leynes, 71570 La Chapelle-de-Guinchay.
> Clean, lively Mâcon-Villages and St-Véran which gain richness with age. Really intelligent winemaking.

Domaine des Deux Roches
71960 Davayé. 22 ha. St-Véran, St-Véran Les Terres Noires, Mâcon-Villages (white), Mâcon (red).
> Broad, buttery St-Véran. The best *cuvées* ferment in 20–50 percent new wood, and they can taste fairly 'oaky', but without being overdone.

Domaine Duperon
Chasselas, 71570 La Chapelle-de-Guinchay.
> Good quality St-Véran, ripe and full.

Domaine Thierry Guerin
71960 Vergisson.
>   Well-made, fairly full St-Véran, and Pouilly-Fuissé of
>   weight and finesse, especially the *cuvée* La Roche.

Domaine Maurice Martin
Davayé, 71960 Pierreclos.
>   Good quality St-Véran.

Domaine Michel Paquet
Davayé, 71960 Pierreclos.
>   Nutty, lanolin wine, no 'sparks', but nice St-Véran.

Martine & Jean-Luc Tissier/Domaine des Crais
Les Vessats, 71570 Leynes. 6 ha. St-Véran, Mâcon (white),
Beaujolais-Villages.
>   The St-Véran Domaine des Crais is an elegant wine, the
>   flavour of which gives an indication of the chalky soil.

Domaine Vincent
Fuissé, 71960 Pierreclos.
>   Rich and full, everything one would expect from Jean-
>   Jacques Vincent.

The following domains are also reliable: Georges Chagny and R
Duperron at Leynes, André Chavet at Davayé, as well as the Lycée
Agricole at Davayé. Again, the Duboeuf selections are impeccable.

Laying Down Burgundy

There are two main advantages in cellaring fine Burgundy: you can drink the wines when they are showing at their best; and you can buy them when they are first offered, at the keenest possible price. It is a sad fact that when a wine becomes ready to drink, it has frequently disappeared from the market, so judicious buying at an early stage is always to be recommended. Only Grands Crus from top quality vintages should be considered for really long-term cellaring, but Premiers Crus make excellent mid-term drinking. Both the Pinot Noir and the Chardonnay make 'fragile' wines which are highly susceptible to temperature fluctuation, so laying down Burgundy should only be considered if you have access to a cool cellar – between 10°C and 15°C is ideal.

Buying Burgundy at Auction

Burgundy bargains can be found at auction since the market is dominated by Bordeaux and many people do not automatically think of the saleroom as a source of supply for good Burgundy. However, there are frequently excellent lots of wine that sell for less at auction than they would on some wine merchants' lists.

By keeping a careful eye on the catalogues, Premier and Grand Cru Chablis can be found at very affordable prices. Overall, few domains have really made their mark in the auction room, with notable exceptions such as Domaine de la Romanée Conti, Henri Jayer and Leflaive, but many high quality domains appear from time to time and give Burgundy-lovers a real chance to acquire their favourite wine at a moderate price.

● ○ ◑ Beaujolais

About 22,000 hectares are under the vine in the Beaujolais, in a region which is 55 km (34 miles) long and 12–15 km (seven to nine miles) wide, with an average altitude of 300 metres (984 feet). There are a few large domains, but many small family properties of four to five hectares (around 2,500 properties of one to four hectares, and 1,400 properties of four to seven hectares).

The system of *vigneronnage* is very strong in the Beaujolais, in which the vigneron cultivates the owner's vineyards, while the owner may provide the vigneron's house, but certainly the vinification equipment, vine plants and treatment materials. The vineyard worker usually provides the vineyard equipment, and he does the work. Normally, the profits on the wine are shared. About 50 percent of Beaujolais properties are worked by vignerons.

The Gamay Noir à Jus Blanc covers 98 percent of the Beaujolais vineyard area (Pinot Noir and Chardonnay are included in the two percent left). It is interesting to note that the ten Beaujolais *crus* can be declassified into Bourgogne, so if you drink a red Burgundy made in these areas, it will be Gamay, and not Pinot Noir, wine, somewhat different from a Bourgogne Rouge from the Côte Chalonnaise.

La taille courte, or Gobelet pruning, is found in the northern area of the *crus* and of Beaujolais-Villages, while *la taille longue*, simple Guyot pruning on wire, is found in Beaujolais Sud. In both cases, there must never be more than 12 buds on a vine, and the density of vine plants must be between 9,000 and 13,000 per hectare.

In red wine vinification, the main difference between the Beaujolais and the rest of Burgundy is that the Gamay is never crushed – there is no *foulage* – and the grapes are thus whole. They are put into fermentation vats, which are usually of wood *chez le vigneron*, but often of concrete at the cooperatives. The *cuves* are not completely filled, so that the accumulation of carbonic gas in the empty space can act as a break on the speed of the fermentation and protect against acetic contamination. Vats of 60 hectolitres are ideal, but in cooperatives they tend to be much larger. The weight of the grapes on top causes some juice to run at the bottom of the vat and this is then pumped over, and sometimes warmed, to get the fermentation going. Sugar to increase the alcohol and sulphur dioxide (an anti-oxidant) are added at this time.

Optimum extraction of bouquet (one of the great charms of Gamay vinified in this way) occurs between 25 and 28°C, and the

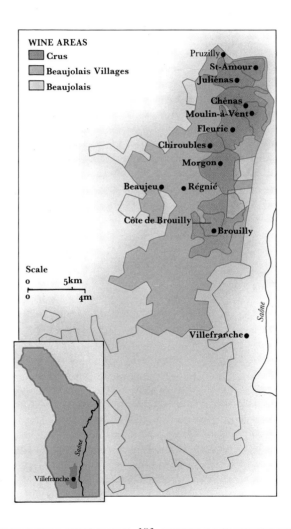

fermentation period lasts four to six days, depending on the ambient temperatures and the way in which the yeasts are working.

In effect, there is a fermentation *within* each whole grape, induced by the CO_2 released by the fermenting juice at the bottom of the vat. This is a variation of a pure carbonic maceration fermentation, when the vat is saturated with added CO_2 and a 10–12 day maceration follows; but the typical Beaujolais procedure described above is both natural and ideally suited to the Gamay. The grapes are pressed to extract the rest of the juice, the wine is put into *cuve* to settle down, and then into *fûts* where a month later the fermentation is usually completed. These casks vary enormously in Beaujolais, from 216 litres, 110 litres or 50–55 litres, to six hectolitres or a *foudre* with an average capacity of 50 hectolitres (this can also be made of concrete in a cooperative).

Before bottling, usually in the spring following the vintage where the *crus* are concerned, some wines are put through a flash-pasteurization for total stability. But small growers do not have these facilities, and firms like Duboeuf prefer to use membrane filters and cold sterile bottling in order to preserve maximum fruit.

The worst faults of Beaujolais are usually an excess of alcohol, with the 'fumes' masking the lovely fresh, fruit aromas, and the over-bolstered body disguising the frank, clean taste. Some of the *négociants* foster a hard, beefy, strong *négoce* style, while some growers' wines are casky and dirty. In large vintages, some wines are often naturally very pale and weak, as the growers give very short *cuvaisons*, or vattings, due to shortage of space. But today, more than ever before, there are lovely examples of pure, lilting Beaujolais just waiting to be selected by wise wine-buyers who recognize good quality.

Beaujolais Nouveau, or Beaujolais Primeur, was a comparatively new phenomenon on the export markets which became increasingly popular during the 1970s. Now, there is evidence that the season for drinking Beaujolais Nouveau is growing ever shorter – the wine is released for sale in shops and wine bars on the third Thursday in November but, by Christmas, most people have lost interest in this vinous diversion, and the signs now are that sales of Nouveau are falling off as December advances. Delicious as it can be, much of it seems overpriced in the early 1990s.

There are many excellent Nouveau wines each year, and the

problems of stability in a wine so rapidly prepared are largely overcome, but it is a pity when good Beaujolais, with the potential to be even better in the following year, is sold and drunk as Nouveau.

Nearly 50 percent of the production of Beaujolais is exported throughout the world. There could not be a more seductive flagship for French exports than this delectable, lively wine.

● ○ ◕   # Beaujolais

1990 production: Beaujolais
               & Beaujolais-Villages
               & Beaujolais *crus*   *1,344,476 hectolitres*

Nearly all Beaujolais is red, although there are very small amounts of white and rosé. Most straight Beaujolais is produced south of Villefranche, on clay and limestone, although it can come from anywhere in the region. Beaujolais Supérieur is rarely seen – it just means that it must have one percent more alcohol than Beaujolais *tout court*. Essentially, simple Beaujolais is best in the year after its birth – then the wise wine-drinker moves on to Beaujolais-Villages.

The following growers all produce delicious Beaujolais: Jean-Paul Brun at Charnay, with astonishing, raspberry-flavoured wine, Philippe Jambon at Corcelles, Château de Bel-Air which is made at the Lycée Viticole de Belleville, Château Gaillard of Jacqueline and Jean-Louis Riche at Denicé, René Riottot at Denicé, Pierre Jomard at Fleurieux-sur-l'Arbresle and René Marchand at Cogny. Amongst the cooperatives, the Beaujolais from the Cave Beaujolaise du Beau Vallon at Theizé have been particularly impressive. The Beaujolais Blanc from the Domaine de l'Eclair (Antoine Clément) is full of verve and fruit, while Beaujolais Rosé from La Cave des Vignerons de Liergues and Georges Texier at Blacé both have a hint of strawberries.

There are 19 cooperative cellars in Beaujolais, in the following communes: Chénas, Fleurie, Chiroubles, Quincié, St-Jean d'Ardières, Gleizé, Liergues, Sain-Bel, Lachassagne, St-Etienne-des-Oullières, Létra, Bully, St-Vérand, Theizé, Le Perréon, Le Bois-d'Oingt, Juliénas, St-Laurent-d'Oingt. They vinify about 300,000 hectolitres of wine a year.

Some of the Principal Beaujolais Producers

Pierre Ferraud & Fils
31 rue Maréchal Foch, 69823 Belleville.
This is an extremely 'serious' *négociant-éleveur*, which manages a number of domains while doing the *élevage* and bottling of others. They look for perfume, finesse and AC character, rather than too-powerful wines which lack individuality. In my view, they succeed admirably, and a Ferraud wine inspires complete confidence.

Loron & Fils
Pontanevaux, 71570 La Chapelle-de-Guinchay.
A large family business formerly selling mainly in bulk, but now more and more in bottle under various brand names. Both domain wines (some very good) and non-*appellation vins de marque*. Their own blends can be a bit clumsy.

Les Vins Mathelin
69830 Châtillon-d'Azergues.
Prizewinning red and white Beaujolais.

Pasquier-Desvignes
St-Lager, 69220 Belleville.
Volume firm for Beaujolais and Mâconnais wines. Produces the Beaujolais brand of Le Marquisat. Overall, dull wines.

Amongst *négociants*, some of the best wines come from Chanut, Louis Tête, Trenel, Fessy/Dessalle, Gobet, Piat, Ferraud, Beaudet, Les Caves de Champclos, and Les Vins Mathelin. Georges Duboeuf is internationally known for quality, and the Eventail de Vignerons Producteurs at Corcelles is a group of independent growers who all make their own wine but come together to bottle and market it.

The best Côte d'Or *négociants* select well in Beaujolais, but some wines seem slightly '*Beaunifiés*', a play on words for which I may not be popular with the burghers of that lovely town.

● ○   St-Amour

1990 production: St-Amour   *17,584 hectolitres*

It may be facetious to say that this is the wine for St-Valentine's Day, but there can be few more pleasurable ways of cementing a relationship than by drinking a bottle of St-Amour *à deux*! It is perhaps best not to go into the reputed origins of the name, since it reflects somewhat badly on the clerics of times past. Suffice it to say that here we are still on a granite base, although it is the only *cru* of the Beaujolais entirely in Saône et Loire. Some years ago, St-Amour had considerable trouble from the outpourings of a factory nearby, which tainted many of the wines – happily, this is now a thing of the past. The white wine made in the commune can be called St-Véran. The wines have a certain sprightliness, which is intriguing, combined with fruit and delicacy – they need sunny years to give them the necessary ripeness. Light vintages can be drunk young, but when conditions are good, a St-Amour of two to three years old is all the more interesting. Unfortunately, there is not a great deal of St-Amour to go around.

The Principal St-Amour Producers

Domaine des Ducs
71570 St-Amour-Bellevue.
     Reliable, rich St-Amour and Chénas.
Domaine Dufour
39160 St-Amour.
     Highly regarded St-Amour which gives a very good lesson in *appellation* taste.
Domaine Elie Mongénie
39160 St-Amour.
     St-Amour that keeps well in ripe years.
Domaine de Mongrin
39160 St-Amour.
     The Duc Frères are responsible for this pretty, soft, flowery wine, the epitome of charm in a St-Amour.

Domaine du Paradis (*Duboeuf*)

71570 St-Amour-Bellevue.

Vines of a good age on sandy, gravelly topsoil produce a rich St-Amour of finesse.

Domaine Guy Patissier (*Eventail*)

39160 St-Amour.

Marked by strong regional flavour, this really packs a punch, but through its depth of *taste*, not through its alcohol imbalance.

Domaine Jean Patissier (*Eventail*)

71570 St-Amour.

Has an equally high reputation – lovely wines with bite and attack – as has Jean-Bernard Patissier with Les Bonnets.

Domaine Francis Saillant

39160 St-Amour.

Very creditable, easy-to-drink St Amour.

Pierre Siraudin/Château de St-Amour

Château de St-Amour, St-Amour-Bellevue, 71570 La Chapelle-de-Guinchay. 13 ha (8 ha *en métayage*). St-Amour, Beaujolais-Villages St-Vérand (red).

The Château de St-Amour is an excellent example of the *appellation*. It is fermented for seven to ten days, according to the nature of the year, and keeps well. The Beaujolais-Villages from St-Vérand ferments for six to eight days, again in order to make a wine which is not ephemeral. For 25 years part of the crop has been sold to Piat, but there is also direct selling in bottle from the château.

Paul Spay/Domaine de la Cave Lamartine

Domaine de la Cave Lamartine, 71570 St-Amour-Bellevue. 6 ha (7 ha *en métayage*). Juliénas Côte de Bessay, St-Amour, Beaujolais St-Amour (white).

This domain possesses good sites, facing south and south-east. It is increasing its bottle sales and its exports to all the usual markets. The vinification is classic, the aim to make wines with regional character and fruit which are delicious for two to three years after the harvest. But Paul Spay is against laying down the *crus* – 'leave that to the Côte d'Or and Bordeaux'!

Georges Duboeuf (St-Amour)
Romanèche-Thorins, 71570 La Chapelle-de-Guinchay.
Other good Duboeuf bottlings in the *appellation* include the
Domaine des Sablons and the Cuvée Poitevin (this is not a
wine which has escaped from the other side of France – M
Poitevin is the vigneron and the *vinificateur*). This is
produced from clay-limestone topsoil, balanced and elegant
and capable of ageing with grace.

● # Juliénas

1990 production: Juliénas   *33,899 hectolitres*

Near St-Amour, the high vineyards of Juliénas give wines which
are really the epitome of what Beaujolais *crus* are all about. They are
wonderfully sturdy, oozing purple fruit when young, positively
crunchy in the mouth, but with a backbone that promises further
development if you can only prevent yourself from pulling the
cork straightaway. There is granite and schist, and the wines have
the *charpente* of the soil. This is the most northerly *cru* of the Rhône
department and it includes some vineyards from the villages of
Jullié (about 80 hectares) and Pruzilly. The slopes of Jullié are very
steep, comparable to those of Chiroubles – no picking machine can
venture up this kind of gradient. Some Juliénas has intriguing spicy
overtones (cinnamon and cloves) to add to the glossy richness.

The Principal Juliénas Producers

Château des Capitans
69840 Juliénas.
Juliénas which usually lasts well in bottle … perhaps a bit
'old style', but not tasted recently.
Cave Coopérative de Liergues
69400 Villefranche.
Founded in 1929, this is the oldest cooperative in the
region. They are great Beaujolais Primeur specialists,

concentrating on producing this fast-turnover, charming wine. It may be fashionable to knock the stuff, but it is still a lovely shot in the arm every November! The firm produces fairly light wines including a delicious roses-and-strawberries rosé.

Caves Coopératives des Grands Vins de Juliénas
69840 Juliénas.

A very 'serious' cooperative, founded in 1961. The Cave sells to *négociants*, direct, and on the export markets – and they do a very good job of work. This is an example of a successful cooperative in the Beaujolais which is also playing a valuable role in today's market.

Domaine René Gonon
69840 Juliénas.

Highly respected wine, which really 'delivers the goods'.

Château de Juliénas/François Condemine
69840 Juliénas.

Owned by François Condemine, this is always remarkable wine, with a scented, delicate nose but immense crunch and bite on the palate – even irony. It keeps beautifully.

Domaine Monnet (*Eventail*)
69840 Juliénas.

This is part of the Château de Juliénas vineyard – the vines face south-south-east and therefore attract the best of the sun. The wine is very fruity, with that Juliénas structure behind it.

Domaine André Pelletier (*Eventail*)
69840 Juliénas.

Les Envaux which is consistently amongst the best Juliénas of each year, full of fruit and *élan*.

Château des Poupets (*Duboeuf*)
69840 Juliénas.

Solid wine, *gardé en fûts*, with character and flavour.

Domaine PBI Sarrau
69840 Juliénas. 6 ha. Fleurie Grand Pré, Morgon Château Gaillard.

These two properties are owned by Pierre, Bernard and Isabelle Sarrau. The wines are bottled at the domain and sold through the firm of Sarrau – an exercise in keeping it in the family! 65 percent is exported, 35 percent sold in

France. Same style and vinification methods as other
properties in the Sarrau group.

Domaine de la Seigneurie de Juliénas (*Duboeuf*)
69840 Juliénas.

This is a domain which is part of the Château de Juliénas
and under the same ownership. Not surprisingly, the
Condemine-Duboeuf connection produces fine wine, with
body and even some tannin (an unusual quality for a
Beaujolais), so a few years in bottle suits it admirably.

● # Chénas

1990 production: Chénas   *16,392 hectolitres*

Chénas produces less wine than any of the other Beaujolais *crus* and
so it is the least known. The name comes from *chênes* as this area
used to be covered by a forest of oaks, but now the vine has taken
over. The vineyards lie on granite between the villages of Chénas
and La Chapelle-de-Guinchay, on either side of the valley of the
Mauvaise and to the north-west of Moulin-à-Vent. Les Rouge-
monts is a Chénas site which is much appreciated. The wines have
pronounced character and repay keeping for a few years in ripe
vintages. They share some tasting qualities with Moulin-à-Vent,
but do not have the silkiness of the 'ultimate' wines of that
appellation. However, Chénas is generous and fruity, not quite as
robust as Morgon – they say it has a bouquet of peonies, but I have
yet to detect that characteristic.

The Principal Chénas Producers

Château Bonnet
71570 La Chapelle-de-Guinchay.

Pierre Perrachon here makes wine with good, fruity,
definite bouquet – perhaps even better than the impression
on the palate.

Domaine Guy Braillon
69840 Chénas.
>Fruity wine, remaining youthful in bottle – lots of body.

Domaine des Brureaux
69840 Chénas.
>Ample, mouth-filling and impressive Chénas from Daniel Robin.

Domaine Louis Champagnon
69840 Chénas.
>Chénas from the village of Les Brureaux; this is superb wine, deep-coloured, full of fruit, all rose petals and crushed grapes.

Château de Chénas (*Eventail*)
69840 Chénas.
>Lovely crunchy fruit – magnificent taste.

Domaine Michel Crozet
Romanèche-Thorins, 71570 La Chapelle-de-Guinchay.
>Chénas from the Coteaux des Brureaux, with vibrant fruit, roundness and body.

Manoir des Journets (*Duboeuf*)
69840 Chénas.
>Old vines here give a wine that is 'a bouquet of flowers lying in a velvet basket', a fanciful description with which I would agree. Basically, it means delightful floral aromas and a velvety texture.

Domaine Hubert Lapierre
Les Gandelins, 71570 La Chapelle-de-Guinchay.
>Wines with good, fruity bouquet and ripe power, which is not the same as excessive alcohol. They also make a special oak-aged *cuvée* of Chénas.

Domaine Jean-Louis Santé
71570 La Chapelle-de-Guinchay.
>Fruity, bouncy, frank Chénas.

● Moulin-à-Vent

1990 production: Moulin-à-Vent   *37,760 hectolitres*

This is the grandest of the ten Beaujolias *crus*, the wine, they say,
which most resembles a Pinot Noir from the Côte d'Or when it is
aged in bottle. Maybe this was true with the '47s, and perhaps it will
be true with the '83s. Much of the vineyard has a soil of crumbly,
pink sand over granite, but the special ingredient is manganese –
there is an old mine under Romanèche-Thorins. Whether this
contributes to the silky power of the wine is a moot point. But fine
Moulin-à-Vent has real breed allied to structure and length. The
appellation does not take its name from a village, but from a sail-less
windmill perched on the granite hillock of the Poncier in the
hamlet of Les Thorins. Don't be surprised if Moulin-à-Vent has
little bouquet when a year old – it needs time in bottle to develop.

The Principal Moulin-à-Vent Producers

Jean Brugne Le Vivier (*Eventail*)
69820 Fleurie.
> Straightforward fruit rather than sheer Moulin style.
> Deliciously rich, ripe and velvety '91.

Domaine des Caves/Famille Delore
Chénas, 69840 Juliénas.
> The sloping vineyards, facing south-south-east, give a
> powerful, generous wine, well able to age.

Domaine Louis Champagnon
69840 Chénas.
> Consistently excellent wines which have the balance to age
> well.

GFA Domaine Desvignes
71570 La Chapelle-de-Guinchay.
> The Château des Jean Loron has belonged to the Desvignes
> family since 1816. The Desvignes are keen on preserving
> aromas so that the wine also has fruity charm and slips
> down easily.

Héritiers Finaz Devillaine (*Eventail*)
Fine violets, fruity nose leads to silky, good and frank taste
– breed rather than blockbuster type.

Domaine Diochon
Romanèche-Thorins, 71570 La Chapelle-de-Guinchay.
Rich and flamboyant Moulin-à-Vent which needs a few
years' bottle-ageing.

Château des Jacques
71570 Romanèche-Thorins.
The largest estate of the *appellation*, with 40 hectares of
vines. It is the pride of the Thorin family and there have
been famed older vintages. The wines keep well, but they
sometimes seem a bit heavy-handed with the alcohol.

Domaine Jacky Janodet
Romanèche-Thorins, 71570 La Chapelle-de-Guinchay.
Very old vines produce rich, solid bottles.

Maurice Labruyère
Les Thorins, 71720 Romanèche-Thorins. 9 ha. Moulin-à-Vent Clos
du Carquelin 1er Grand Cru Classé.
The Clos du Carquelin is a renowned name in Moulin-à-
Vent. Maurice Labruyère represents the fourth generation
of his family to produce the wine here and he is also
President of the Union des Viticulteurs du Moulin-à-Vent.

Alphonse Mortet/Les Fargets (*Eventail*)
Romanèche-Thorins, 71570 La Chapelle-de-Guinchay.
Lovely fresh fruit and no exaggerated chaptalization.

Château du Moulin-à-Vent/Domaine des Héritiers Tagent
Romanèche-Thorins, 71570 La Chapelle-de-Guinchay.
Owned by the Bloud family, this is one of the three largest
estates in the *appellation*. Wood-ageing. Textbook Moulin-
à-Vent, ideal for laying down. Depth and richness.

Clos du Moulin-à-Vent (*Duboeuf*)
Romanèche-Thorins, 71570 La Chapelle-de-Guinchay.
Right in the shadow of the windmill, this is a Moulin
which can age and take on the flavours of Pinot Noir.

Moulin-à-Vent des Hospices
The Bourisset family manage the vineyards of the Hospices
de Romanèche and the wine is usually quite hefty.

Château Portier/Michel Gaidon
Romanèche-Thorins, 71570 La Chapelle-de-Guinchay.
    I have found this rather alcoholic, at least in some vintages.
Thorin
Pontanevaux, 71570 La Chapelle-de-Guinchay.
    Owns Château des Jacques in Moulin-à-Vent and Château
    de Loyse. Also sells under the name of Faye in
    supermarkets. Not my favourite Beaujolais.
Domaine de la Tour du Bief/Comte de Sparre (*Duboeuf*)
69840 Chénas.
    Georges Duboeuf does a domain-bottling of this wine from
    the commune of Chénas. The soil is sandy, the style is full
    and robust. The Domaine de la Rochelle is in the same
    family.
Union des Viticulteurs Romanèche-Thorins at Chénas
69840 Chénas.
    Fruity, but tends to be thick in style, without real Moulin
    silkiness.

● Fleurie

1990 production: Fleurie   *48,047 hectolitres*

Fleurie is blessed with the most evocative name of all the ten
Beaujolais *crus*, easy to say, even easier to drink. The wines are
charming and full of fruit – and there are enough of them to go
round. Between Chiroubles and Moulin-à-Vent the underlying
granite gives Fleurie its *ampleur* – a fine bottle is at its most seductive
between 18 months and three years old. Fleurie's perfume and
crushed fruit should jump out of the glass at you.

The Principal Fleurie Producers

Domaine Paul Bernard
69820 Fleurie.
    Rich, full and sweetly juicy Fleurie.

Domaine René Berrod-les-Roches du Vivier
69820 Fleurie.

Top quality Fleurie, Moulin-à-Vent and Beaujolais-Villages. Drinking these bottles can give a frisson of pure pleasure which seems peculiar to the best wines of Beaujolais.

Cave Coopérative des Grands Vins de Fleurie
69820 Fleurie.

A very well run cooperative, with good, true Fleurie. Their two top *cuvées* are the Cuvée Presidente Marguerite (named after a wonderful lady, Mlle Marguerite Chabert, who used to preside over the Cave), a perfumed, 'feminine' Fleurie, and the Cuvée du Cardinal Bienfaiteur, which is more powerful and can take some bottle-age.

Domaine Michel Chignard
69820 Fleurie.

Les Moriers is a good wine, full of crunchy fruit.

Domaine Monrozier
Les Moriers, 69820 Fleurie. 9 ha.

The domain borders the *cru* of Moulin-à-Vent, north of the commune of Fleurie. This is a property which makes Fleurie designed to keep for a few years, rather than for instant drinking. A Swiss *négociant* takes a good chunk of the production.

Domaine de Montgenas (*Eventail*)
69820 Fleurie.

Really copybook Fleurie, full of ripe fruit and juicy texture.

Domaine du Point du Jour
69820 Fleurie.

Guy Depardon makes clean, *appellation*-character wine.

Domaine des Quatre Vents (*Duboeuf*)
69820 Fleurie.

Owned by Dr Darroze, this exemplary Fleurie is distributed by Duboeuf and a Swiss *négociant*, but bottled at the property.

Quinson
69820 Fleurie.

Large producers of Beaujolais; but not for me – too 'thick' in style.

Georges Duboeuf (Fleurie)

Romanèche-Thorins, 71570 La Chapelle-de-Guinchay.

Other Fleuries, bottled and sold by Duboeuf, are Château Couhard, Clos de la Pointe du Jour, Château des Déduits, Domaine de Fanfotin, Domaine du Haut-Poncié, Clos du Pavillon and 'La Madonne', an important *climat* of 50 hectares with 20 owners. It is beautifully sited overlooking the village of Fleurie on sandy topsoil – the statue of the Virgin Mary is perched on a little chapel in view of the whole vineyard. Here, the nose is meant to be of peaches and peonies, but it is true crushed red fruit.

Other Fleurie Sites

These include La Chapelle des Bois and La Roilette. Mostly the wines are very good (such as Sylvain Fessy's La Roilette), but some are spoilt by excessive alcohol, as if the winemakers have sought to gild the lily. A pity, as it destroys the essential fruit character of Fleurie, indeed, of all Beaujolais. As elsewhere, this was noticeable in '83, when the natural alcohol was of a good level, so there was no need for heavy-handed chaptalization. Recently, the situation has improved greatly, with alcohol levels tightly controlled. The Fleuriatons have a fine reputation, worth guarding.

Oak-ageing in the cellars of Fleurie

● Chiroubles

1990 production: Chiroubles   *20,221 hectolitres*

This is the most ethereal of all the *crus*, light and fragrant, as airborne as the height of its vineyards. It is the *cru* one drinks first of all the ten – I have nostalgic memories of downing bottles of it in February and March in the Paris bistros where returning skiers met to swap stories of derring-do on the slopes. Chiroubles is ready before all the other *crus*, with developed bouquet and enormous charm when the rest are still at the dumb stage. There is a marvellous viewpoint at La Terrasse de Chiroubles where, from a height of 750 metres (2,460 feet) you can see the whole of Beaujolais, the River Saône and, on the horizon, the Jura topped by the snowy Alps and even Mont Blanc on clear days. The Terrasse and surrounding hills are themselves often dusted with snow in January and February. Although this is the highest in altitude of the *crus*, the vineyards are still firmly based on granite. All in all, the Chiroublons are very lucky to have such a delicious commodity which 'sells itself' at such a young age.

The Principal Chiroubles Producers

Domaine Cheysson-les-Farges
69115 Chiroubles.
   Archetypal Chiroubles, which means it is delicious and
   gouleyant – utterly gulpable.
Domaine Desmures Père & Fils (*Duboeuf*)
69115 Chiroubles.
   Another jewel in the Duboeuf crown, a triumph of
   teamwork between a family of growers and winemakers
   and the perfect technique and cleanliness of professional
   bottling.
Château de Javernand (*Duboeuf*)
69115 Chiroubles.
   M Fourneau, President of the *cru*, owns this property. The
   wine is extraordinarily 'Chiroubles', with a 'floaty' taste,
   but a lovely kernel of fruit. Sandy topsoil and steep slopes.

Domaine Gérard-Roger Méziat
69115 Chiroubles.
> Delightful Chiroubles, true to the *appellation*'s role as a giver of pleasure.

Domaine Georges Passot (*Eventail*)
69910 Villié-Morgon.
> Divine, scented Chiroubles nose – a lovely mouthful of ethereal fruit. La Grosse Pierre is always one of the best wines of the *appellation*.

Château de Raousset (*Duboeuf*)
69115 Chiroubles.
> The property possesses 20 hectares of Chiroubles, as well as 12 hectares of Fleurie and 13 hectares of Morgon. Granite-based vineyards, the soil here has a little less clay than at Morgon. The average age of the vines is 25–30 years. The Duboeuf bottling of this well-known property is impeccable, as one would expect.

Domaine René Savoye (*Eventail*)
69115 Chiroubles.
> Another Chiroubles which gives a real lift-off.

La Maison des Vignerons à Chiroubles
69115 Chiroubles.
> Delicious, light, textbook Chiroubles – quaff it in huge quantities when it is six months to a year old.

Eventail de Vignerons Producteurs (Chiroubles)
Corcelles-en-Beaujolais, 69220 Belleville.
> Other excellent examples of the *appellation*, available through the Eventail, are those of Christian Lafay and Philippe Gobet.

● # Morgon

1990 production: Morgon   *63,596 hectolitres*

Morgon makes the most wine, after Brouilly, amongst the ten Beaujolais *crus*. The actual village of Bas-Morgon is not nearly as important as Villié-Morgon, but between the two lies the splendid

Mont du Py, whence come the most exciting wines. The underlying soil is granite, but a distinctive feature of Morgon is the disintegrating schist called *roche pourrie*.

The wines from the best parts of the *appellation* have such an individual bouquet that they have created a verb – *morgonner*. But this pronounced nose is a product of the best sites and finest winemaking, and needs time to develop, because very young Morgon (for example, in the spring after the vintage) tends to be rather dumb of bouquet in comparison with the other *crus*. However, given time in bottle, the robust, generous, fleshy character of the *cru* really shows its paces. There are rich, fine flavours at two to four years old and, in great years, exotic flavours in wines far older. Descriptions such as wild cherry and sherry are bandied about, but if I ever found a taste of sherry in my mature Morgon (which I have not), I think I would be worried!

The best *climats* are Le Py, La Roche Pilée, Bellevue, Les Pillets and Les Charmes, but frequently the wines are mixed between these favoured sites and others.

The Principal Morgon Producers

Georges Brun (*Eventail*)
69910 Villié-Morgon.
  Morgon Le Clachet that is terrific at two years.
Domaine de la Chanaise
69910 Villié-Morgon.
  Dominique Piron emphasizes the fruit in his Morgon, perhaps more than the body.
Paul Collonge
69910 Villié-Morgon. 3·64 ha in production. Beaujolais-Villages, Morgon, Morgon Les Charmes, Régnié.
  The vineyards are well placed, facing south and south-east. The wines are robust, generous and keep well – M Collonge calls the bouquet 'kirsch and framboise', which is 'typically Morgon'. Direct selling in France and exports.
Domaine de Colonat
69910 Villié-Morgon.
  Bernard Collonge produces very fruity wine which likes

some bottle-age to show its paces.

Domaine Jean Descombes (*Duboeuf*)

69910 Villié-Morgon.

This is, obviously, one of the best Morgons, with three-quarters of the vines more than 30 years old. In 1985, I had the pleasure of tasting in Descombes' cellars, and a bottle of his '76 was heavenly, all chocolate, truffles and warm cocoa! The wines are still as good.

Louis Claude Desvignes

La Voûte-au-Bourg, 69910 Villié-Morgon. 15 ha (8 ha worked). Vines are scattered over the commune: 4·5 ha are in the best *climats* of Morgon Côte du Py and Morgon Javernières.

A family domain, worked *de père en fils* for seven generations – since 1712! They follow traditional methods and aim for keeping wines typical of Morgon. They bottle after six to twelve months.

Sylvain Fessy

69823 Belleville.

The Cuvée André Gauthier displays exemplary crunchy fruit.

Domaine Louis Genillon (*Eventail*)

69910 Villié-Morgon.

Good Morgon, which lasts well. Louis Desvignes is another member of the *équipe de l'Eventail*, but his Javernières is more supple and ready earlier.

Domaine Lieven (*Duboeuf*)

69910 Villié-Morgon.

Associated with Château de Raousset, the property is owned by the Princesse de Lieven (Madame Charles Piat) and her delightful, raspberry-scented Morgon-Charmes is bottled at the domain by Georges Duboeuf. The wine can also be sold under the Château de Bellevue label.

Another Duboeuf bottling is the solid, full Domaine des Versauds.

Domaine des Pillets

69910 Villié-Morgon.

Gérard Brisson produces Morgon with a lovely fruity, deep bouquet, and a highly commendable, full, juicy taste. In ripe vintages, the wines are splendid at three to four years.

Château de Pizay

69220 St-Jean d'Ardières. 53 ha. Morgon, Régnié, Beaujolais Rouge, Blanc.

This is a beautiful property, whose vineyards lie partly in Morgon, partly in Beaujolais-Villages territory. Their Côte du Py is lighter than the wine of Pierre Savoye, but has great finesse. The reason for this is that the Pizay vineyards are on the other side of the Côte, near the foot of the slope – Morgon from St-Joseph is like that too. They also make 2,500 cases of enticing Beaujolais Blanc each year.

Domaine de Ruyère

69910 Villié-Morgon.

Paul Collonge makes good Morgon, not ultra flavoursome, but pleasing.

Domaine Savoye (Pierre Savoye)

'Sur la Côte du Py', 69910 Villié-Morgon. 14 ha. Beaujolais, Morgon, Morgon Côte du Py.

This is a splendid domain, principally on the Côte du Py, where the schistous rock is called *pierre bleue*, which in effect becomes ochre in colour as it decomposes and gives that elusive quality to the wine – *un vin qui 'morgonne'*. Pierre Savoye, the son-in-law of Jean Descombes (who could be called the honorary grandfather of Morgon) makes splendid Côte de Py here. It has a wonderful colour and formidable taste, an experience for all those who wish to taste 'true' Morgon. These wines keep. They even *terroitent*, due to the mineral content of the soil.

Domaine Jacques Trichard

69910 Villié-Morgon.

Typical Morgon, with fine fruit, sometimes a bit hard in youth but promising well.

Régnié

1990 production: Régnié   *36,799 hectolitres*

Régnié was officially granted its status as Beaujolais' tenth *cru* in December 1988. The *appellation* lies between Morgon and Brouilly, and is based on a relatively light soil, a sandy granite similar to that found in Chiroubles. It claims to be the first Beaujolais location where the Romans planted the vine, indeed the name Régnié derives from an early Roman resident, a nobleman called Reginus. The best Régniés are supple, delicate, scented wines, redolent of strawberries and redcurrants. Those from the southern end of the commune, near Brouilly, are the lightest and freshest; those coming from closer to Morgon in the north have more substance.

The Principal Régnié Producers

Château du Basty
69430 Lantignié. 12 ha (5 ha *en métayage*). Beaujolais-Villages, Regnié.
   Light but stylish Beaujolais Régnié.

Domaine des Braves
Régnié-Durette, 69430 Beaujeu.
   One of the best of this *cru*, deep and vibrant.

Domaine Jean & Yves Durand
69430 Régnié-Durette.
   Light but well-crafted Régnié and Brouilly.

Domaine de la Gérarde
69430 Régnié-Durette.
   Stylish wine, a regular medal-winner at competitions.

Domaine Joel Rochette
Le Chalet, 69430 Régnié-Durette.
   Light, appealing Régnié and Beaujolais-Villages.

Château de la Tour Bourdon (*Duboeuf*)
69430 Régnié.
   Old vines, but a wine which is delicious for the summer
   after the vintage.

Côte de Brouilly

1990 production: Côte de Brouilly   *18,021 hectolitres*

In the context of the Côte d'Or, anything that is *Côte de* is not as good as the straight name, ie Côte de Beaune is not as good as Beaune itself. But Côte de Brouilly is most certainly one up the ladder from plain Brouilly, due to the fact that its vineyards are on the slopes of Mont Brouilly. But, as there is far less Côte de Brouilly than Brouilly, not so many people discover it. It is interesting to note that Côte de Brouilly has a higher minimum alcohol level than the other *crus* – 10·5 percent instead of ten percent – but in all cases, if the name of the *climat* or vineyard is added, it has to be 11 percent. Mont Brouilly rises to 500 metres (1,640 feet), with the vines on all sides (therefore some sites are better exposed than others), on a base predominantly of granite.

The *appellation* is spread over the communes of Odenas, St-Lager, Cercié and Quincié. I have seen Mont Brouilly described as a sort of giant mole-hill placed like a lighthouse at the head of Beaujolais – the person who coined that mixed metaphor must have imbibed a good deal of its wine. Côte de Brouilly has tremendous projection of fruit, rich, savoury and grapey.

The Principal Côte de Brouilly Producers

Domaine L Bassy
Odenas, 69830 St-Georges de Reneins.
   Deliciously juicy Côte de Brouilly.
Domaine de Chavanne
69460 Brouilly.
   Claudius Geoffray makes excellent wine, with massive fruit on the nose and the impression of crunching grapes as you drink.
Domaine de Conroy
69460 Brouilly.
   Wine of balance and charm and great drinkability made by Jean de St-Charles. The vines are right on the *pierre bleue*, the porphyry of the old volcano that is now Mont Brouilly.

Domaine Guy Cotton
Odenas, 69830 St-Georges de Reneins.

    Lovely wines with fruit and guts.

Domaine Delachanal
69460 Odenas. 5·2 ha, half of which are in Brouilly, half in Côte de Brouilly. Three-quarters are old vines on the southern side of the hill of Brouilly. 20,000 bottles per annum, 7,500 magnums in Côte de Brouilly.

    Traditional vinification in wooden vats and bottling in March of the following year. Vatting is usually six to seven days here (M Charmette describes it as *vinification type Bordelaise*!), so this is not ephemeral Côte de Brouilly. Sells to *négociants*, as well as to private clients, and exports to Switzerland. Makes a speciality of amusing labels, 'personalized' presents designed for customers, such as the Cuvée des Pompistes, Cuvée des Douaniers, and even the Cuvée des Bordelais!

André Large (*Eventail*)
69460 Odenas.

    Delicious, gulpable wine, usually ready a little earlier than that of Verger (qv).

Domaine du Petit Pressoir
69460 Brouilly.

    Marcel and Daniel Mathon make juicy, tempting wine.

Château Thivin
69460 Odenas.

    Mme Veuve Claude Geoffray is responsible for superb Côte de Brouilly. It has a wonderful gutsy, fruity nose, lovely fruit and no hardness – yet body – on the palate. Terrific wine.

Domaine Lucien & Robert Verger (*Eventail*)
69220 St-Lager.

    Their L'Ecluse has a nose of violets, which is very marked in this vineyard – another wine of superb fruit. The name is curious, with its evocation of running water, because the vineyard is right on the slopes and there has never been a stream here.

● Brouilly

1990 production: Brouilly   *73,413 hectolitres*

Brouilly produces much more wine than any of the other ten *crus* and so it inevitably has a high profile in cafés, bistros and brasseries. Some people say, rather cruelly, that it is just a glorified Beaujolais-Villages, but good Brouilly has more substance and finish, and the more solid examples keep longer than a straight *villages*. The *appellation* is spread over six communes: Odenas, St-Lager, Cercié, Charentay, Quincié and St-Etienne-la-Varenne. In fact, many producers make both Brouilly and Beaujolais-Villages. Brouilly is a totally legitimate *cru*, because the vines grow on granite and schist, called locally *gore* and *morgon*. Brouilly is frank and without complication, a heady glass of the grape in liquid form.

The Principal Brouilly Producers

Château du Bluizard
St-Etienne-la-Varenne, 69460 St-Etienne-les-Ouilliers.
> Jean de St-Charles makes round, rich wines, supple and tempting – he also produces Beaujolais-Villages.

Château de la Chaize
69460 Odenas. 94 ha (60 ha *en métayage*). Brouilly Château de la Chaize. All vineyards within the parish of Brouilly.
> The Marquise de Roussy de Sales reigns over the largest integrated private wine estate in Beaujolais and Burgundy, which supports 24 families – the property includes extensive woods. The Château, built in 1676 following the plans of Mansart and Le Nôtre, is of great classical symmetry. On form (for it is occasionally inconsistent), the wine is no less impressive, sold at a premium price but luscious and full, brimming with Brouilly fruit. Enormous attention to detail goes into making this fine Brouilly, which has the body and fruit in good vintages to last three to five years. Length of vatting is five to seven days, and the wine is stocked in wooden *foudres* and then in stainless steel for optimum freshness.

Vins Fessy

69220 St-Jean d'Ardières.

A bit patchy, but certainly some good wines.

Jean Lathuilière

69220 Cercié-en-Beaujolais.

Seductively fruity, prizewinning Brouilly-Pisse-Vieille, much prettier than its horrid name.

Domaine de la Roche (*Duboeuf*)

43260 St-Etienne-la-Varenne.

This vineyard is on steep slopes 420 metres (1,380 feet) high – the yields are small and the work difficult on a mixture of gravel and sand. The wine is relatively light and 'floaty', for young drinking. The domain also makes Beaujolais-Villages.

Domaine André Ronzière (*Eventail*)

Charentay, 69220 Belleville.

Really rich Brouilly, no doubt due to the many old vines.

Domaine Ruet

69220 Cercié-en-Beaujolais.

Jean-Paul Ruet makes most respectable wine.

Domaine Patrick & Martine Vermorel/Domaine de la Fully

Chambon, 69460 Blacé.

Really wonderful fruit – all that a beautifully-handled, frank wine should be. The Beaujolais-Villages also excels.

Domaine de Vuril

Charentay, 69220 Belleville.

Georges Dutraive is responsible for very commendable Brouilly.

Eventail de Vignerons Producteurs (Brouilly)

Corcelles-en-Beaujolais, 69220 Belleville.

The Verger family has fine Brouilly, sold through the Eventail.

Beaujolais-Villages

1990 production: Beaujolais-Villages   *332,451 hectolitres*

The following villages have the right to the *appellation*: in the Saône et Loire – Leynes, St-Amour-Bellevue, La Chapelle-de-Guinchay, Romanèche-Thorins, Pruzilly, Chânes, St-Vérand and St-Symphorien d'Ancelles; in the Rhône – Juliénas, Jullié, Emeringes, Chénas, Fleurie, Chiroubles, Lancié, Villié-Morgon, Lantignié, Beaujeu, Régnié, Durette, Cercié, Quincié, St-Lager, Odenas, Charentay, St-Etienne-la-Varenne, Vaux, Le Perréon, St-Etienne-des-Oullières, Blacé, Arbuissonnas, Salles, St-Julien, Montmelas, Rivolet, Denicé, Les Ardillats, Marchampt and Vauxrenard.

All these villages lie between Villefranche-sur-Saône in the south and the border with the Mâconnais in the north. It is by far the best zone for Beaujolais, and although the Villages wines do not have the sheer individuality of the *crus*, they have more projection and body than straight Beaujolais.

It is a ravishingly pretty area, with rolling, vine-covered hills and somewhat sleepy villages, particularly in the afternoon. The roads twist and turn and dip, and no one should attempt high speeds. There is granite, schist and pebbles, with sandstone and limestone breaking out more often in the southern villages. Beaujolais-Villages is delicious in the spring following the vintage and for the next two years.

The Principal Beaujolais-Villages Producers

Paul Beaudet
Pontanevaux, 71570 La Chapelle-de-Guinchay. 15 ha. Chénas Château des Vignes, Beaujolais-Villages Clos du Rochettes.

> A wide range of Beaujolais and Mâconnais wines. You always get a good bottle from this firm, although perhaps not the scintillating best.

Chanut Frères
71570 Romanèche-Thorins.

> Good quality Beaujolais with plenty of extract, particularly in Moulin-à-Vent and Morgon.

Château de Corcelles
Corcelles-en-Beaujolais, 69220 Belleville.

Light, pretty wine, in a well-designed bottle. The vineyards are on flat land, and not in the best part of the hills.

Domaine Dalicieux
Vernette, 71570 Leynes. Beaujolais-Villages, Mâcon-Villages.

Excellent wines, both white and red.

Vins Dessalle
69220 St-Jean d'Ardières.

Négociant whose range of Beaujolais wines are also seen under the label Sylvain Fessy. Results are patchy.

Georges Duboeuf
Romanèche-Thorins, 71570 La Chapelle-de-Guinchay. 5 ha. Pouilly-Fuissé (commune of Chaintré) 4 ha, 25,000 bottles; Beaujolais Blanc (commune of Chaintré) 1 ha, 8,000 bottles.

The domain, good as it is, must inevitably be dwarfed by the vast Duboeuf *négociant* empire, one of the great wine trade success stories of this century. Georges Duboeuf, through sheer hard work, a deep knowledge of his region and a sure touch for the genuine, has done more than anyone else for the spread of the true taste of Beaujolais and Mâconnais wines. Stocks now run to four to five million bottles. Some of the wines he chooses are bottled at the individual domains, the rest go to his ultra-modern plant. What are the secrets? He buys all his requirements very early, and so tends to get top quality. He also practises no *acténisation*, or flash pasteurization, and relies on Kieselguhr membrane filters and cold sterile bottling. As a result, Duboeuf wines are always fresh and fruity.

Château de la Grand'Grange
Le Perréon, 69830 St-Georges de Reneins.

M Chamussy at Le Perréon produces round, ripe wine.

Claude & Michelle Joubert
Lantignié, 69430 Beaujeu. 13 ha. Beaujolais-Villages Lantignié, Côte de Brouilly, Juliénas, Régnié.

This is a very reliable domain which has been built up lovingly by Claude and Michelle Joubert. The average age of the vines undoubtedly contributes to the full, deep fruit of the wines. The Beaujolais-Villages is made by semi-carbonic maceration, while the Juliénas receives a traditional vatting of eight to ten days. The Jouberts were first known for their rich, full Villages, but the Juliénas is rapidly catching up.

Château de Lacarelle

69460 St-Etienne-des-Oullières. 150 ha (100 ha currently planted in the communes of St-Etienne-des-Oullières and St-Etienne-La-Varenne.)

The family of the Comte Durieu de Lacarelle has been making wine here for more than 200 years. They produce aromatic and supple wines which are delicious to drink when young.

GAEC René & Christian Miolane

Le Cellier, 69460 Salles-Arbuissonnas. 19 ha (5 ha *en métayage*). Beaujolais-Villages: Classique, Cuvée de la Côtebras, Cuvée des Chasseurs, Rosé.

The Miolanes have had vineyards on the same slope for three centuries, which gives a pleasant sense of continuity. René Miolane now runs the property with his son, his daughter and his son-in-law. The wines are solid for Villages and are not of the ephemeral, here-this-minute-gone-the-next variety. They sell across the board to private clients and wholesalers, but exports account for 60–70 percent of the total volume.

Domaine Monternot

69460 Blacé-en-Beaujolais.

This is excellent Villages from Blacé, with fruit, style and body.

Domaine de Montmeron (*Duboeuf*)

69430 Lantignié.

More old vines give a wine of individuality.

Robert Sarrau/Caves de l'Ardières

69220 Belleville.

Domain wines reliable, but also an important *négociant*.
They distribute the wines of PBI Sarrau (qv).

Domaine de la Sorbière

69430 Quincié.

Pleasant Villages is made by Jean-Charles Pivot, lighter than some but very gulpable.

Domaine St–Sorlin

René Jacquet makes wine which finishes with a fruity flourish.

Louis Tête

St-Didier-sur-Beaujeu, 69430 Beaujeu. 3·5 ha. Moulin-à-Vent, Régnié, Beaujolais-Villages.

This is the small family property of Louis Tête, the highly respected *négociant* in Beaujolais wines, whose selections are always prime examples of their kind. The wines are made at low temperature to conserve maximum fruit, but so that the finished bottles have good structure too.

Domaine des Trois Coteaux

69430 Quincié.

Jean-Philippe Perron makes very frank, fruity Villages at Quincié.

Château Varennes (*Piat*)

Totally tempting, with a glorious bouquet and a really attractive flavour.

Georges Duboeuf (Beaujolais-Villages)

Romanèche-Thorins, 71570 La Chapelle-de-Guinchay.

These include the Domaine du Colombier, Domaine des Buillats, Domaine du Potet, which ages well, Château de la Tour, Domaine des Trois Coteaux, Château des Vierres and the Domaine de la Treille, again a Villages which can be kept a year or two.

Eventail de Vignerons Producteurs (Beaujolais-Villages)

Corcelles-en-Beaujolais, 69220 Belleville.

The Eventail produces high-quality Beaujolais-Villages from Paul Fortune, André Jaffre, André Depardon, Roger & Jean-Luc Tissier, Guy Patissier, André Ronzière and Jacques Montange.

A–Z of Burgundy Producers

The A–Z section is an alphabetical list of some 600 Burgundy producers (whether growers, *négociants* or *négociants-éleveurs*) and provides an index to those recommended in the Wines and Villages section.

For **Chablis**, **Côte Chalonnaise**, the **Mâconnais** and **Beaujolais**, on looking up an individual domain or *château* readers will be referred to the relevant area and village/*appellation* in the Wines and Villages (W&V) section, where details can be found of holdings (where available) and wine-making methods, together with an assessment of the wines.

For **Côte d'Or** producers, the total area of land cultivated, details of vineyard holdings, and a description of the winemaking and wine styles are included here in the A–Z. The wines are listed in the following order: Grand Cru, Premier Cru, *Village* and Regional, with each category divided by a full stop. Figures for holdings *en métayage* or *en fermage* are in addition to the main holdings figure. Recommended wines are in small capital letters, indicating that a more specific reference to the wine can be found under the relevant village/*appellation* in Wines and Villages.

For example, Domaine Michel Gaunoux (a Côte d'Or producer) has two wines recommended in its entry on page 267 of the A–Z: the Grand Cru Corton-Renardes and a Pommard Premier Cru, Grands Epenots. More information on these wines can be found (under Domaine Michel Gaunoux) on page 124 in the Aloxe-Corton section, and on page 137 in the Pommard section, of Wines and Villages.

If you are unsure which *appellation* a recommended Grand Cru wine belongs to, the list on the following page will help.

Côte d'Or Grands Crus	Village/Appellation
Bâtard-Montrachet	Puligny-Montrachet
Bienvenues-Bâtard-Montrachet	Puligny-Montrachet
Bonnes Mares	Morey-St-Denis
Chambertin	Gevrey-Chambertin
Chambertin Clos de Bèze	Gevrey-Chambertin
Chapelle-Chambertin	Gevrey-Chambertin
Charmes-Chambertin	Gevrey-Chambertin
Chevalier-Montrachet	Puligny-Montrachet
Clos des Lambrays	Morey-St-Denis
Clos de la Roche	Morey-St-Denis
Clos St-Denis	Morey-St-Denis
Clos de Tart	Morey-St-Denis
Clos de Vougeot	Vougeot
Corton (also: Corton-Bressandes, Corton Clos du Roi, Corton-Perrières, Corton-Pouget, Corton-Renardes, etc)	Aloxe-Corton
Corton-Charlemagne	Pernand-Vergelesses
Criots-Bâtard-Montrachet	Chassagne-Montrachet
Echézeaux	Flagey-Echézeaux
Grands Echézeaux	Flagey-Echézeaux
Griotte-Chambertin	Gevrey-Chambertin
Latricières-Chambertin	Gevrey-Chambertin
Mazis-Chambertin	Gevrey-Chambertin
Mazoyères-Chambertin	Gevrey-Chambertin
Le Montrachet	Puligny-Montrachet
Musigny	Chambolle-Musigny
Richebourg	Vosne-Romanée
La Romanée	Vosne-Romanée
Romanée-Conti	Vosne-Romanée
Romanée-St-Vivant	Vosne-Romanée
Ruchottes-Chambertin	Gevrey-Chambertin
La Tâche	Vosne-Romanée

Bertrand Ambroise

Prémeaux-Prissey, 21700 Nuits-St-Georges. 7 ha (8 ha *en métayage*). Grand Cru: Corton. I^{ers} Crus: Nuits-St-Georges: Rue de Chaux, Vaucrains. Nuits-St-Georges, Côte de Nuits-Villages, Bourgogne Rouge, Blanc and Aligoté.

Basic Bourgogne Pinot Noir and Côte de Nuits-Villages which are not impressive, even in years like 1988 and 1989. The Nuits-St-Georges Premier Cru Rue de Chaux '87 seemed 'dirty', cutting the fruit.

Bernard Amiot

21220 Chambolle-Musigny. 3·5 ha (2 ha *en métayage*). I^{ers} Crus: Chambolle-Musigny: Les Charmes, Les Châtelots, Chambolle-Musigny. CHAMBOLLE-MUSIGNY, **Bourgogne Rouge and Aligoté.**

Good straight Chambolle-Musigny.

Pierre Amiot

Morey-St-Denis, 21220 Gevrey-Chambertin. 7 ha (3 ha *en métayage*). Grands Crus: Charmes-Chambertin; Les Bonnes Mares, Clos des Lambrays, CLOS DE LA ROCHE, **Clos St-Denis, Clos de Tart *monopole*. I^{ers} Crus: Gevrey-Chambertin Les Combottes; Morey-St-Denis: Aux Charmes, Les Millandes, Les Ruchots. Gevrey-Chambertin, Morey-St-Denis, Bourgogne Aligoté, Bourgogne Grand Ordinaire.**

Remarkably good wines with a bouquet of undergrowth and truffles. The Clos de la Roche is particularly fine and the '84 Les Combottes was astonishing for the vintage. Occasionally the wines are just good and fail to 'flash lights' at you. The grapes are 50 percent destemmed and the wines aged in 15 percent new wood.

Amiot-Bonfils

13 rue du Grand Puits, Chassagne-Montrachet, 21190 Meursault. 9 ha (7·4 ha *en métayage*). Grand Cru: Le Montrachet. I^{ers} Crus: Puligny-Montrachet Les Demoiselles; Chassagne-Montrachet: Les Caillerets, Les Champgains, Clos St-Jean (red and white), Les

Macherelles, La Maltroie, Les Vergers (red and white).
Chassagne-Montrachet, Bourgogne Blanc and Aligoté.
Traditionally-vinified wines aged in 25 percent new oak. I hardly
ever see these, occasionally in France (which accounts for 45 percent
of Guy Amiot's market), but the wines are well made.

Robert Ampeau

**6 rue de Cromin, 21190 Meursault. 1ᵉʳˢ Crus: Savigny-lès-
Beaune: Fourneaux, Lavières;** BEAUNE CLOS DU ROI; **Volnay
Santenots;** BLAGNY LA PIÈCE SOUS LE BOIS; AUXEY-DURESSES
LES ECUSSEAUX; MEURSAULT: CHARMES, **La Pièce sous le Bois,**
PERRIÈRES; PULIGNY-MONTRACHET LES COMBETTES. POMMARD,
Meursault.

Robert Ampeau and his son Michel work immensely hard and
produce some astonishing wines. At first, it was the whites which
were renowned, but now the reds are excellent too. The whites last
beautifully, with explosive flavours, heady bouquets and vanillin
textures – they are frequently in full flight while other wines of the
same *appellation* are tiring. The reds ooze gamey fruit – I like the
Blagny and Auxey, and even the Savignys, while they are still quite
young and precocious, but obviously the Pommard, Beaune Clos
du Roi and Volnay Santenots last longer. An Ampeau bottle is
always a treat, but they are not seen as much as they should be – M
Ampeau does not much like selling his wines!

Pierre André

**Château de Corton-André, 21420 Aloxe-Corton. 30 ha.
Grands Crus: Clos de Vougeot; Corton-Charlemagne;
Corton Château de Corton-André, Corton Clos du Roi,
Corton-Combes, Corton Hautes Mourottes, Corton-
Pougets. 1ᵉʳˢ Crus: Aloxe-Corton Les Chaillots; Savigny-
lès-Beaune Clos des Guettes. Gevrey-Chambertin;
Pernand-Vergelesses; Ladoix: white, Clos des Chagnots;
Savigny-lès-Beaune: Clos des Godeaux, Clos des
Guettottes; Côte de Nuits-Villages.**

Pierre André is both a *négociant* and an important proprietor of
vineyards. The labels depict the beautiful, flamboyantly-tiled roofs
of Burgundy. M André founded and owns the firm of La Reine
Pédauque. I am afraid that I do not get on at all with the wines; if

they are clean and without fault, they are also neutral and lack all individuality. Sales in France are big – exports are much smaller.

Domaine Marquis d'Angerville

Volnay 21190 Meursault. 14 ha. 1ers Crus: VOLNAY: **Caillerets,** CHAMPANS, CLOS DES DUCS, **Fremiets, Taillepieds; Meursault Santenots. Pommard, Bourgogne Rouge and Blanc.**

This was one of the first great Burgundy estates to domain-bottle and its standards have never slipped. The emphasis is on finesse and elegance, and the wines usually have a long, lingering finish. They are made in wooden vats and matured in oak barrels which are renewed every five years. Exports account for 65 percent of turnover, and are to all the traditional markets. The d'Angerville family has contributed enormously to both quality and authenticity in wine production in Burgundy, and for that Burgundy-lovers must always be grateful. The Marquis d'Angerville is the sole owner of the Clos des Ducs.

Domaine de l'Arillière

See W&V, Mâconnais, Pouilly-Fuissé.

Domaine Arlaud Père & Fils

21700 Nuits-St-Georges.

Wines perhaps made to attract a commercial following, rather than for someone seeking real individuality.

Domaine de l'Arlot

Prémeaux, 21700 Nuits-St-Georges. 13·25 ha. Grand Cru: Romanée-St-Vivant. 1ers Crus: NUITS-ST-GEORGES: CLOS DE L'ARLOT **(red and** WHITE**),** CLOS DES FORÊTS ST-GEORGES. **Côte de Nuits-Villages.**

A relatively new domain owned by Axa Millésimes, also owners of Château Pichon-Longueville-Baron and Château Petit-Village (amongst others) in Bordeaux. There is clearly a similar dedication to quality here, with very skilled winemaking from Jean-Pierre de Smet, who produces refined red and white Nuits-St-Georges.

Domaine Comte Armand
21630 Pommard.
The domain's sole vineyard is POMMARD CLOS DES EPENEAUX.
French-Canadian Pascal Marchand makes wine of great extract,
aged in 50 percent new wood, usually needing at least six to eight
years to mature. Some fine old bottles too.

Domaine Arnoux Père & Fils
**21200 Chorey-lès-Beaune. 23 ha (including 10 ha in
Chorey).**
Mostly rather rustic reds.

Domaine Robert Arnoux
**Route Nationale, 21700 Vosne-Romanée. 12 ha. Grands
Crus:** CLOS DE VOUGEOT; **Echézeaux,** ROMANÉE-ST-VIVANT.
1ers Crus: VOSNE-ROMANÉE: **Les Chaumes,** LES SUCHOTS;
**Nuits-St-Georges: Corvées Pagets, Les Procès. Vosne-
Romanée Hautes Maizières, Vosne-Romanée,
Nuits-St-Georges.**
Rewarding wines on the whole. Occasionally could have more
concentration.

Maison Auvigue
See W&V, Mâconnais, Pouilly-Fuissé.

Domaine Bachelet
**Rue de la Petite Issue, 21220 Gevrey-Chambertin. 7 ha.
Grand Cru:** CHARMES-CHAMBERTIN. **1er Cru: Gevrey-
Chambertin Les Corbeaux. Gevrey-Chambertin, Côtes de
Nuits-Villages, Bourgogne Rouge and Aligoté.**
Confusion with the domain at Dezize is understandable as these
wines also used to sell under the name Bernard Bachelet! Bernard
Bachelet is the father of Denis, who now manages the property
here. The wines are good quality, made in a well-coloured, mouth-
filling style: impressive '86s for the year, rather lean '87s, ripe but
austere '88s. *Village* wines very reliable, but an '89 Gevrey-
Chambertin Premier Cru Les Corbeaux was on the rustic side and
lacking in 'class'. The Charmes-Chambertin can be splendid.

Domaine Bernard Bachelet
Dezize-les-Maranges, 71150 Chagny.
Not to be confused with the Domaine Bachelet at Gevrey-Chambertin whose wines are far superior.

Domaine Jean-Claude Bachelet
39410 St-Aubin.
Pretty, well-made St-Aubin whites and reds.

Domaine Bachelet-Ramonet
Chassagne-Montrachet, 21190 Meursault. 12·45 ha. Grands Crus: Bâtard-Montrachet, Bienvenues-Bâtard-Montrachet. 1er Cru: Chassagne-Montrachet (red and white). Puligny-Montrachet (white), Chassagne-Montrachet (red and white), Bourgogne Aligoté, Bourgogne Passe-Tout-Grains.
A domain with very well situated vineyards, but sadly making unexciting wine at the moment.

Domaine Ballot-Millot
21190 Meursault.
Good quality Meursaults in particular, using a modest proportion of new wood (about 25 percent). Seems to be equally at home with red and white wines, in a range embracing a myriad of *appellations*.

Daniel Barraud
See W&V, Mâconnais, Pouilly-Fuissé.

Domaine André Bart
24 rue de Mazy, 21160 Marsannay-la-Côte. 13·5 ha (3·85 ha en *métayage*). Grands Crus: Bonnes Mares; Chambertin Clos de Bèze. 1er Cru: Fixin-Hervelets. Chambolle-Musigny, Santenay (red and white), Côte de Nuits-Villages.
Uninspiring wines.

Domaine Barthod-Noëllat
Chambolle-Musigny, 21220 Gevrey-Chambertin. 1ers Crus: Chambolle-Musigny: Les Charmes, Chambolle-Musigny.

CHAMBOLLE-MUSIGNY, **Bourgogne Rouge.**
Gaston Barthod's wines are now sold under the label of Ghislaine
Barthod, his daughter; the wines are the same. A ripe, supple
Bourgogne Rouge and lovely, scented Chambolle-Musigny,
unfiltered and modestly oaked. Exceptional wines in 1990.

Thomas Bassot
5 quai Dumorey, 21700 Nuits-St-Georges.
Négociants. See Jean-Claude Boisset.

Domaine L Bassy
See W&V, Beaujolais, Côte de Brouilly.

Château du Basty
See W&V, Beaujolais, Régnié.

Domaine Philippe Batacchi
11 rue du Gaizot, 21220 Gevrey-Chambertin. 4·5 ha (1·5 ha
en métayage). **Grand Cru: Clos de la Roche. 1ᵉʳ Cru:**
Morey-St-Denis. Fixin, Gevrey-Chambertin, Morey-St-
Denis, Côte de Nuits-Villages, Bourgogne Rouge.
Named Domaine Clos Noir since 1989.

Paul Beaudet
See W&V, Beaujolais, Beaujolais-Villages.

Château de Beauregard
See W&V, Mâconnais, Pouilly-Fuissé.

Adrien Belland
Place du Jet d'Eau, 21590 Santenay. 11 ha. Grands Crus:
Chambertin; Corton Clos de la Vigne au Saint, CORTON-
GRÈVES, **Corton-Perrières. 1ᵉʳˢ Crus:** CHASSAGNE-MONTRACHET
MORGEOT CLOS CHARREAU; **Santenay Clos des Gravières,**
SANTENAY COMME. **Aloxe-Corton, Puligny-Montrachet,**
Santenay.
An archetypal, fragmented Burgundian domain, but this one is
well run – always a feat when the vineyards are so scattered – from
southern Santenay right up to Chambertin. M Adrien Belland is

now helped by one of his sons and they follow a policy of destalking, long vatting, fermentation with *chapeau flottant* and *pigeage* twice a day, ageing in oak casks and bottling after 20–22 months. Recent vintages have impressed me and I will watch their progress with interest. M Belland sells to just about everyone, which could be called a safe policy – private clients, restaurants, *négociants* in France, and all the usual markets abroad.

Joseph Belland
21590 Santenay.
Quite good wines but less dimension and interest than those of Adrien Belland.

Domaine Belleville
See W&V, Côte Chalonnaise, Rully.

Bénas Frères
See W&V, Mâconnais, Mâcon.

Domaine Paul Bernard
See W&V, Beaujolais, Fleurie.

Domaine René Berrod-les-Roches du Vivier
See W&V, Beaujolais, Fleurie.

Domaine Bertagna
21640 Vougeot. 11 ha (17 ha *en métayage*). Grands Crus: Chambertin; Clos St-Denis; Clos de Vougeot. 1ers Crus: Chambolle-Musigny; Vougeot: Clos de la Perrière, Les Cras, Petit Vougeot, Vougeot (white); Vosne-Romanée Les Beaux Monts; Nuits-St-Georges Murgers. Chambolle-Musigny, Vougeot Clos Bertagna, Hautes Côtes de Nuits (red), Bourgogne Rouge.
A fine 'clutch' of Vougeot vineyards that have been rather up and down in quality in the past two decades. The Reh family (of the Von Kesselstatt estate in Trier, Germany) acquired the domain in 1982 and the wines look very promising once again from 1988. Vougeot Clos de la Perrière and Vosne-Romanée Les Beaux Monts are wines of finesse and breed, regularly amongst their best bottles.

Domaine Denis Berthaut
21220 Fixin. 8 ha (5 ha *en métayage*). 1er Cru: Fixin. Fixin, Gevrey-Chambertin, Bourgogne Rouge.
Vinification with long *cuvaison* and, as so often at Fixin, wines that are on the rustic side.

Domaine Pierre Bertheau
Chambolle-Musigny, 21220 Gevrey-Chambertin.
I have limited experience, but this is a serious domain making good wine at all levels.

Domaine Besancenot-Mathouillet
78 faubourg St-Nicholas, 21200 Beaune. 6 ha (5 ha *en métayage*). Grand Cru: Corton-Charlemagne. 1ers Crus: BEAUNE: Bressandes, CENT-VIGNES, CLOS DU ROI, GRÈVES, à l'Ecu, THEURONS, Toussaints. PERNAND-VERGELESSES (red and white), Aloxe-Corton, Beaune, Bourgogne Rouge and Aligoté.
An important, well-run domain with some classic Beaune, and wines which show very good typicity between *climats*. Occasional bottles which are not quite clean.

Maison Albert Bichot
6 bis boulevard Jacques Copeau, 21200 Beaune. 41·36 ha. Domaine du Clos Frantin, Vosne-Romanée, 15 ha. Grands Crus: Chambertin; Clos de Vougeot; Echézeaux, Grands Echézeaux, Richebourg; Corton-Charlemagne; Corton. 1ers Crus: Vosne-Romanée Les Malconsorts; Aloxe-Corton Les Fourniers. Vosne-Romanée, Gevrey-Chambertin, Nuits-St-Georges.
A huge firm concentrating on exports. It has a multitude of *sous-noms*, including Paul Bouchard and Jean Bouchard (not to be confused with other Beaune Bouchards), Léon Rigault, Rémy Gauthier and Lupé Cholet. Most of these are very dreary Burgundies indeed. I am happiest with the firm's Chablis wines, from the Domaine Long-Depaquit, especially the splendid La Moutonne. *See also* W&V, Chablis.

Domaine Billard-Gonnet
21630 Pommard.
Beaune and Pommard in a very firm style. Keepers, but not really up to the class of their *appellations*.

Domaine Pierre Bitouzet
11 rue de Citeaux, 21420 Savigny-lès-Beaune. 3 ha (1 ha *en métayage*). Grand Cru: Corton-Charlemagne. 1ᵉʳˢ Crus: Aloxe-Corton Valozières; Savigny-lès-Beaune: Lavières, Les Talmettes.
Small property, best known for exceptional Corton-Charlemagne; also good white Savigny-lès-Beaune. Fairly oaky wines to taste, though M Bitouzet says he only uses one-third new wood.

Domaine Bitouzet-Prieur
Volnay, 21190 Meursault.
Quality Meursaults; Volnay-Taillepieds which repays cellaring.

Domaine Simon Bize & Fils
21420 Savigny-lès-Beaune. 10 ha (7 ha *en métayage*). 1ᵉʳˢ Crus: SAVIGNY-LÈS-BEAUNE: Fournaux, AUX GUETTES, LES MARCONNETS, Talmettes, LES VERGELESSES. Savigny Grands Liards, Savigny-lès-Beaune (red and white), Bourgogne Rouge and Blanc.
An extremely serious family estate, passed from father to son for 150 years. Patrick Bize is now making the wine, with great respect for the *fruit* and no excess weight or camouflage. He seems to have the right formula for this weight of wine – ten-day fermentations, about 18 months in oak before bottling. Since 1985 he has upped the new oak, but it is absorbed by the fruit. Bravo. Snap up the Savigny Les Vergelesses if you can. Entrancing white too.

Domaine Blain-Gagnard
21190 Chassagne-Montrachet. 6·6 ha. Grands Crus: BÂTARD-MONTRACHET, Criots-Bâtard-Montrachet. 1ᵉʳˢ Crus: CHASSAGNE-MONTRACHET: La Boudriotte, Cailleret, Clos St-Jean, MORGEOT. Pommard, Volnay, Chassagne-Montrachet (red and white).
Small amounts of wine from numerous *appellations*. Connected

with Delagrange-Bachelet, Jean-Marc Blain-Gagnard makes refined, perfumed and concentrated white wines, and also a stylish red Clos St-Jean. Occasionally I feel there is a bit too much oak.

Château du Bluizard
See W&V, Beaujolais, Brouilly.

Domaine Marcel Bocquenet
21700 Nuits-St-Georges.
A minute domain with a good reputation.

Domaine Henri Boillot
Volnay, 21190 Meursault. 21·6 ha. Ier Cru: Pommard. Volnay, Puligny-Montrachet.
Ample Pommards, LES JAROLIÈRES and Rugiens in particular. The wines are also seen under the Jean Boillot label.

Domaine Jean-Marc Boillot
21630 Pommard. 4 ha (6 ha *en métayage*). I^ers Crus: Beaune Montrevenots; Pommard: Jarolières, Rugiens, Saucilles; Volnay: Carelle sous la Chapelle, Pitures, Ronceret; Puligny-Montrachet: Champ Canet, Combettes, Referts, Truffières. Pommard, Volnay, Meursault, Puligny-Montrachet, Chassagne-Montrachet, Bourgogne Rouge and Aligoté.
Well-made wines. True-to-type perfumed Volnays in a lighter style, which show that *macération à froid*, fermentation temperatures up to 32°C and three *pigeages* a day do not have to produce 'heavy' wines; and broad, supple Côte de Beaune whites which could do with less oak at the *village* level, but which respect the *appellation* character nonetheless.

Domaine Lucien Boillot & Fils
21220 Gevrey-Chambertin. 6·5 ha (7 ha *en fermage* and *en métayage*). I^ers Crus: Gevrey-Chambertin: Champonnets, Cherbaudes, Les Corbeaux; Nuits-St-Georges Prûliers; Beaune Epenottes; Pommard: Les Croix Noires, Fremiers; Volnay: Les Angles, Caillerets, Brouillards. Fixin, Gevrey-Chambertin, Volnay, Côte de Nuits-Villages,

Bourgogne Rouge and Blanc.
Now run by Lucien Boillot's sons Pierre and Louis. Quality at this estate is clearly improving: pure, fruity, Pinot-style Beaune Epenottes and Volnay Les Angles; solid, workmanlike Gevrey-Chambertins, with a distinctive, concentrated Premier Cru Les Corbeaux in '89 and '90.

Domaine Pierre Boillot
21190 Meursault.
Low yield Meursaults of considerable concentration and judicious oaking. The whites can 'hit the bull's-eye'.

Jean-Claude Boisset
2 rue des Frères Montgolfier, 21700 Nuits-St-Georges.
This is a *négociant* with only 30 years behind it and sales of 13 million bottles a year. Names now under the Jean-Claude Boisset aegis include: Lionel J Bruck, Thomas Bassot, Charles Viénot, Morin, and Pierre Ponnelle. (The Domaine Claudine Deschamps wines are also sold entirely by Boisset, mostly to French wholesalers.) I am afraid these Burgundies give me absolutely no 'lift' at all.

Domaine Boisson-Vadot
21190 Meursault.
Meursaults made from old vines, with extended lees contact and ageing in up to one-third new wood. If the *village* wines are sometimes too lean, the Genevrières can be a particularly refined wine with real texture on the palate.

Domaine André Bonhomme
See W&V, Mâconnais, Mâcon.

Domaine Bonneau du Martray
Pernand-Vergelesses, 21420 Savigny-lès-Beaune. 11·1 ha.
Grands Crus: Corton-Charlemagne **(white); Corton (red).**
A very well run domain, with vineyards mid-slope on the Montagne de Corton. The owner, the Comte Jean le Bault de la Morinière, comes down from Paris every weekend. For their great Corton-Charlemagne, stainless steel vats are used for the first, tumultuous stage of the fermentation, thereby keeping the

temperature below 20°C, and then the wines finish fermenting in one-third new oak barrels. The Corton-Charlemagne is a rich, nutty experience – all the expected years are superb, but even more modest vintages, like '84 and '87, are intense, wonderful drinking over a decade after their birth. The Corton is vinified in open oak vats and the *élevage* is in a mixture of new, second and third year oak *pièces*. There is elegance in these wines, and weight too in years like '83, '85, '86, '88, and '90. Up to 92 percent of production is exported to 19 different countries, but in France the only sales are to restaurants which have been awarded Michelin stars.

Château Bonnet
See W&V, Beaujolais, Chénas.

Domaine Bonnot-Lamblot
21420 Savigny-lès-Beaune.
Solid Savigny-lès-Beaune; forceful rather than friendly.

Bouchard Aîné & Fils
36 rue Ste-Marguerite, 21200 Beaune. 21·12 ha (7·15 ha worked, Domaine Marion, Fixin). Grand Cru: Chambertin Clos de Bèze. 1ers Crus: Fixin Clos du Chapitre; Mercurey: Clos la Marche, Les Vasées. Fixin Mazière, Fixin Clos Marion, Beaune Les Sceaux, Mercurey, Mercurey Blanc, Côte de Nuits–Villages, Bourgogne Côte Chalonnaise.
Of course, Bouchard Aîné are first and foremost very important Beaune *négociants*, so it may surprise people to discover that their main holdings are on the Côte Chalonnaise, indeed their most reliable and rewarding wines are those from Mercurey. They stress the importance of limited yields, and follow a policy of long maceration in open wood *cuves* and maturing in Allier oak barrels – a third new each year. The wines usually keep well and are often *tastevinés*, but they are seen more frequently in the region than on export markets. Bouchard Aîné also buy the grapes and vinify for the Domaine Marion, which includes Chambertin Clos de Bèze. The *négociant* wines puzzle me somewhat, as sometimes they are rather good, and at other times best avoided. A pity, as the better wines certainly win friends for them.

Bouchard Père & Fils

Au Château, 21202 Beaune. 100 ha (13 ha *en métayage*).
Grands Crus: CHAMBERTIN La Romanée; Corton-
Charlemagne; LE CORTON; CHEVALIER-MONTRACHET, Le
Montrachet. 1ers Crus: Nuits-St-Georges: Clos St-Marc,
Clos des Argillières; Aloxe-Corton; Savigny-lès-Beaune
Les Lavières; BEAUNE: Cent Vignes, Clos de la Mousse,
Clos St-Landry, Du Château (red and white), GRÈVES VIGNE
DE L'ENFANT JESUS, Marconnets, Teurons; Pommard;
VOLNAY: CAILLERETS ANCIENNE CUVÉE CARNOT, FREMIETS, CLOS
DE LA ROUGEOTTE, Taillepieds; Meursault-Genevrières.
Savigny-lès-Beaune, Pommard, Bourgogne Aligoté
Bouzeron.

A considerable family firm, selling their Burgundies around the
world. In the *négociant* business, they manage to combine quantity
with quality, within the bounds of the possible, for when one is in
the market for 1,000 cases of an *appellation*, you cannot expect the
individuality of a small, specialist estate. But the domain wines of
BPF, known as the Domaines du Château de Beaune, are very good
indeed, and it is only a pity that on some export markets they do not
have the distribution or reputation that they should. BPF has
always been in the vanguard of technical advance, and has a
splendid new computer-controlled vinification plant, necessary for
the huge amount of grapes it now buys in. But the traditional side is
well preserved, with the domain wines being kept in beautiful
convent cellars, and enormous investment in new wood barrels;
indeed the domain whites now finish their fermentation in oak.
Some of the domain wines are really good, although others have
not lasted as well as one might have hoped, '78s for example.

Domaine Jean-Marc Bouley

21190 Volnay. 12·19 ha. 1ers Crus: Beaune Reversées;
Pommard: Fremiers, Pezerolles, Rugiens; Volnay:
Caillerets, Carelles, Clos des Chênes, Ronceret, Volnay.
Pommard, Volnay, Bourgogne Hautes Côtes de Beaune,
Bourgogne Rouge, Blanc and Aligoté, Bourgogne Passe-
Tout-Grains.

The estate's wines were sold in bulk until Jean-Marc Bouley started
domain-bottling in 1985. He now makes wines from 17 *appel-*

lations, but principally from Volnay and Pommard. Vinification aims at maximum extract and colour to make *vins de garde*, and the *village* and Premier Cru wines are aged in 30–50 percent new oak. Perfumed Volnays, Pommards appropriately with more muscle; all the wines have plenty of *matière*, but possibly too much tannin, especially for some of the Volnays. They promise much from cask; we have yet to see how harmoniously they mature.

Pierre Bourée & Fils
21220 Gevrey-Chambertin. 4 ha. Grand Cru: Charmes-Chambertin. 1ᵉʳ Cru: Beaune Epenottes. Gevrey-Chambertin Clos de la Justice *monopole*.

This is a small *négociant* now run by Pierre Bourée's nephew M Vallet. A very large number of *appellations* is made from both Côtes, the *négociant* wines (the vast majority) being vinified from purchased grapes. People seem to 'discover' the wines every few years, but they are not really to my taste, seeming too alcoholic and top-heavy, although others like the style. The firm is sole owner of Gevrey-Chambertin Clos de la Justice, which is usually of a higher quality than its *village* designation implies.

Domaine Denis Boussey
Monthélie, 21190 Meursault.
Well-made red and white wines.

Domaine Michel Bouzereau
3 rue Planche Meunière, 21190 Meursault. 11 ha *en métayage*. 1ᵉʳˢ Crus: Beaune: Les Epenottes, Les Vignes Franches; Meursault-Genevrières; Puligny-Montrachet Les Champs-Gains. Pommard Les Cras, Volnay Les Auxy, Meursault Les Grands Charrons, Meursault Les Tessons, Bourgogne Rouge, Blanc and Aligoté.

Good quality '90s. Fine Genevrières and flavoursome Puligny-Montrachet Les Champs-Gains, but Meursault Les Tessons is the best value with a bouquet of limes and plenty of sheen and finesse.

Domaine P Bouzereau
15 place Europe, 21190 Meursault.
Meursault '88 should taste better than Bourgogne Blanc!

Domaine Hubert Bouzereau-Gruère
21190 Meursault.
Middle-of-the-road white Burgundy, although the red SANTENAY
has impressed in the past, as has the CORTON-BRESSANDES.

Domaine Yves Boyer-Martenot
**21190 Meursault. 1·46 ha (7 ha *en fermage*). 1ᵉʳˢ Crus:
Meursault: Charmes, Genevrières, Perrières. Pommard;
Auxey-Duresses; Meursault: Les Narvaux, l'Ormeau, Le
Pré de Manche; Bourgogne Rouge, Blanc and Aligoté.**
Very 'hit and miss'. Of two '89s tasted in 1992, a *village* Meursault
Les Narvaux was elegant and attractive, but the Premier Cru
Genevrières suggested careless cellar handling; it was flat and dirty.

Domaine Guy Braillon
See W&V, Beaujolais, Chénas.

Domaine des Braves
See W&V, Beaujolais, Régnié.

Domaine Jean-Claude Brelière
See W&V, Côte Chalonnaise, Rully.

Domaine Bressand
See W&V, Mâconnais, Pouilly Fuissé.

Domaine Michel Briday
See W&V, Côte Chalonnaise, Rully.

Lionel J Bruck
6 quai Dumorey, 21700 Nuits-St-Georges.
Négociant dealing with 44 hectares in the Côte d'Or, including the
six hectare domain of the Château de Vosne-Romanée, a parcel of
Corton Clos du Roi, and 6·8 hectares of Premier Cru Savigny-lès-
Beaune Les Guettes. *See also* Jean-Claude Boisset.

Jean Brugne Le Vivier
See W&V, Beaujolais, Moulin-à-Vent.

Georges Brun
See W&V, Beaujolais, Morgon.

Domaine des Brureaux
See W&V, Beaujolais, Chénas.

Domaine Georges Bryczek
**Morey-St-Denis, 21220 Gevrey-Chambertin. 3·2 ha. 1ᵉʳ
Cru:** Morey-St-Denis Clos-Sorbés. Morey-St-Denis.
Good quality Morey-St-Denis.

Domaine Buisson-Battault
21190 Meursault.
Better whites than reds.

Domaine Alain Burguet
**18 rue de l'Eglise, 21220 Gevrey-Chambertin. 3·5 ha (2·5 ha
en fermage). Gevrey-Chambertin,** Gevrey-Chambertin
Vieilles Vignes**, Bourgogne Rouge.**
Very good rather than great. Alain Burguet vinifies with plenty of
pigeage and long *cuvaisons* of two to three weeks, aiming to make
wines which can be drunk, as he puts it, 'at ten, 20 or 40 years of age,
depending on the vintage'.

Domaine Cacheux-Blée
**Route Nationale, Vosne-Romanée, 21700 Nuits-St-
Georges.**
Tiny property. I have no experience of it myself, but it has a fine
reputation.

Roger Caillot & Fils
21190 Meursault.
An earthy, workaday '89 Meursault Les Tessons and a *village*
quality Puligny-Montrachet Les Folatières from the same vintage
hardly inspire confidence! Others have been more impressed.

Calvet
21200 Beaune.
This is a large *négociant*, much in evidence on the boulevard around

Beaune. I have to say that it produces some of the most disappointing Burgundies I have ever encountered.

Domaine Camus Père & Fils
21220 Gevrey-Chambertin. 17.15 ha. Grands Crus: Chambertin, Charmes-Chambertin, Latricières-Chambertin, Mazis-Chambertin, Mazoyères-Chambertin. Gevrey-Chambertin, Bourgogne Rouge, Rosé and Aligoté, Bourgogne Grand Ordinaire.
Sometimes good, rarely more. I have never had a wine from this domain that reflected the quality of the vineyard holdings. Alas!

Domaine Luc Camus
21420 Savigny-lès-Beaune. 3·7 ha (3 ha *en fermage*). 1ers Crus: Savigny-lès-Beaune: Gravains, Lavières, Narbantons; Beaune Clos du Roi. Savigny-lès-Beaune (red and white), Bourgogne Rouge, Blanc and Aligoté.
Bourgogne Blanc with a good depth of fruit and a firm, vivid Savigny-lès-Beaune Vieilles Vignes with plenty of character.

Domaine Capitain-Gagnerot
21550 Ladoix-Serrigny.
Can be good value in the more modest *appellations*.

Château des Capitans
See W&V, Beaujolais, Juliénas.

Domaine Capron-Manieux
21420 Savigny-lès-Beaune.
White and red Savigny which have promise but are sometimes a bit rustic – perhaps the red could spend less time in cask? At their best when drunk young. Finot-like Pernand-Vergelesses.

Domaine Louis Carillon
21190 Puligny-Montrachet. 12 ha. Grand Cru: BIENVENUES-BÂTARD-MONTRACHET. **1ers Crus: Puligny-Montrachet: Les Champs Canet, Les Champs Gains, Les Combettes, Les Perrières, Les Referts. Puligny-Montrachet, Chassagne-Montrachet (red and white), Mercurey, Côte de Beaune-**

Villages, Bourgogne Rouge and Aligoté.
Carillons have been making wine since 1632, and know their *métier* very well. They sell direct, export and deal with *négociants*. Their white wines are matured in oak barrels for a year, then spend three to six months in stainless steel or enamel-lined containers before bottling. The red grapes are entirely or partially destalked, according to the character of the year, vatting/fermentation takes eight to ten days, and the *élevage* is the same as for the whites. The Pulignys have elegance and style.

Domaine Denis Carré
Meloisey, 21190 Meursault. 1ers Crus: Pommard; Auxey-Duresses. Meursault Les Tillets, St-Romain (red), Bourgogne Hautes Côtes de Beaune (red and white).
Rather lean and sturdy style of reds; Carré's best wine is his broad, earthy *village* Meursault Les Tillets.

Domaine Guy Castagnier
Morey-St-Denis, 21220 Gevrey-Chambertin.
Good wines in the scrumptious, fruity style, even in less than propitious years – therefore drink relatively young.

Domaine Cathiard-Molinier
Vosne-Romanée, 21700 Nuits-St-Georges.
A domain that seems to be getting smaller, in all senses of the word. A great pity.

Cave Coopérative de Buxy
See W&V, Côte Chalonnaise, Montagny.

Cave Coopérative La Chablisienne
See W&V, Chablis.

Cave Coopérative de Clessé
See W&V, Mâconnais, Mâcon.

Cave Coopérative des Grands Vins de Fleurie
See W&V, Beaujolais, Fleurie.

Cave Coopérative d'Igé
See W&V, Mâconnais, Mâcon.

Cave Coopérative de Liergues
See W&V, Beaujolais, Juliénas.

Cave Coopérative de Lugny
See W&V, Mâconnais, Mâcon.

Cave Coopérative de Prissé
See W&V, Mâconnais, St-Véran.

Cave Coopérative de Viré
See W&V, Mâconnais, Mâcon.

Caves Coopératives des Grands Vins de Juliénas
See W&V, Beaujolais, Juliénas.

Domaine des Caves/Famille Delore
See W&V, Beaujolais, Moulin-à-Vent.

Les Caves des Hautes Côtes Groupement de Producteurs
Route de Pommard, 21200 Beaune. 500 ha in 70 *appellations.* **Principal holdings in** Hautes Côtes de Nuits **and** Hautes Côtes de Beaune.
This is a group of 200 producers who sell to *négociants*, the export markets and directly to the public. Their vinification has improved greatly in recent years, and the *élevage* now includes 3,000 oak *pièces*. The wines are fruity, fresh and charming, and good value. This is a very good source of supply for Burgundy's generic wines.

Château de la Chaize
See W&V, Beaujolais, Brouilly.

Jean-Noël Chaland
See W&V, Mâconnais, Mâcon.

Domaine Yves Chaley
Curtil-Vergy, 21220 Gevrey-Chambertin. 13 ha.
Bourgogne Hautes Côtes de Nuits Rouge, Blanc and Pinot
Beurot, Bourgogne Aligoté.
A well-situated domain, vital in the Hautes Côtes. Traditional methods, with the reds kept 18 months in a combination of oak *foudres* and up to one-third new barrels. The white wines are in stainless steel tanks, and are slowly fermented at 18°C in order to obtain both maximum perfume and freshness. Good value wines.

Château de Chambolle-Musigny
21220 Chambolle-Musigny. 4 ha. Grands Crus: Bonnes
Mares; MUSIGNY. 1ers Crus: Chambolle-Musigny: Les
Amoureuses, Les Fuées. CHAMBOLLE-MUSIGNY.
Frédéric Mugnier makes the wines at this domain in a style which brings out all that is best in Chambolle: scent, subtlety, laciness of texture and great persistence. His wines are getting better and better; the '87s were excellent, and '88, '89 and '90 promise to be a very great trio.

Domaine du Château de Chamilly
See W&V, Côte Chalonnaise, Mercurey.

Domaine du Château de Chamirey
See W&V, Côte Chalonnaise, Mercurey.

Domaine Louis Champagnon
See W&V, Beaujolais: Moulin-à-Vent, Chénas.

Champy Père & Cie
5 rue du Grenier à Sel, 21200 Beaune.
Until 1990 both *négociant* and proprietor (founded in 1720, it might be the oldest *négociant* of all), but now solely a *négociant*. Louis Jadot purchased Champy in 1989 and, whilst retaining the vineyard holdings, sold the *négociant* side of the business in 1990. The principal owners are now Henri and Pierre Meurgey, though Jadot retains an 18 percent interest. The wines used to be rather thick and heavy, but were made in a much lighter style during the 1980s when, however, if they were 'correct', they were also unexciting.

The first vintage produced under the new ownership is the '90 and, with the Meurgeys now supervising purchase and *élevage*, the wines already have more polish and elegance.

Domaine de la Chanaise
See W&V, Beaujolais, Morgon.

Emile Chandesais
See W&V, Côte Chalonnaise, Rully.

Domaine Chandon de Briailles
21420 Savigny-lès-Beaune. 13 ha. Grands Crus: Corton (white), Corton-Charlemagne, Corton Clos du Roi, CORTON-BRESSANDES**, Corton Les Maréchaudes. 1ers Crus: Pernand-Vergelesses, Pernand Ile des Vergelesses; Aloxe-Corton Les Valozières; Savigny-lès-Beaune Les Lavières. Savigny-lès-Beaune.**

Owned by Comte Aymard-Claude de Nicolay and his children, who are related to the Chandons of Champagne fame, this is an estate with excellent vineyards (and a magnificent French garden). Winemaking methods are traditional, and sometimes one finds a very good bottle, but there is a feeling that with a little tighter control or technical help, things could be even better. Recent tastings have not changed that view.

Chanson Père & Fils
10 rue Paul-Chanson, 21201 Beaune. 44 ha. 1ers Crus: PERNAND-VERGELESSES**: Les Caradeux,** LES VERGELESSES**; Savigny-Dominode, Savigny-Marconnets (red and white);** BEAUNE**: Champimonts (red and white), Clos des Fèves, Clos des Marconnets, Clos des Mouches (red and white),** CLOS DU ROI**,** GRÈVES**, Teurons.**

Chanson is one of those Beaune houses combining an important *négoce* business with ownership of some very fine vineyards. Recent vintages of the domain wines have seemed very good, although some of the *négociant* wines are dull.

Chanut Frères
See W&V, Beaujolais, Beaujolais-Villages.

Savigny-lès-Beaune

Chanzy Frères/Domaine de l'Hermitage
See W&V, Côte Chalonnaise, Bouzeron.

Maurice Chapuis
**21420 Aloxe-Corton. 1 ha (9 ha *en fermage*). Grands Crus:
Corton, CORTON-CHARLEMAGNE, Corton-Languettes,
Corton-Perrières. 1ᵉʳ Cru: Aloxe-Corton. Aloxe-Corton,
Bourgogne Blanc.**

M Chapuis is in charge of this highly respected domain, which
combines selling to *négociants* with direct selling locally and on the
export markets. There has been recent modernization and construction of new cellars. Total destalking for Pinot Noir, ten-day
fermentations on average, and *élevage* in barrels (15 percent new
each year) for 18 months to two years. Obviously, there is a rush to
buy his excellent Corton-Charlemagne (drink earlier than the
Louis Latour or Bonneau du Martray versions). Less successful reds.

Domaine François Charles
Nantoux, 21190 Meursault. 11 ha (1 ha *en métayage*). 1ᵉʳˢ

Crus: Beaune Les Epenottes; Volnay Les Frémiets. Pommard, Volnay Clos de la Cave, BOURGOGNE HAUTES CÔTES DE BEAUNE **(red and white), Bourgogne Aligoté, Bourgogne Passe-Tout-Grains.**
Notably good Hautes Côtes de Beaune.

Domaine Charlopin-Parizot
21160 Marsannay. 5 ha (5·5 ha *en fermage***). Grands Crus: Charmes-Chambertin; Clos St-Denis. Marsannay (red and white), Gevrey-Chambertin, Morey-St-Denis, Chambolle-Musigny, Vosne-Romanée, Bourgogne Rouge.**
A somewhat puzzling domain, with highs and lows of quality.

Château de la Charrière
21590 Santenay.
Concentrated, long-lived Santenays of very good quality are made by Jean Girardin; look out for LES GRAVIÈRES especially.

Domaine Chartron/Chartron & Trébuchet
13 Grande Rue, Puligny-Montrachet, 21190 Meursault. 8·2 ha. Grand Cru: Chevalier-Montrachet. 1ᵉʳˢ Crus: Puligny-Montrachet: Clos de la Pucelle, Clos du Cailleret (red and white), Les Folatières. Bourgogne Rouge, Blanc, Aligoté.
Created in 1984, this *négociant-éleveur* specialises in white wines and distributes the production of Domaine Chartron. The *négociant* wines are good, if not long-lasting; they are vinified in a light but elegant style and bottled early. In lesser vintages, however, they can be light to a fault and there is occasionally a slight 'oiliness' in the flavour. My favourite wines from the domain are the Premier Cru Clos de la Pucelle and the Chevalier-Montrachet. The *négociant* side produces Le Montrachet with a finish of nougat. The firm buys in must direct from the press and vinifies the wines itself.

F Chauvenet
6 route de Chaux, 21700 Nuits-St-Georges. Grands Crus: Charmes-Chambertin; Echézeaux; Corton-Charlemagne; Corton; Bienvenues-Bâtard-Montrachet. Rully.
A large *négociant*, now taking a very dynamic place on the market. Other names include Louis Max, Marc Chevillot, Poulet Père &

Fils and Guy Leblanc. It has important holdings in the Yonne, notably the Domaine de Pérignon, known for its Passe-Tout-Grains. The wines are fair, but with a distinct 'house-style'.

Jean Chauvenet
21700 Nuits-St-Georges.
Fullish, solid Nuits-St-Georges; on the whole very good (Les Bousselots and Les Vaucrains), without being top class.

Domaine de Chavanne
See W&V, Beaujolais, Côte de Brouilly.

Domaine Anne-Marie Chavy
Puligny-Montrachet, 21190 Meursault.
Much is sold to *négociants*. Good domain-bottled whites.

Domaine des Chazelles
See W&V, Mâconnais, Mâcon.

Château de Chénas
See W&V, Beaujolais, Chénas.

Domaine de Chervin
See W&V, Mâconnais, Mâcon.

Domaine Chevalier
Buisson, 84110 Vaison-la-Romaine.
See W&V, Côte d'Or, Ladoix-Serrigny.

Domaine Georges & Michel Chevillon
21700 Nuits-St-Georges. 6·5 ha (2 ha *en métayage*). 1ᵉʳˢ Crus: Nuits-St-Georges: Aux Champs Perdrix, Porets, St-Julien, Nuits-St-Georges, Les St-Georges. Vosne-Romanée, Nuits-St-Georges, Bourgogne Rouge, Passe-Tout-Grains.
Cousins of Robert Chevillon, who also makes Nuits-St-Georges. Wines with a good reputation, though without the class of Robert's. Two '88s tasted in 1992 give some cause for concern over cellar management; the *village* Nuits-St-Georges and the Champs Perdrix had coarse flavours and little Nuits AC character.

Domaine Robert Chevillon
**68 rue Felix Tisserand, 21700 Nuits-St-Georges. 13 ha. 1ᵉʳˢ
Crus:** NUITS-ST-GEORGES: LES CAILLES, **Les Perrières, Les
Roncières, Les St-Georges,** LES VAUCRAINS.

A comparatively recent estate (in Burgundian terms) which
established an excellent reputation during the 1980s. Traditional
vinification, with quite long fermentations depending on vintage,
followed by a maceration of the wine and skins for several days.
Open *cuves*, and *pigeage* and *remontage* every day. 80 percent of the
total production is bottled at the domain, the rest is sold to local
négociants. Exports to a spread of countries. Robert Chevillon's
wines are at the top of the Nuits-St-Georges ladder, consistently
elegant expressions of their vintage and *terroir*.

Domaine Cheysson-les-Fargues
See W&V, Beaujolais, Chiroubles.

Domaine Georges Chicotot
21700 Nuits-St-Georges.

Strong, dark wines based on the methods of Guy Accad (long cold
maceration before fermentation and then a prolonged vatting on
the skins). They are flattering when tasted young, but have yet to
convince that they age gracefully.

Domaine Michel Chignard
See W&V, Beaujolais, Fleurie.

Domaine Jean Chofflet
See W&V, Côte Chalonnaise, Givry.

Domaine André Chopin & Fils
Comblanchien, 21700 Nuits-St-Georges.

Quite firm wines, but tastings are not frequent enough for a real
pattern to emerge.

Domaine Daniel Chopin-Groffier
Prémeaux 21700 Nuits-St-Georges.

Clean, frank, well-made wines with an emphasis on elegance rather
than concentration. Warmly fruity Côte de Nuits-Villages, sweet

and pretty Chambolle-Musigny. The Clos Vougeot has a good reputation, but the '89 did not warrant its Grand Cru pedigree.

Domaine Chouet–Clivet
21190 Meursault.
Straightforward Meursaults, often rather angular.

Domaine Bruno Clair
5 rue du Vieux Collège, 21160 Marsannay-la-Côte. 20 ha. Grand Cru: Chambertin Clos de Bèze. 1ers Crus: GEVREY-CHAMBERTIN: **Clos de Fontenay** *monopole*, CLOS ST-JACQUES, **Les Cazetiers, Gevrey-Chambertin;** SAVIGNY-LÈS-BEAUNE LA DOMINODE. MARSANNAY **Rouge, Blanc and** ROSÉ, FIXIN, **Morey-St-Denis en la Rue de Vergy (red and white), Chambolle-Musigny Veroilles, Vosne-Romanée Champs Perdrix, Bourgogne Rouge, Blanc and Aligoté, Crémant de Bourgogne.**
The young team here is an example of the most encouraging aspect of Burgundy today – unblinkered, hardworking and conscientious. The wines are very pure in their Pinot character, stressing refinement and aromatic persistence rather than sheer *puissance*, and the use of oak is accordingly moderate – 35 percent maximum for the Grands Crus. Bruno Clair feels there is potential for more white wine production in the northern Côte de Nuits, but his experiments with Pinot Blanc and Chardonnay are not yet entirely convincing.

Domaine Michel Clair
21590 Santenay. 5·53 ha (5·17 ha *en fermage*)**. 1ers Crus: Santenay: Clos de Beaurepaire, Clos de la Combe, Clos de Tavanne, Gravières, Passe-Temps. Santenay: red, white, Clos Genets; Bourgogne Aligoté, Crémant de Bourgogne.**
Quite a pretty style, with wines that do not become as earthy as some Santenays.

Domaine Henri Clerc
Puligny-Montrachet, 21190 Meursault. Grands Crus: Bâtard-Montrachet, Bienvenues-Bâtard-Montrachet, Chevalier-Montrachet. 1ers Crus: Puligny-Montrachet: Combettes, Folatières. Blagny La Pièce sous le Dos d'Ane,

Puligny-Montrachet (red and white), Bourgogne Rouge, Blanc and Aligoté.

Form here can be a bit 'hit and miss', but when on target the *village* and Premier Cru Pulignys are thoroughly enjoyable in a soft, full and peachy style. In a good vintage the Grands Crus often have considerable weight to them, but lack a little breed to put them right in the top rank.

Domaine Georges Clerget

Gilly-lès-Citeaux, 21640 Vougeot. 3 ha. 1ers Crus: Vougeot; Chambolle-Musigny. Morey-St-Denis, Chambolle-Musigny, Vosne-Romanée Les Violettes, Bourgogne Rouge.

Small domain. His best wines can be a lovely combination of gamey Pinot and Côte de Nuits spice.

Domaine Michel Clerget

21640 Vougeot.

Tiny domain; some good wines.

Domaine Raoul Clerget

St-Aubin, 21190 Meursault. 17 ha. Domaine du Pimont 12 ha: St-Aubin Le Charmois (red and white), Chassagne-Montrachet Les Chaumées (red), Chassagne-Montrachet (white). Clerget 5 ha: St-Aubin Frionnes.

A family domain; at the same time the Clergets are *négociants*. They regard lengthy wood-ageing as important for red wines, and the whites, too, often show oak influence when they are young. I have had delicious whites, but others have not been as lucky and attention should be paid to what could be less than perfect wood.

Domaine Y Clerget

Volnay, 21190 Meursault. 5·15 ha. 1ers Crus: Pommard Rugiens; Volnay: Caillerets, Clos du Verseuil, Carelle Sous la Chapelle, Santenots, Volnay. Meursault, Bourgogne Rouge.

This must be the family of growers with the oldest history in Burgundy – with skills passed down from father to son in Volnay since 1270. Clergets abound, but this branch goes right back to the source. The red wines have the balance and style to keep well, especially in the loftier *climats*. However, an '89 Meursault Chevalières was coarse. The domain uses 25 percent new wood for all its wines.

Domaine du Clos des Lambrays
21220 Morey-St-Denis. 10 ha. Grand Cru: Clos des Lambrays. 1ᵉʳ Cru: Morey-St-Denis. Morey-St-Denis.
The *monopole* Clos des Lambrays was purchased by Louis and Fabien Saier in 1979 and they started to replant the vineyard in 1980. Under the previous owners nothing had been done for decades, and the average age of the vines was 70 years, a most unhealthy state of affairs. The vineyard is very well situated and was granted Grand Cru status in 1981, but this elevation seems premature based on its performance during the 1980s. The '88, which should have been outstanding, was not a bad wine as such, but it certainly lacked both Grand Cru class and the quality of the vintage. We must live in hope, for there were some splendid vintages in the 1940s and 1950s.

Domaine Julien Coche-Debord
21190 Meursault.
Good quality without being exciting; Premiers Crus more reliable than the *village* wines.

Domaine Jean-François Coche-Dury
21190 Meursault. 7 ha (8·5 ha *en métayage*). Grand Cru: Corton-Charlemagne. 1ᵉʳˢ Crus: Monthélie; Volnay; Auxey-Duresses; Meursault-Perrières. Meursault (red and white), Bourgogne Rouge, Blanc and Aligoté, Bourgogne Grand Ordinaire.
This domain has sold wine under its own label since 1973 and now must be considered in the very top rank in Meursault. M Coche-Dury always uses natural yeasts, allowing his fermentations to start in their own time. He prefers not to make wines of over 13 percent alcohol. Stunning white wines – '82s and '86s drunk recently have been heavenly – and the red Auxey-Duresses is almost a miracle from such young vines. This winemaker truly has a magic touch.

Domaine Fernand Coffinet
Chassagne–Montrachet, 21190 Meursault.
Minute estate, but very good wines; notably the Bâtard-Montrachet.

Domaine Pierre Cogny
See W&V, Côte Chalonnaise, Rully.

Domaine Marc Colin
Chassagne–Montrachet, 21190 Meursault.
Very good whites, with depth and backbone, especially St-Aubin La Chatenière.

Société Michel Colin-Deléger
Chassagne–Montrachet, 21190 Meursault.
Colin-Deléger's wines also appear under the simpler name of Michel Colin. Very classy winemaking: stylish, beautifully-balanced white Burgundies with real 'race' and finesse, and the capacity to age too; the Chassagne-Montrachet Les Chaumées is particularly good. All the vines are worked *en métayage* and *élevage* is in 20 percent new oak; eight to ten months for the white wines, 12–15 for the reds.

Domaine Jean Collet & Fils
See W&V, Chablis.

Paul Collonge
See W&V, Beaujolais, Morgon.

Domaine de Colonat
See W&V, Beaujolais, Morgon.

Domaine de la Condemine
See W&V, Mâconnais, Mâcon.

François Condemine
See W&V, Beaujolais, Juliénas.

Domaine Jean–Jacques Confuron
Prémeaux 21700 Nuits-St-Georges. 7 ha. Grands Crus: Romanée-St-Vivant; Clos de Vougeot. 1ers Crus: Vosne-Romanée Les Beaux Monts; Nuits-St-Georges: Boudots, Chaboeufs; Chambolle-Musigny. Chambolle-Musigny, Nuits-St-Georges, Côte de Nuits-Villages, Bourgogne Rouge and Aligoté.

Sturdy wines whose extract and 'thickness' tend to blur *appellation* character, hence not for lovers of refined Pinot. There is 60 percent new wood for the Grands Crus, 40 percent for the Premiers Crus and *village* wines.

Domaine J Confuron-Cotetidot
Vosne-Romanée, 21700 Nuits-St-Georges.

Jack Confuron and his oenologist son Jean-Pierre are both dedicated winemakers and well-known disciples of the controversial oenologist Guy Accad. They make their wines from very ripe grapes which are cold-macerated for eight to ten days before undergoing a relatively cool fermentation (25–28°C), and barrel-ageing is in a maximum of 20 percent new wood. Their 'showiness' from cask (the sweetness of bouquet in particular) has led to doubts as to whether they will be true-to-type Burgundies when mature; but they have plenty of backbone and a seven year-old '85 Nuits-St-Georges had both the seductive ripeness of the vintage as well as the distinctive 'earthiness' wanted from a good Nuits. Especially good Echézeaux which is lacy, layered and with a lovely projection of flavours.

Domaine de Conroy
See W&V, Beaujolais, Côte de Brouilly.

Château de Corcelles
See W&V, Beaujolais, Beaujolais-Villages.

Domaine Roger Cordier
See W&V, Mâconnais, Pouilly-Fuissé.

Château de Coreaux
See W&V, Mâconnais, St-Véran.

Domaine Edmond Cornu

21550 Ladoix. 8 ha (4·15 ha *en métayage*). Grand Cru: Corton-Bressandes. 1ᵉʳˢ Crus: Ladoix Corvées; Aloxe-Corton Moutottes. Ladoix, Aloxe-Corton, Savigny-lès-Beaune, Chorey-lès-Beaune (red and white), Bourgogne Rouge.

Rather variable in quality, but some good buys at this domain.

Coron Père & Fils

See W&V, Mâconnais, Mâcon.

Domaine Corsin

See W&V, Mâconnais, Pouilly-Fuissé.

Domaine Guy Cotton

See W&V, Beaujolais, Côte de Brouilly.

Domaine Jean Coulon

See W&V, Côte Chalonnaise, Rully.

Domaine de Courcel

21630 Pommard. 8·4 ha. 1ᵉʳˢ Crus: POMMARD: EPENOTS, Croix Noires, GRAND CLOS DES EPENOTS, Fremières, Rugiens. Pommard, Bourgogne Rouge.

Another old-established family domain to make the *parvenus* shudder; more than four centuries lie behind this estate. Extraordinary wine, deeply coloured and intensely concentrated, the result of long vatting and several *pigeages* each day to obtain the maximum extraction. No destalking, or only partial destalking, according to the year, and two years in new wood before bottling. These are wines that have a good heart of flavour even in lesser vintages; in great years they require, and repay, keeping – indeed I wish I had more Rugiens '78 in my cellar.

Domaine Michel Crozet

See W&V, Beaujolais, Chénas.

Domaine Louis Curveux

See W&V, Mâconnais, Pouilly-Fuissé.

Domaine Dalicieux
See W&V, Beaujolais, Beaujolais-Villages.

Domaine Pierre Damoy
Rue de Lattre de Tassigny, 21220 Gevrey-Chambertin.
5·7 ha. Chambertin, Chambertin Clos de Bèze.
A domain owning untold riches – the biggest single share of Chambertin and Clos de Bèze plus Chapelle and the Gevrey-Chambertin *monopole* Clos du Tamisot. Memorable old wines. Occasional good bottles recently, but far too many misses.

Domaine Darnat
20 rue des Forges, 21190 Meursault. 2 ha. I^{ers} Crus:
MEURSAULT: CLOS RICHEMONT *monopole*, Gouttes d'Or.
Meursault: Les Pelles, Les Charrons, Le Meix Tavaux;
Bourgogne Blanc and Aligoté.
The Domaine Darnat has belonged to the same family for more than a century and their one good wine, Clos Richemont, has enjoyed an excellent reputation for a long time. The wine is exported to the USA and UK, and in France there are private clients – I have also seen the Clos Richemont sold under the Sélection Jean Germain label. Vinification owes nothing to 'new' methods, Vincent Darnat being convinced that fermentation and ageing must be carried out in oak barrels (very few of them new) for the wines to preserve all their character. And they most certainly do, even after years in bottle. There is always great flavour, and it would be a pity to drink the Clos Richemont too young. Unfortunately, there is very little of it.

Domaine Jean Dauvissat
See W&V, Chablis.

Domaine René & Vincent Dauvissat
See W&V, Chablis.

Château de Davenay
See W&V, Côte Chalonnaise, Montagny.

David & Foillard
69830 St-Georges-de-Reneins.
Probably the largest *négociants* in the Rhône.

Domaine Jean Defaix
See W&V, Chablis.

Domaine Delachanal
See W&V, Beaujolais, Côte de Brouilly.

Domaine Delagrange-Bachelet
Chassagne-Montrachet, 21190 Meursault.
This tiny, quality domain has been handed down to the next generation, although 82 year-old Edmond Delagrange still has a few ares of vines. The vineyards have gone to Blain Gagnard, Fontaine-Gagnard and Gagnard-Delagrange.

Domaine Marius Delarche
21420 Pernand-Vergelesses. 6·5 ha (1·5 ha *en métayage*). Grands Crus: Corton-Charlemagne; Corton-Renardes. 1ers Crus: Pernand-Vergelesses: des Vergelesses, Ile des Vergelesses. Pernand-Vergelesses (red and white) Bourgogne Rouge and Aligoté.
Corton-Charlemagne and Corton-Renardes that are reliable in good vintages.

Maison Delaunay
Château de Charmont, L'Etang-Vergy, 21220 Gevrey-Chambertin. 10 ha. Bourgogne Hautes Côtes de Nuits **(red and white).**
This is a family firm of *commissionaires en vins*, who work entirely on the export markets. Their strength is in their tasting and selecting ability, so any Burgundy bought from them really tastes of its *appellation*. They cover the whole of the region, from Dijon down to the Beaujolais. Since 1989 Delaunay have also become proprietors in the Hautes Côtes de Nuits, these wines being sold under the name of Château de Charmont. 30 percent of the white Hautes Côtes de Nuits is fermented in new oak. *See also* W&V, Côte Chalonnaise, Montagny.

Domaine Georges Deléger
Chassagne-Montrachet, 21190 Meursault.
Very small estate producing perfumed CHASSAGNE-MONTRACHET whites and a good red Chassagne. Minute quantities of excellent Chevalier-Montrachet too.

André Delorme
See W&V, Côte Chalonnaise, Rully.

Domaine Lucien Denizot
See W&V, Côte Chalonnaise, Montagny.

Domaine Jacques Depagneux
See W&V, Mâconnais, Mâcon.

Domaine André Depardon
See W&V, Mâconnais, St-Véran.

Michel Derain
See W&V, Côte Chalonnaise, Givry.

Domaine Jean Descombes
See W&V, Beaujolais, Morgon.

Domaine Desmures Père & Fils
See W&V, Beaujolais, Chiroubles.

Vins Dessalle
See W&V, Beaujolais, Beaujolais-Villages.

GFA Domaine Desvignes
See W&V, Beaujolais, Moulin-à-Vent.

Louis Claude Desvignes
See W&V, Beaujolais, Morgon.

Propriété Desvignes
See W&V, Côte Chalonnaise, Givry.

Domaine des Deux Roches
See W&V, Mâconnais, St-Véran.

Héritiers Finaz Devillaine
See W&V, Beaujolais, Moulin-à-Vent.

Jean-Pierre Diconne
Auxey-Duresses, 21190 Meursault. 1ᵉʳ Cru: Auxey-Duresses Les Duresses. **Auxey-Duresses, Meursault, Bourgogne Rouge and Blanc, Bourgogne Passe-Tout-Grains.**
Particularly good red and white Auxey-Duresses.

Domaine Diochon
See W&V, Beaujolais, Moulin-à-Vent.

Maison Doudet-Naudin
21420 Savigny-lès-Beaune. 4·83 ha. Grands Crus: Corton-Charlemagne; Corton Les Maréchaudes. 1ᵉʳˢ Crus: Pernand-Vergelesses Fichots; Aloxe-Corton; Savigny-lès-Beaune Les Guettes, Savigny-lès-Beaune Redrescul; Beaune Clos du Roy. Aloxe-Corton Les Boutières, Savigny-Liards, Bourgogne Blanc.
This house is known above all for its *négociant* wines, which tend to divide opinion. The style is big, rich, dark and jammy, with alcoholic backbone – consequently, the wines last, but I find it easier to recognize a Doudet-Naudin wine than to identify its commune. Their own wines receive long vinifications in oak *cuves*, with partial destalking according to the character of the year.

Jean-Paul Droin
See W&V, Chablis.

Maison Joseph Drouhin
7 rue d'Enfer, 21200 Beaune. 55 ha (3 ha *en fermage*). Côte d'Or 22·7 ha, Chablis 35·3 ha. Grands Crus: Chambertin Clos de Bèze, Griottes-Chambertin; **Bonnes Mares, Musigny; Clos de Vougeot;** Echézeaux, Grands Echézeaux; **Corton-Charlemagne; Corton-Bressandes;** Le Montrachet **(Domaine Marquis de Laguiche); Chablis Les Clos**

Vaudésirs. 1ᵉʳˢ Crus: Chambolle-Musigny, Chambolle-Musigny Amoureuses; Beaune, BEAUNE CLOS DES MOUCHES **(red and white); Volnay Clos des Chênes; Chablis. Chorey-lès-Beaune, Chablis.**
Maison Joseph Drouhin, run by Robert Drouhin, is a highly-reputed Beaune *négociant*, but also an important domain proprietor – many people forget how much it owns in Chablis. The maison combines tradition with new developments and is always willing to try fresh techniques if they are improvements. The red wines are fermented in open *cuves* with floating *chapeau*, and go through long macerations at controlled temperatures. The white grapes are pressed slowly, the last pressings are not used, and fermentation takes place in 228-litre casks. The white and red Beaune Clos des Mouches are flagships, but all the wines are to be highly recommended. The Chablis is influenced by oak and is delicious. The *négoce* business buys in grapes and turns them into wine with the same care it gives those of its own domain. The business only sells AC Bourgogne wines and has never created a *vin de marque*. *See also* W&V, Chablis.

Domaine Drouhin Laroze
21220 Gevrey-Chambertin.
This estate has well-placed parcels in Latricières-Chambertin, Chapelle-Chambertin and Chambertin Clos de Bèze, as well as plots in some of the best parts of the Clos de Vougeot. Recently, however, the Clos de Vougeots have been weak (overcropping?) and the Chambertins are also light. Some of the wines age well, for eight to ten years anyway, but they should be drunk youngish.

Georges Duboeuf
See W&V, Beaujolais, Beaujolais-Villages. For *négociant* details *see* Beaujolais: St-Amour, Fleurie, Beaujolais-Villages.

Roger Duboeuf
See W&V, Mâconnais, Pouilly-Fuissé.

Robert Dubois & Fils
Prémeaux, 21700 Nuits-St-Georges. 9 ha (9 ha *en fermage* and *en métayage*). 1ᵉʳˢ Crus: Chambolle-Musigny Les

Combottes; Nuits-St-Georges: Clos des Argillières, Les Porêts St-Georges; Beaune Blanche Fleur. Vosne-Romanée Les Chalandins, Nuits-St-Georges, Savigny-lès-Beaune Les Golardes, Côte de Nuits-Villages. Bourgogne Rouge, Blanc, Rosé and Aligoté, Bourgogne Passe-Tout-Grains.

A family domain, with Régis Dubois now in charge – they would like to widen their range of *appellations* even further. They follow the practice of heating the must to 40°C for four hours before fermentation in order to extract colour and aromas, then cooling to 28°C for a traditional Burgundian vinification. The wines are certainly keepers, but I have not appreciated them as much as some, always finding something slightly 'tainted' about them – I am not sure whether it is the heating or the tastes from some barrels which cause this. Exports account for 60 percent of sales, but there is also an important private clientele in France.

Domaine P Dubreuil-Fontaine Père & Fils
Pernand-Vergelesses, 21420 Savigny-lès-Beaune. 19 ha. Grands Crus: Corton-Charlemagne; CORTON-BRESSANDES, CORTON CLOS DU ROI, **Corton-Perrières. 1ᵉʳˢ Crus: Pernand Ile des Vergelesses; Savigny-Vergelesses.** PERNAND-VERGELESSES**: (red and white),** CLOS BERTHET **(red and white), Aloxe-Corton, Bourgogne Rouge and Aligoté.**

Bernard Dubreuil manages this excellent domain, which sells half its wines on the export markets and half in France. Vinification is traditional in wood *cuves*, with a floating *chapeau* of skins which is pushed down into the fermenting must (*pigeage*) twice each day. The aim is for wines which will keep, but only in those years with ageing potential. His family knows all there is to know about Pernand, and is especially proud of its Clos Berthet (which the family owns in its entirety) and of its Corton-Bressandes.

Domaine Duchet
21200 Beaune.

The red wines have a reputation for keeping well.

Domaine des Ducs
See W&V, Beaujolais, St-Amour.

Dufouleur Frères
1 rue de Dijon, 21701 Nuits-St-Georges. 7 ha. Grands Crus: Clos Vougeot Les Grands Maupertuis; Musigny. Mercurey, Mercurey Champs Martin, Mercurey Clos l'Evêque, Côte de Nuits-Villages Les Vaucrains.

Dufouleur is a name that is certainly *du métier* because a *fouleur* is a man who treads the grapes to crush them. This is a large *négociant* business, exporting all over Europe, with the domain activity somewhat dwarfed by the *négociant* side. Vinification is traditional in oak vats, with long vatting and floating *chapeau* of skins. Destalking only takes place in certain, well-defined cases. Some of the wines are kept in *fûts* – the firm selects and buys the oak two years beforehand so that it can be aged. They are particularly proud of their Clos Vougeot.

Dufouleur Père & Fils
17 rue Thurot, 21700 Nuits-St-Georges.

This *négociant* markets a wide range of wines and spirits from Burgundy, the Rhône and Bordeaux. The *négociant* wines are fairly dull, but they do also distribute the wines of Domaine Guy Dufouleur.

Domaine Guy Dufouleur
19 place Monge, 21700 Nuits-St-Georges. 20 ha. 1ers Crus: Nuits-St-Georges: En-La-Châine-Carteaux, Clos des Perrières, Les Crots, Les Poulettes. Nuits-St-Georges, SANTENAY CLOS GENÊTS, BOURGOGNE HAUTES CÔTES DE NUITS, **Bougogne Grand Ordinaire.**

The Santenay Clos Genêts and Bourgogne Hautes Côtes de Nuits are to be recommended.

Domaine Dufour
See W&V, Beaujolais, St-Amour.

Domaine Pierre Dugat
21220 Gevrey-Chambertin. 6 ha. Grand Cru: CHARMES-CHAMBERTIN. **1er Cru:** GEVREY-CHAMBERTIN CHAMPEAUX. **Gevrey-Chambertin.**

Pierre Dugat ferments his wines in open cement vats with a manual *pigeage*, and they age in 20 percent new oak for the *village* Vieilles Vignes and the Premier Cru, 30 percent for the Charmes. Very well made wines, full yet elegant.

Domaine Dujac
7 rue de la Bussière, Morey-St-Denis, 21220 Gevrey-Chambertin. 11·5 ha. Grands Crus: Charmes-Chambertin; Clos de la Roche, Clos St-Denis, Bonnes Mares; **Echézeaux. 1ᵉʳˢ Crus:** Gevrey-Chambertin Aux Combottes; Morey-St-Denis**; Chambolle-Musigny; Vosne-Romanée Les Beaumonts. Morey-St-Denis, Chambolle-Musigny, Bourgogne Rouge.**

Jacques Seysses bought this domain in 1968 and has since built it up to be one of the most notable on the Côte de Nuits through a combination of hard work and intelligent winemaking. He took the trouble to qualify as an oenologist at the University of Dijon and is always willing to experiment, although he still conserves everything that is good in traditional techniques. There is no destalking here, a rarity nowadays. The Grands and Premiers Crus are matured in new barrels, the *village* wines in *fûts* that have only been used once. The wines are fined with whites of egg and bottled after 15 months, without filtration. Great character is therefore preserved in all the *appellations*. The domain exports 90 percent of production.

Domaine Duperon
See W&V, Mâconnais, St-Véran.

Domaine Duplessis
See W&V, Chablis.

Domaine Jean & Yves Durand
See W&V, Beaujolais, Régnié.

Domaine Dureuil-Janthial
See W&V, Côte Chalonnaise, Rully.

Jean Durup/Domaine de l'Eglantière
See W&V, Chablis.

Domaine Duvernay
See W&V, Côte Chalonnaise, Rully.

Domaine Maurice Ecard & Fils
21420 Savigny-lès-Beaune. 12·5 ha. 1ers Crus: Savigny-lès-Beaune: Les Cloux, Les Jarrons, Les Narbantons, Les Peuillets, Les Serpentières. Savigny-lès-Beaune.
Savigny-lès-Beaunes which have been very impressive recently. Aged in up to 25 percent new barrels. The Premier Cru Les Serpentières lasts well and all the wines combine great red fruit quality with sound structure.

Domaine René Engel
3 place de la Mairie, Vosne-Romanée, 21700 Nuits-St-Georges. 7 ha. Grands Crus: Clos Vougeot; Echézeaux, GRANDS ECHÉZEAUX. 1er Cru: Vosne-Romanée Les Brûlées. Vosne-Romanée, Glapigny Bourgogne.
This is a domain which includes some precious land in a very good part of Clos Vougeot. There are great old bottles of Engel wines and now Philippe Engel is restoring the estate's fine reputation. A stainless steel sorting table has been in place since 1987 and Grands Crus are put into 30 percent new barrels. There are both open and closed vats for fermentations – the enamel-lined vats give elegant, austere wines, while the wooden *cuves* contribute richness.

Domaine Frédéric Esmonin
21220 Gevrey-Chambertin. 3 ha (5 ha *en métayage*). Grands Crus: Griottes-Chambertin, Mazy-Chambertin, Ruchottes-Chambertin. 1ers Crus: Gevrey-Chambertin: Les Corbeaux, Estournelles St-Jacques, Lavaux St-Jacques. Gevrey-Chambertin Clos Prieur.
Wines of great extract and promise.

Domaine Michel Esmonin
21220 Gevrey-Chambertin.
Very good Gevrey-Chambertin Clos St-Jacques.

Maison J Faiveley
8 rue du Tribourg, 21702 Nuits-St-Georges. 97 ha (13 ha

en fermage). **Grands Crus: Chambertin Clos de Bèze, Latricières-Chambertin, Mazis-Chambertin; Clos de Vougeot; Echézeaux; Corton Clos des Cortons Faiveley. 1ers Crus: Gevrey–Chambertin La Combe aux Moines;** NUITS-ST-GEORGES: CLOS DE LA MARÉCHALE, **Les Porêts St Georges. Rully Les Villeranges, Mercurey Clos Rochette, Mercurey Clos des Myglands, Mercurey La Framboisière.** François Faiveley has taken the domain wines of this important *négociant* right to the top. The policy revolves around very long vinifications (three weeks, even a month in some years), avoiding high temperatures in order to preserve aroma. Fermentation takes place in enamel-lined metal *cuves* which are equipped with a cooling system by means of running water down the sides of the *cuves* (seen more often in Bordeaux than in Burgundy). The wines are aged in oak *pièces* for 18 months, with Grands and Premiers Crus in new oak. There is light fining with egg white, and the wines are kept for a minimum of six months after bottling before being sold. The aim is to make aromatic wines which keep. France takes just over half the production. Maison Faiveley is a very large owner in Mercurey, its properties including the Clos des Myglands. Faiveley also buys in grapes and makes wine itself – notably in Morey-St-Denis (only 15 percent of the production is not from the domain). Faiveley wines have great flavour, and the Mercureys are very good value for what you get. I'm not quite as enamoured of the whites as of the stunning reds. The family business has existed since 1825.

Domaine Jean Faurois
Vosne-Romanée, 21700 Nuits-St-Georges.
This domain no longer exists as Jean Faurois has retired, and the vines have reverted to, or been taken over by, Domaine Méo-Camuzet.

Domaine Jeanne Ferret
See W&V, Mâconnais, Pouilly-Fuissé.

Pierre Ferraud & Fils
See W&V, Beaujolais.

Sylvian Fessy
See Vins Dessalle and W&V, Beaujolais, Morgon.

Vins Fessy
See W&V, Beaujolais, Brouilly.

Domaine William Fèvre
See W&V, Chablis.

Domaine Jean–Philippe Fichet
2 rue Sudot, 21190 Meursault. 1ers Crus: Meursault Les Perrières; Volnay Champans. Meursault, Volnay, Bourgogne Rouge and Blanc. (All *en métayage* **or** *en fermage***).**

Little track record as yet from this new, young producer; but early efforts look promising, especially his whites. Distinctive 'stony' Meursault Les Perrières, slightly austere style in the Volnays, good Bourgogne Rouge and even better Bourgogne Blanc.

Domaine Fleurot–Larose
21590 Santenay. 6·8 ha. Grands Crus: Le Montrachet, Bâtard-Montrachet. 1ers Crus: Chassagne-Montrachet Abbaye de Morgeot (red and white); Santenay.

A large domain. They make a good red Santenay Clos du Passetemps.

Domaine de la Folie
See W&V, Côte Chalonnaise, Rully.

Domaine Fontaine–Gagnard
19 route de Santenay, 21190 Chassagne-Montrachet. 4·44 ha. Grands Crus: Bâtard-Montrachet, Criots-Bâtard-Montrachet. 1ers Crus: Chassagne-Montrachet: Caillerets, Clos St Jean (red), La Maltroie, Morgeot (red and white), Vergers, Chassagne-Montrachet**; Pommard Rugiens; Volnay Clos des Chênes.**

Very good quality whites especially. The whites spend about a year in wood and the reds 18 months, with a maximum of 25 percent new oak. Richard Fontaine is in charge.

Domaine Michel Forest
See W&V, Mâconnais, Pouilly-Fuissé.

SCEA Domaine Forey Père & Fils
2 rue Derrière le Four, 21700 Vosne-Romanée. 4·5 ha (1·5 ha *en métayage***). Grand Cru: Echézeaux. 1ᵉʳˢ Crus: Vosne-Romanée; Nuits-St-Georges. Vosne-Romanée, Nuits-St-Georges, Bourgogne Rouge and Blanc.**
The red wines spend 12–18 months in 30–40 percent new oak. Good wines, especially from Vosne-Romanée.

Domaine Jean-Claude Fourrier
21220 Gevrey-Chambertin.
The wines are not nearly as wondrous as in the time of Fernand Pernot, the great-uncle of the current owner (whose '69 Griotte and Clos St-Jacques are amongst the most amazing Burgundies of my life). A few have breed and cherry-like qualities; however, there is a 'hit and miss' element here, and often the cellars seem to give the wines a taint. A real pity, as the vineyards are so superb. More concentration and cleanliness are urgently needed.

Société Civile du Château de Fuissé
See W&V, Mâconnais, Pouilly–Fuissé.

Domaine Jean-Noël Gagnard
21190 Chassagne-Montrachet. 8·5 ha. Grand Cru: Bâtard-Montrachet. **1ᵉʳˢ Crus:** Chassagne-Montrachet: Les Caillerets, **Les Chenevottes, Clos de la Maltroye, Clos St-Jean (red),** Morgeot **(red and white), Chassagne-Montrachet; Santenay Clos de Tavannes (red). Chassagne-Montrachet Les Mesures, Bourgogne Rouge and Aligoté.**
The whites have always been exceptionally good from this domain, but the reds deserve attention too. The wines are real keepers and M Gagnard is a true guardian of his region's winemaking reputation. His daughter Caroline is now helping him run the domain.

Domaine Gagnard-Delagrange
Chassagne-Montrachet, 21190 Meursault. 3·8 ha (1 ha *en métayage***). Grands Crus: Le Montrachet, Bâtard-**

Montrachet. I^{ers} Crus: Volnay-Champans; Chassagne-Montrachet La Boudriotte, Clos St-Jean, Morgeot.
CHASSAGNE-MONTRACHET **(red and white).**
Jacques Gagnard no longer looks after all his vineyards as he has given some parcels to members of his family (Domaine Blain-Gagnard and Domaine Fontaine-Gagnard) *en métayage*. A renowned estate, where standards remain high.

Vincent Gallois/Domaine de la Vallée aux Sages
See W&V, Chablis.

Domaine des Gandines
See W&V, Mâconnais, Mâcon.

Domaine Jean Garaudet
21630 Pommard.
Very good Pommards and Beaune Clos des Mouches.

Domaine du Gardin
See W&V, Côte Chalonnaise, Givry.

Abel Garnier
21190 Meursault.
Small *négociant* specialising in Meursault, where he also has four hectares of vines.

Domaine François Gaunoux
23 rue du 11 novembre, 21190 Meursault. 8·4 ha. Grand Cru: Corton-Renardes. I^{ers} Crus: Beaune Le Clos des Mouches; Pommard: Les Grands Epenots, Les Epenots, Les Rugiens; Volnay Les Clos des Chênes; Meursault La Goutte d'Or. Pommard, Meursault Le Clos de Tavaux *monopole*, **Bourgogne Rouge and Blanc.**
Brother of Michel Gaunoux of Pommard.

Domaine Michel Gaunoux
Rue Notre Dame, 21630 Pommard. 7 ha. Grand Cru:
CORTON-RENARDES. **I^{ers} Crus: Beaune: Les Boucherottes, Les Epenottes;** POMMARD: **Les Arvelets, Les Charmots, Les**

Combes, GRANDS EPENOTS**, Rugiens. Beaune, Bourgogne Les Sorbins.**
Those wishing to try the wines of this domain will probably have to go to France, as very little is exported – top French restaurants and a following of private customers have got there first. Methods are more than traditional, with treading carried out by a *pigeur* in each wooden *cuve*. Many growers say they wish to produce *vins de garde*, but this domain really achieves it, especially with the very good Pommard Grands Epenots.

Domaine Gay Père & Fils
21200 Chorey-lès-Beaune.
See W&V, Côte d'Or, Chorey-lès-Beaune.

Domaine Geantet-Pansiot
3 route de Beaune, 21220 Gevrey-Chambertin. 0.5 ha (10·5 ha *en fermage*). Grand Cru: CHARMES-CHAMBERTIN**. Ier Cru:** GEVREY-CHAMBERTIN LE POISSENOT**. Marsannay Champs Perdrix, Gevrey-Chambertin Vieilles Vignes, Bourgogne Rouge, Bourgogne Passe-Tout-Grains.**
Rich and classy Le Poissenot; all the wines seem to have moved up a gear with the excellent '90s.

Domaine Pierre Gelin
2 rue du Chapitre, 21220 Gevrey-Chambertin. 16 ha *en métayage*. Grands Crus: Chambertin Clos de Bèze, Mazis-Chambertin. I^{ers} Crus: Fixin: Clos du Chapitre, Clos Napoleon, Les Hervelets. FIXIN**, Gevrey-Chambertin, Bourgogne Aligoté, Bourgogne Passe-Tout-Grains.**
Good wines, but ones which do not, personally, engender a great deal of enthusiasm.

Domaine Louis Genillon
See W&V, Beaujolais, Morgon.

Château Génot-Boulanger
25 rue de Citeaux, 21190 Meursault. 19 ha. I^{ers} Crus: Beaune-Grèves; Pommard; Volnay; Chassagne-Montrachet Les Vergers; Mercurey (red). Pommard,

Volnay, Meursault, Mercurey (white).
Charles Génot makes whites which need a few years to look their
best – Les Vergers is floral and smoky, becoming plumper on
contact with air. The wines can be a bit patchy, however, and I have
been less impressed with the reds under this banner.

Domaine Alain Geoffroy
See W&V, Chablis.

Domaine de la Gérarde
See W&V, Beaujolais, Régnié.

Domaine Henri Germain
Rue Forges, 21190 Meursault.
Do not expect much of a *frisson* from these; Meursaults more
reliable than the Chassagnes.

Domaine Jacques Germain
**Château de Chorey-lès-Beaune, 21200 Beaune. 17 ha. 1ers
Crus:** BEAUNE: **Les Boucherottes; Cent-Vignes, Les Cras,**
LES TEURONS, **Vignes-Franches.** PERNAND-VERGELESSES
(WHITE), CHÂTEAU DE CHOREY-LÈS-BEAUNE, **Bourgogne
Château Germain (red and white).**
François Germain now makes the wines at this domain founded 100
years ago by his great-grandfather. The wines are uniformly
excellent, whether they be simple Chorey-lès-Beaune or grand
Beaune Les Teurons. The emphasis is on finesse and perfume,
making every vintage a pleasure to drink. Vinification is in wood
cuves with quite long vattings of 10–15 days. There is no destalking,
except in years where the grapes are either rather unripe or affected
by rot. The *élevage* is partly in new wood – the amount varies with
the *cru*, with the Beaune Premiers Crus being matured in 50 percent
new barrels, the Chorey-lès-Beaune 25 percent and the Pernand-
Vergelesses 20 percent. Exports account for 75 percent of sales, with
Switzerland and the UK the best customers.

Maison Jean Germain
**9 rue de la Barre, 21190 Meursault. 0·76 ha (1 ha *en
métayage*). St-Romain Clos sous le Château;** MEURSAULT: **La**

Barre, MEIX CHAVAUX**; Puligny-Montrachet: Corvées des Vignes, Les Grands Champs.**

An impeccably-run small domain with a man at the helm who really knows how to make fine white Côte de Beaune wines. There is a 'handmade' quality about the enterprise, with a very old press, but new oak barrels for ageing. M Germain is not a devotee of unnecessarily high alcohol – he likes his wines to be around 12·8 percent. The wines are bottled at 11–18 months. They are fruity and supple when quite young, but last beautifully due to the perfect techniques of *élevage*. Jean Germain is also a *négociant* and exports under the name of the Société l'Elevage et Conditionnement des Vins Fins. In this instance the wines really merit the term *fins*!

Emilian Gillet
See W&V, Mâconnais, Mâcon.

Domaine Armand Girardin/Le Royer Girardin
Route Autun, 21630 Pommard. 5 ha (1.5 ha *en métayage*).
1ers Crus: Beaune: Montrevenots, Clos des Mouches;
Pommard: Charmots, Epenots, Grands Epenots, Rugiens.
Pommard, Bourgogne Rouge.

The running of this estate is gradually being taken over by Armand Girardin's daughter, Aleth Le Royer Girardin, and the latter name will be seen increasingly on the labels. Rich and fruity Pommard Grands Epenots '89; not absolutely top class, but will make a very good drink. However, the same year's Rugiens (under the Royer Girardin name) was weak and dull by comparison.

Domaine Jacques Girardin
Chassagne-Montrachet, 21190 Meursault.
Red Morgeot which has a lovely fresh fruit nose and is most pleasant, if not of marked distinction.

Jean Girardin
See Château de la Charrière.

Domaine Vincent Girardin
21590 Santenay. Savigny-lès-Beaune, Santenay, Maranges.
Good winemaking and pretty wines.

Domaine Girard-Vollot
21420 Savigny-lès-Beaune. 1ᵉʳ Cru: Savigny-lès-Beaune Les Peuillets. Pernand-Vergelesses, Aloxe-Corton, Savigny-lès-Beaune, Bourgogne Rouge and Blanc.
Straight Savigny and Les Peuillets which both have good fruit projection on the nose and satisfying taste.

Domaine Bernard Glantenay
Volnay, 21190 Meursault. 1 ha (7 ha *en fermage*). 1ᵉʳˢ Crus: Pommard: Rugiens, Saussilles; Volnay: Brouillards, Caillerets, Clos des Chênes, Santenots; Puligny-Montrachet. POMMARD, VOLNAY, Bourgogne Rouge and Aligoté, Bourgogne Passe-Tout-Grains.
Bernard Glantenay makes very good wine from a fine array of vineyards. They are fairly firm in style, and need several years before they begin to show well.

Domaine René Gonon
See W&V, Beaujolais, Juliénas.

Domaine Michel Goubard
See W&V, Côte Chalonnaise, Montagny.

Domaine Goud de Beaupuis
Château des Moutots, 21200 Chorey-lès-Beaune. 10 ha. 1ᵉʳˢ Crus: Ladoix Les Hautes Mourottes; Aloxe-Corton Valozières; Savigny-Vergelesses; Beaune: Clos St-Anne, Clos des Vignes Franches, Grèves; Pommard: Epenots, La Chanière. Aloxe-Corton, Chorey-lès-Beaune, Bourgogne Château des Moutots, Bourgogne Aligoté.
A family domain since 1787, there seems to be a thriving direct sale business to the public, although the wines are also exported and sold to restaurants in France. They believe in the virtue of old vines to 'assure quality'. Vinification is in oak *cuves* with slow maceration to develop aromas. The grapes are destalked and the wines aged in oak barrels for two years before bottling. The wines are not to my taste, as the alcohol seems to be all-dominant, masking AC character.

Domaine Henri Gouges
7 rue du Moulin, 21700 Nuits-St-Georges. 1ᵉʳˢ Crus: Nuits-St-Georges: **Les Chaignots,** Clos des Porets *monopole*, Les Pruliers, Les St-Georges, Les Vaucrains. **Nuits-St-Georges.** For a number of years, up to and including 1988, this domain was making weak and uninspiring wines. Since 1989, however, things have improved enormously and the wines (in '89, '90 and '91) once again have the depth and class that made this name so famous.

Domaine Bertrand de Gramont
21700 Nuits-St-Georges.
Tiny quantities of very good quality Nuits-St-Georges.

Château de la Grand'Grange
See W&V, Beaujolais, Beaujolais-Villages.

Domaine des Granges
See W&V, Mâconnais, Mâcon.

Domaine Alain Gras
21190 St-Romain.
Very good quality Auxey-Duresses and St-Romain.

Domaine René Gras Boisson
21190 St Romain. 6 ha. Meursault, Auxey-Duresses (white), St-Romain (red and white)**, Bourgogne Aligoté.**
Very good quality red and white St-Romain made by Mme Gras Boisson's son, Alain Gras (qv), in the same style as his own wines.

Château de la Greffière
See W&V, Mâconnais, Mâcon.

Château Gris
21700 Nuits-St-Georges.
Owned by Lupé-Cholet, now part of Maison Albert Bichot. *See also* W&V, Côte d'Or, Nuits-St-Georges.

Domaine Albert Grivault
7 place de Murger, 21190 Meursault. 4·8 ha. 1ᵉʳˢ Crus:

Meursault Clos des Perrières, Meursault Perrières;
Pommard Clos Blanc; Meursault.
Michel Bardet, the son of the owner Mme Bardet-Grivault, now
runs this property. Whites are fermented at 16°C and aged in one-
third new oak. Very classy Meursaults with Puligny-like finesse.

Domaine Jean Grivot
**6 rue de la Croix Rameau, 21700 Vosne-Romanée. 11·26 ha
(2·77 ha *en métayage*). Grands Crus:** Clos de Vougeot;
Echézeaux; Richebourg. **1ers Crus: Chambolle-Musigny La
Combe d'Orvaux; Vosne-Romanée: Beaux Monts,
Brûlées, Chaumes, Les Reignots, Les Rouges, Suchots;**
Nuits-St-Georges: **Boudots,** Lavières, Pruliers, **Roncières.
Vosne-Romanée, Nuits-St-Georges. Bourgogne Rouge,
Grand Ordinaire, Bourgogne Passe-Tout-Grains.**
Guy Accad has been advising on viticulture here since 1982, and on
vinification since 1987. Very good wines, though the Grands Crus
lack the gloss and opulence of the finest. A maximum of 20 percent
new wood is used for the first year's ageing. Etienne Grivot aims to
make wines with the structure to age well, but which are
harmonious enough to be drunk young too. Not surprisingly, it is
difficult to satisfy both of these aims, but nearly all the domain's
wines seem to age well.

Domaine Robert Groffier
**4 route des Grands Crus, 21220 Morey-St-Denis. 8 ha.
Grands Crus: Chambertin Clos de Bèze;** Bonnes Mares. **1ers
Crus:** Chambolle-Musigny: Les Amoureuses, **Les Hauts-
Doix, Les Sentiers. Gevrey-Chambertin, Bourgogne.**
Prior to 1975 Groffier used to sell his wine to Piat for *élevage* and
bottling, and, if the '71 Les Amoureuses is anything to go by,
Groffier made very good wine and Piat did a good job too. After a
long patchy period the '87s turned out well and the '88s are
excellent: elegant, glossy wines. Things are looking up.

Domaine Anne & François Gros
**21700 Vosne-Romanée. 4·5 ha. Grands Crus: Clos Vougeot;
Echézeaux; Richebourg. Vosne-Romanée, Chambolle-
Musigny, Bourgogne Rouge.**

François is the second brother of Jean Gros; his daughter Anne makes the wine here and runs the property with her father. There is some vexation at the recent appearance of the wines of Domaine Anne-Françoise Gros under that name.

Domaine Anne-Françoise Gros
La Garelle, Route d'Ivry, 21630 Pommard. 4 ha. Grands Crus: Echézeaux; Richebourg. 1ᵉʳˢ Crus: Vosne-Romanée Maizières, Aux Réas. Bourgogne Hautes Côtes de Nuits.
Anne-Françoise Gros is the only daughter of Jean Gros. She is married to François Parent (Domaine Parent-Gros, Pommard) but produces the Côte de Nuits wines from the vineyards she inherited under her maiden name; an understandable source of confusion with the wines of her cousin Anne and uncle François!

Domaine Gros Frère & Soeur
21700 Vosne-Romanée. Grands Crus: Clos Vougeot; Grands Echézeaux; Richebourg. Vosne-Romanée, Bourgogne Hautes Côtes de Nuits.
The 'frère et soeur' here are the brother and sister of Jean Gros: Gustave (deceased) and Colette, but the domain is now run by Bernard, Jean Gros' second son. Very good wines, if not quite up to the superb quality of Domaine Jean Gros.

Domaine Jean Gros
3 rue des Communes, 21700 Vosne-Romanée. 10 ha (8 ha *en fermage*). Grands Crus: Clos Vougeot**; Richebourg. 1ᵉʳ Cru:** Vosne-Romanée Clos des Réas**. Vosne-Romanée, Chambolle-Musigny, Nuits-St-Georges, Bourgogne Hautes Côtes de Nuits, Bourgogne Rouge.**
An excellent domain (now managed by Jean's son Michel) where your expectations of grand names are fulfilled. Inevitably the vineyards have been split up in true Burgundian fashion so that even the Burgundians are confused. The large (7 ha) Hautes Côtes de Nuits vineyard was planted some 20 years ago and its wine is sold under the label of Michel Gros. Traditional methods are followed, with 100 percent new oak for the Grands Crus and Premiers Crus, 30–50 percent for the *villages*. Try to obtain some of these superb wines as they will not disappoint.

Domaine Thierry Guerin
See W&V, Mâconnais, St-Véran.

Domaine Guffens-Heynen
See W&V, Mâconnais, Pouilly-Fuissé.

Domaine Adrien Guichard
See W&V, Mâconnais, Mâcon.

Domaine Guillemard-Dupont & Ses Fils
21190 Meloisey.
Based at Meloisey in the Hautes Côtes de Beaune, these vignerons make strawberry-scented Pommard, balanced and unfettered by excess alcohol. The wine has a raw flavour when young and a lovely after-taste.

Domaine Pierre Guillemot
21420 Savigny-lès-Beaune. 7·6 ha. 1ers Crus: SAVIGNY-LÈS-BEAUNE: LES JARRONS, LES NARBANTONS, LES SERPENTIÈRES. SAVIGNY-LÈS-BEAUNE **(red and** WHITE**), Bourgogne Rouge.**
Very good wines with a pure Savigny taste of strawberries. M Guillemot really knows what his *appellation* should represent.

Domaine Guillemot-Michel
See W&V, Mâconnais, Mâcon.

Domaine Antonin Guyon
21420 Savigny-lès-Beaune. 47 ha. Grands Crus: Charmes-Chambertin; Corton-Charlemagne; Corton-Bressandes, Corton Clos du Roy, Corton-Renardes. 1ers Crus: Pernand-Vergelesses, Aloxe-Corton, Volnay Clos des Chênes, Meursault-Charmes. Gevrey-Chambertin, Chambolle-Musigny, Pernand-Vergelesses, Savigny-lès-Beaune, Chorey-lès-Beaune, Beaune, Hautes Côtes de Nuits, Bourgogne Aligoté.
In the past, I often found wines of finesse and *appellation* style from this domain. Then there seems to have been a disappointing patch, although I have not seen the '88s, '89s and '90s.

Domaine Haegelen-Jayer
47 rue Croix Remeau, 21700 Vosne-Romanée. 5 ha. Grands Crus: Clos de Vougeot; Echézeaux. 1ᵉʳ Cru: Nuits-St-Georges Les Damodes. Chambolle-Musigny, Vosne-Romanée.

M Haegelen-Jayer aims to make wines with plenty of extract, with four days' *macération à froide* and three weeks' *cuvaison*. The wines spend 18 months in 50 percent new wood, are given a light egg-white fining and are not filtered. They are well made. The *village* and Premier Cru wines are fruity and solid without being coarse; the Echézeaux and Clos de Vougeot are rich and supple; very good without being in the grandest league.

Domaine Thierry Hamelin
See W&V, Chablis.

Domaine Heresztyn
27 rue Richebourg, 21220 Gevrey-Chambertin. 10 ha. Grand Cru: Clos St-Denis. 1ᵉʳˢ Crus: Gevrey-Chambertin: Les Champonnets, Les Corbeaux, Les Goulots, La Perrière; Morey-St-Denis Les Millandes. Gevrey-Chambertin, Bourgogne Rouge and Blanc.
A domain that is 'on the up'.

Hospices de Beaune
See W&V, Côte d'Or, Hospices de Beaune.

Domaine des Hospices de Nuits-St-Georges
Rue Henri Challand, 21700 Nuits-St-Georges. 11 ha, of which 8·5 ha are Nuits-St-Georges 1ᵉʳ Cru and Nuits-St-Georges. Also owns vineyards in Vosne-Romanée and Prémeaux-Prissey.

The Hospices de Nuits is a charitable foundation which dates from the year 1270 and, as with the Hospices de Beaune, its principal concern is the provision of retirement homes for the elderly. The main financial support for this comes from the annual sale of fine wines, which usually takes place on the Sunday before Palm Sunday. As with its counterpart in Beaune, all depends on the *élevage*. When tasting the wines from barrel, they can seem too heavily chaptalised and I wonder whether the use of 100 percent new oak, irrespective of the vintage, is wise.

Domaine Bernard Hudelot
21700 Villars-Fontaine.
See W&V, Côte d'Or, Hautes Côtes de Nuits.

Domaine Alain Hudelot-Noëllat
21640 Vougeot. 12 ha. Grands Crus: Clos Vougeot; RICHEBOURG, ROMANÉE-ST-VIVANT. **1ers Crus:** VOSNE-ROMANÉE: **Les Malconsorts,** LES SUCHOTS; CHAMBOLLE-MUSIGNY LES CHARMES; **Nuits-St-Georges Les Murgers; Vougeot. Vosne-Romanée,** CHAMBOLLE-MUSIGNY.
Absolutely lovely wines.

Jaboulet-Vercherre
5 rue Colbert, 21201 Beaune. 12 ha. Grand Cru: Corton-Bressandes. 1ers Crus: Beaune Clos de l'Ecu *monopole*, **Bressandes (white); Pommard Clos de la Commaraine** *monopole*; **Volnay-Caillerets; Puligny-Montrachet Les Folatières (white); Santenay Grand Clos Rousseau (red). Savigny-lès-Beaune Les Vermots (red and white), Pommard Les Petits Noizons.**
Négociants and domain owners. I find it difficult to identify *appellation* character in their *négoce* wines – a case of house style dominating the nuances.

Lucien Jacob
21420 Echevronne. 12 ha *en fermage*. **1er Cru: Savigny-Vergelesses (red and white). Savigny-lès-Beaune,** BOURGOGNE HAUTES CÔTES DE BEAUNE, **Bourgogne Aligoté.**
Well-made, fruity wines; good quality without being exceptional. The Hautes Côtes de Beaune, however, is excellent.

Château des Jacques
See W&V, Beaujolais, Moulin-à-Vent.

Paul & Henri Jacqueson
See W&V, Côte Chalonnaise, Rully.

Maison Louis Jadot

5 rue Samuel Legay, 21200 Beaune. 40 ha. Grands Crus: Corton-Charlemagne; Corton, CORTON-POUGETS**;** CHEVALIER-MONTRACHET LES DEMOISELLES**. 1ers Crus:** BEAUNE**:** BOUCHEROTTES**,** LES BRESSANDES**, Les Chouacheux, Clos des Couchereaux,** CLOS DES URSULES**,** THEURONS**; Puligny-Montrachet Les Folatières. Pernand-Vergelesses Clos de la Croix de Pierre.**

A very important *négociant* business which was sold to the owners of its American importer Kobrand in 1985. However, M André Gagey remained in charge, which was a good thing for everybody. Now, after 45 years with the company – he made his first wine there in 1947 and took over as chairman in 1954 – he will be handing over the running of Louis Jadot to his equally capable son Pierre Henry at the end of 1992. The Jadot family owns plots in some very prestigious vineyards in the Côte de Beaune, and these were substantially enlarged during the 1980s through the acquisition of a large portion of the Clair Daü vineyards in the Côte de Nuits in 1985, and of Maison Champy's vineyards in 1989. Jadot also makes and markets the wines of the Domaine du Duc de Magenta. The white wines are fermented in oak barrels and aged similarly for 12–18 months. The red wines are traditionally vinified in open wooden vats with a floating *chapeau* of skins, *pigeage* and ageing in oak barrels for 18 months to two years. The wines are exported around the world, as well as being sold in France. The standard is high and the wines age gracefully. The grandest names are much sought after, and justifiably, but I have a particular weakness for their Beaune Boucherottes and the Chouacheux. The quality of the reds is perhaps less even than that of the whites; the latter are consistently fine and the best of them are quite glorious.

Maison Jaffelin

Caves du Chapitre, 2 rue Paradis, 21200 Beaune.

An old-established *négociant* which was bought by Joseph Drouhin in 1969, but which still runs its business separately. Maison Jaffelin owns no vineyards itself, though the Jaffelin family still owns small parcels in Clos Vougeot, Beaune Les Bressandes and Beaune Les Avaux. The wines do not excite me at all.

Domaine Jacky Janodet
See W&V, Beaujolais, Moulin-à-Vent.

Château de Javernand
See W&V, Beaujolais, Chiroubles.

Domaine Georges Jayer
**21700 Vosne-Romanée. Grand Cru: Echézeaux.
Nuits-St-Georges.**

Georges Jayer is Henri Jayer's brother. His style is somewhat lighter than Henri's and less oaky, with an Echézeaux that has great refinement and persistence of flavour.

Domaine Henri Jayer
21700 Vosne-Romanée. 6 ha. Grands Crus: ECHÉZEAUX; **Richebourg. 1ᵉʳˢ Crus: Vosne-Romanée: Les Brûlées, Cros Parentoux; Nuits-St-Georges Les Murgers. Vosne-Romanée,** NUITS-ST-GEORGES.

Henri Jayer claims an official 'cessation d'activité – retraité depuis 1989'. Retired or not, he continues to advise a number of domains and his splendidly rich, opulent wines will be around for a long time to come. M Jayer is a veritable magician – he made some of the most exciting wines on the entire Côte d'Or. The depth of flavour and sheer impact of fruit are remarkable. His recipe appears simple: the grapes are sorted on the vine; complete destalking; cold-maceration for five days before the start of fermentation (natural yeasts only); fining with fresh egg whites; maturing of all wines, except for the straight *villages*, in new oak; bottling by gravity; five *analyses* during the *élevage*. Above all, perhaps, yields are kept low, which is the secret of concentration in Burgundy. Henri Jayer also made the wines of his brother Georges, but with this label they are often sold earlier than his own. Nephew Emanuel Rouget is following in the family footsteps and, in addition, the Méo-Camuzet domain now falls into this winemaking stable.

Domaine Jacqueline Jayer
21700 Vosne-Romanée. Grand Cru: ECHÉZEAUX. **1ᵉʳˢ Crus:** VOSNE-ROMANÉE: **Les Reignots,** LES ROUGES. **Vosne-Romanée,** NUITS-ST-GEORGES.

Now under the same winemaking 'hat' as the Domaine Jean Grivot, the wines being made by Etienne Grivot. Very good wines, even in a vintage like '82, which elsewhere was often overcropped.

Domaine Robert Jayer-Gilles
21700 Magny-lès-Villiers. 9 ha. Grand Cru: Echézeaux. 1ᵉʳ Cru: Nuits-St-Georges Les Damodes. Côtes de Nuits-Villages, Hautes Côtes de Nuits.
Robert Jayer makes exemplary wines, even at modest AC level. The prices are far from modest, but this producer always 'delivers the goods'; lots of oak, but the fruit and extract to take it.

Domaine Jeannin-Naltet Père & Fils
See W&V, Côte Chalonnaise, Mercurey.

Charles Jobard
Auxey-Duresses, 21190 Meursault.
See W&V, Côte d'Or, Auxey-Duresses.

François Jobard
2 rue Leignon, 21190 Meursault.
Serious winemaker whose Meursaults are both flavoursome and elegant. Sometimes the use of oak creates lack of balance when young and, for maximum pleasure, vintages like '88 should not be broached too early.

Domaine Joblot
See W&V, Côte Chalonnaise, Givry.

Domaine Philippe Joliet
21220 Fixin. 5·18 ha. FIXIN CLOS DE LA PERRIÈRE.
Both the Manoir and the Clos de la Perrière vineyard were created by the monks of the Abbey of Citeaux in the 12th century. Methods are traditional, with partial destalking according to the year (20–60 percent). Long vatting (18–20 days) produces wines which keep, certainly the case with the '83 and the '81. *Négociants* receive 35 percent, 35 percent is sold on export markets and 30 percent goes in direct sales. You will not find delicacy here at Fixin, but certainly a wine to be drunk in cold weather from big glasses.

Domaine Jean Joliot & Fils
Nantoux, 21190 Meursault. 11 ha. 1er Cru: Beaune-Boucherottes. Pommard, Meursault, HAUTES CÔTES DE BEAUNE, Bourgogne Aligoté, Bourgogne Passe-Tout-Grains, Crémant de Bourgogne.
A highly regarded domain in the Hautes Côtes de Beaune – the Joliot family have always had vines: 'le souvenir se perd dans la nuit des temps', as they say. Apart from the Hautes Côtes wines, there are also small slices of grander *appellations*, but there is no doubt that the more modest wines are very good value, with the authentic taste of Burgundy. Traditional methods are the order of the day, but modified each year according to the quality of the vintage. The aim is to make wines of perfume and finesse allied to reasonable body, maintaining a balance between alcohol, tannin and acidity so that the wines can age according to their place in the hierarchy, ie you would keep a Pommard longer than a Hautes Côtes de Beaune.

Claude & Michelle Joubert
See W&V, Beaujolais, Beaujolais-Villages.

Domaine du Marquis de Jouennes d'Herville
See W&V, Côte Chalonnaise, Mercurey.

Manoir des Journets
See W&V, Beaujolais, Chénas.

Domaine Michel Juillot
See W&V, Côte d'Or, Pernand-Vergelesses/Côte Chalonnaise, Mercurey.

Château de Juliénas
See W&V, Beaujolais, Juliénas.

Domaine de la Juvinière
Clos de Langres, Corgoloin, 21700 Nuits-St-Georges. 24 ha.
Owned by La Reine Pédauque, the Beaune *négociants*.

Labouré-Roi
21700 Nuits-St-Georges.
A *négociant* and small domain owner. The wines are reliable, not
exciting, but some of the domain wines are good. I have been
impressed by the wines of the René Manuel estate, which they
distribute. The Meursault is oaky and rich, and the unusual red
Meursault has a gamey, fruity character to it. They also usually have
a good white Auxey-Duresses, an *appellation* which is worth
finding when Meursault and Puligny look too expensive. Watch
out also for the Domaine Chantal Lescure wines.

Maurice Labruyère
See W&V, Beaujolais, Moulin-à-Vent.

Château de Lacarelle
See W&V, Beaujolais, Beaujolais-Villages.

Domaine Henri Lafarge
See W&V, Mâconnais, Mâcon.

Domaine Michel Lafarge
Volnay, 21190 Meursault 9·35 ha. Iers Crus: Beaune-Grèves;
Volnay: **Clos du Château des Ducs,** Clos des Chênes,
**Volnay. Volnay, Meursault, Bourgogne Rouge and
Aligoté, Bourgogne Passe-Tout-Grains.**
This is a meticulous family domain, making wine with both care
and intelligence. Complete destalking is practised, and rigorous
selection of the grapes if there is an element of rot in the vintage.
Vinification lasts approximately ten days and the wine is aged in
oak *pièces* for 18 months – about a third of the crop goes into new
barrels. Connoisseurs of fine Burgundy around the world now
know that a Volnay from Michel Lafarge is a treat indeed – but
then, this family has been domain-bottling for 50 years. In years like
1988, a comparison between the Clos du Château des Ducs and the
Clos des Chênes is revelatory.

Domaine des Comtes Lafon
**Clos de la Barre, 21190 Meursault. 13 ha. Grand Cru:
Montrachet. Iers Crus: Monthélie Les Duresses;** Volnay:

Champans, Clos des Chênes, SANTENOTS DU MILIEU;
MEURSAULT: CHARMES, GENEVRIÈRES, GOUTTE D'OR, PERRIÈRES.
MEURSAULT CLOS DE LA BARRE, MEURSAULT DÉSIRÉE,
Meursault.
A superb domain making the kind of Burgundy I like. The reds age
for two years in 30 percent new wood, the whites in up to 40
percent new oak for 21 months – in one of the coolest cellars in
Burgundy. There is no filtration here, and both red and white wines
usually need years to be at their best. Dominique Lafon is
continuing the fine winemaking tradition of his father René, and
there is no greater reputation in Burgundy to uphold.

Domaine Lafouge
21190 Auxey-Duresses.
Both quality and value in red and white Auxey-Duresses.

Domaine Marquis de Laguiche
Puligny-Montrachet, 21190 Meursault.
See W&V, Côte d'Or, Puligny-Montrachet.

Domaine Laleure-Piot
**Pernand-Vergelesses, 21420 Savigny-lès-Beaune. 9 ha.
Grands Crus: Corton-Charlemagne; Corton-Bressandes,
Corton-Rognet. 1ers Crus:** PERNAND-VERGELESSES: LES
VERGELESSES, ILE DES VERGELESSES, PERNAND-VERGELESSES **(red
and** WHITE**); Savigny-lès-Beaune Vergelesses. Pernand-
Vergelesses (red and white), Chorey-lès-Beaune, Côte de
Nuits-Villages Les Bellevues,** BOURGOGNE ALIGOTÉ,
Bourgogne Passe-Tout-Grains.
Particularly attractive white wines, but very good all round.

Michel Lamanthe
39410 St-Aubin.
See W&V, Côte d'Or, St-Aubin.

Domaine Lamarche
**9 rue des Communes, 21700 Vosne-Romanée. 4·5 ha (8 ha
worked). Grands Crus: Clos de Vougeot; Echézeaux,
Grands Echézeaux, La Grand'Rue. 1ers Crus:** VOSNE-

Romanée: **Les Chaumes**, Les Malconsorts**, Les Suchots.
Vosne-Romanée, Bourgogne Rouge and Aligoté,
Bourgogne Passe-Tout-Grains.**
A remarkable estate, with some 'golden' land: it is the sole owner of
La Grand'Rue, sandwiched between La Tâche and the Romanées,
and also has Grands Echézeaux, Echézeaux and the Premier Cru Les
Malconsorts. It aims to make wines which keep, wherever possible.
Some appear somewhat rustic and alcoholic when young, but I
have had fine old bottles from here, and quality is certainly
improving under François Lamarche.

Lamblin & Fils
See W&V, Chablis.

Hubert Lamy
**St-Aubin, 21190 Meursault. 9·5 ha (4 ha *en métayage*).
Grand Cru: Criots-Bâtard-Montrachet. 1er Cru:** St-Aubin
(red and white)**. St-Aubin (red and white), Puligny-
Montrachet, Chassagne-Montrachet (red and white),
Santenay, Côte de Beaune-Villages, Hautes Côtes de
Beaune, Bourgogne Rouge and Aligoté.**
The Lamy family have been vignerons since 1640, and in this case
experience has really resulted in knowledge of the subject. They
know that St-Aubin is ignored by many, so are committed to
'reducing quantity to increase quality'. In this they succeed quite
admirably, whether it is in the *village* wines or in the grander
appellations. The whites have a stylish, acacia-like quality, while the
reds are tannic when young, maturing to become a delicious
mouthful. The red grapes are not destalked, and vatting lasts for 10–
15 days, so you can safely lay down some bottles. They sell to
private customers in France, Belgium and Switzerland, but
England and the USA are also the happy recipients of some of
these wines.

Domaine Lamy-Pillot
**31 route de Santenay, 21190 Chassagne-Montrachet. 6 ha
(12 ha partly owned, partly *en fermage* or *en métayage*). 1ers
Crus: Blagny La Pièce sous le Bois; St-Aubin: Les Castets,
Les Combes; Chassagne-Montrachet: Boudriotte, Clos St-**

Jean, Morgeot. St-Aubin: Argillières, Les Pucelles; Chassagne-Montrachet, Chassagne-Montrachet Champs de Morgeot; Santenay Les Charrons; Bourgogne Rouge, Bourgogne Aligoté La Capitaine, Bourgogne Bas de Madrid, Crémant de Bourgogne.

René Lamy has built up this domain via a succession of plots scattered over a wide variety of *appellations*. Some of the wines are rather hard when young and need ageing. There could be a problem with barrels here, which would explain some rather 'off' odours. But other wines have been successful, and there are old vines in the Boudriotte.

Domaine Aimé Langoureau
39410 St-Aubin.
See W&V, Côte d'Or, St-Aubin.

Denise & Hubert Lapierre
See W&V, Beaujolais, Chénas.

André Large
See W&V, Beaujolais, Côte de Brouilly.

Domaine Laroche
See W&V, Chablis.

Jean Lathuilière
See W&V, Beaujolais, Brouilly.

Maison Louis Latour
18 rue des Tonneliers, 21204 Beaune. 47 ha. Grands Crus: Chambertin; ROMANÉE-ST-VIVANT; CORTON-CHARLEMAGNE; CORTON: **Bressandes, Chaumes, Clos de la Vigne au Saint, Clos du Roi,** GRANCEY, **Grèves, Perrières, Pougets;** CHEVALIER-MONTRACHET LES DEMOISELLES. 1ers **Crus:** PERNAND-VERGELESSES: ILE DES VERGELESSES, **Pernand-Vergelesses;** ALOXE-CORTON: LES CHAILLOTS, LES FOURNIÈRES; BEAUNE: **Clos du Roi, Cras, Grèves, Perrières,** VIGNES FRANCHES; **Volnay-Mittants. Aloxe-Corton, Volnay.**

A *négociant* and a domain owner of excellent reputation, dedicated to producing fine bottles of Burgundy for the French market and around the world. Their methods have not changed with the times: the grapes are still harvested and transported in traditional wicker baskets; the vinification of the reds takes place in open wooden vats with treading of the floating cap; and they are aged for approximately 18 months in oak barrels. The whites are fermented and aged in oak barrels and bottled after approximately 12 months. But if the methods are traditional, all the modern techniques of oenological analysis are also called upon. Apart from the illustrious domain wines, Côte d'Or red wines are bought young, in barrel, while the whites are bought as grapes and vinified by the firm. The *élevage* of these wines then takes place in Latour's cellars, side-by-side with the wines of the domain. The white wines are superlative, and while the reds can go through tricky moments, they do age well. The firm has pasteurized its red wines since the early part of this century. I think it is worth commenting that I have tasted many Burgundian wines which were *not* pasteurized but which were also perfectly disgusting! On the other hand, I wonder if pasteurization is really necessary, and would find it very interesting to make a study of similar wines, made with and without the process, tasting them over a number of years to monitor their development. *See also* W&V, Côte Chalonnaise, Montagny.

Domaine Latour Giraud

6 Route Nationale, 21190 Meursault. 10 ha. 1ers Crus: Meursault: Caillerets (red), Charmes, Genevrières, Perrières, Poruzot; Puligny-Montrachet Champ Canet; Pommard; Volnay Clos des Chênes, Maranges La Fussière. Meursault, Bourgogne Blanc.

Some good wines, but far too patchy, with evidence of oxidation at bottling and perhaps sloppy cellar work. White wines best, especially in the Premiers Crus.

Domaine Philippe Leclerc

13 rue Halles, 21220 Gevrey-Chambertin.

A span of very good Gevrey wines, all kept in 100 percent new oak. Compare them with brother René's domain, where there is very little new wood.

Domaine René Leclerc
28 route Dijon, 21220 Gevrey-Chambertin.
A range of Gevreys which leaves me much less impressed than those of brother Philippe, some wines tasting 'dirty'.

Domaine Leflaive
Place des Marronniers, 21190 Puligny-Montrachet. 21 ha.
Grands Crus: Le Montrachet, BÂTARD-MONTRACHET,
BIENVENUES-BÂTARD-MONTRACHET, CHEVALIER-MONTRACHET.
1ers Crus: PULIGNY-MONTRACHET: LES COMBETTES, CLAVOILLON,
LES PUCELLES. PULIGNY-MONTRACHET, **Bourgogne Rouge and**
Blanc.
This is a splendid old family domain (whose reputation has never been higher). Although Vincent Leflaive is still very much *présent*, the running of the domain is gradually being taken over by his daughter Anne-Claude, a qualified oenologist, and his nephew Olivier Leflaive. Vincent Leflaive considers absolute cleanliness in the cellar one of the most vital parts of white winemaking. The wines are bottled after about 18 months following an *élevage* in oak *pièces* and small stainless steel vats. Let yourself be seduced by their honeyed smoothness – if you have not already succumbed to the heady bouquet! At this stage, I do not want to be definite about criticism over a lack of concentration in wines of the late 1980s; they tasted well in cask and we need to see them with bottle-age.

Olivier Leflaive Frères
Place du Monument, 21190 Puligny-Montrachet. 7·5 ha.
1ers Crus: Meursault Poruzots; Chassagne-Montrachet
Chaumées. Puligny-Montrachet, Chassagne-Montrachet
(red and white), Bourgogne Rouge, Blanc and Aligoté.
Olivier Leflaive helps to run the superb family domain and also manages his own *négociant* business specialising in white wines, which are excellent, but with a few very good reds too. Top flight *élevage* by a young team.

Domaine François Legros
7 rue François Mignotte, 21700 Nuits-St-Georges.
Barely any track record, as M Legros only made his first vintage in 1988; but he is clearly committed, so worth watching.

Domaine Lejeune

La Confrérie, 21630 Pommard. 6 ha. 1ᵉʳˢ Crus: POMMARD:
RUGIENS, LES ARGILLIÈRES, **Poutures. Bourgogne Rouge,
Blanc and Aligoté.**

Unusual vinification method using part *macération carbonique*,
which gives the wines a very marked 'fruit', but also long *cuvaison*
and a high proportion of new oak, both of which make for a fairly
tannic frame as well. Wines which will keep.

Domaine Lequin Roussot

21590 Santenay. 13·50 ha *en fermage*. **Grands Crus: Corton
Les Languettes; Bâtard-Montrachet. 1ᵉʳˢ Crus: Chassagne-
Montrachet Morgeot (red and white); Santenay: La
Comme, Clos Rousseau, Le Passe-Temps. Nuits-St-
Georges, Côte de Beaune-Villages, Pommard,** SANTENAY,
Bourgogne Rouge.

This is a classic example of a fragmented Burgundian vineyard – the
Lequins have to rush up and down the Côte at vintage time, which
accounts for some patchy quality perhaps. But they make fine
wines as well, and that is quite a feat. Fermentations are relatively
long, with *foulages* and *remontages*. The *élevage* is in oak barrels, a
fifth of which are new. The wines have plenty of verve and keep
well, and their AC character is not masked by an excess of oak.

Domaine Leroy & Leroy-Négociant

**Auxey-Duresses, 21190 Meursault. 4·27 ha. Grands Crus:
Chambertin; Musigny; Clos de Vougeot. Pommard,**
AUXEY-DURESSES, **Meursault.**

A high profile *négociant* with very solid long-lasting wines, much
praised by some. Lalou Bize-Leroy, the owner, has decided views
and these emphatic (and expensive) wines are a reflection of her
commitment and personality. Domaine Leroy also now includes
the Domaine Charles Noëllat (in Vosne-Romanée) and Domaine
Remy (in Gevrey-Chambertin), and it will be fascinating to see
these wines develop in bottle.

Domaine Chantal Lescure

Now managed by the *négociant* Labouré-Roi. The domain's
BEAUNE CHOUACHEUX is often good. *See* Labouré-Roi.

Domaine Thierry Lespinasse
See W&V, Côte Chalonnaise, Givry.

Domaine Lieven
See W&V, Beaujolais, Morgon.

Domaine Xavier Liger-Belair
21700 Nuits-St-Georges.

For a long time the Liger-Belairs have been letting out their vineyards *en métayage*, but it is possible that sometime during the 1990s a new generation of the family may start making wine from the family properties again. These include some excellent parcels in Clos Vougeot, Richebourg and Nuits-St-Georges Premier Cru.

Domaine Georges Lignier
41 Grande Rue, 21220 Morey-St-Denis. 14 ha (15 ha *en métayage*). Grands Crus: Bonnes Mares, CLOS DE LA ROCHE, CLOS ST-DENIS. 1ers Crus: Gevrey-Chambertin Les Combottes; MOREY-ST-DENIS CLOS DES ORMES. Gevrey-Chambertin, Morey-St-Denis, Chambolle-Musigny, Bourgogne Rouge and Aligoté, Bourgogne Passe-Tout-Grains.

Traditional methods and *élevage* in 100 percent new oak for the Grands Crus, 20 percent for the Premiers Crus. The Premier Cru Clos des Ormes is always particularly good value. Lovely wines.

Domaine Hubert Lignier
45 Grande Rue, 21220 Morey-St-Denis. 6·2 ha (1·4 ha *en métayage*). Grands Crus: Charmes-Chambertin; CLOS DE LA ROCHE. 1ers Crus: Gevrey-Chambertin; Morey-St-Denis; Chambolle-Musigny. Gevrey-Chambertin, Morey-St-Denis, Chambolle-Musigny, Bourgogne Rouge and Aligoté, Bourgogne Passe-Tout-Grains.

Morey-St-Denis of quality, with excellent Clos de la Roche. Hubert Lignier uses a lot more new wood for his Premier Cru and *village* wines than Georges Lignier, and I sometimes feel that the new oak masks the Pinot.

Domaine Long-Depaquit
See W&V, Chablis.

Loron & Fils
See W&V, Beaujolais.

Lupé-Cholet
17 avenue Général de Gaulle, 21700 Nuits-St-Georges.
28·57 ha. Iᵉʳˢ Crus: Chablis Vaillons; NUITS-ST-GEORGES
CHÂTEAU GRIS *monopole*. Clos de Lupé (Bourgogne Rouge
***monopole*).**
Lupé-Cholet is a *négociant*, now merged with the huge Bichot of Beaune, the largest exporter of Burgundy. But it also owns two *monopoles* on the Côte de Nuits, although one only carries the Bourgogne Rouge *appellation*. Methods are traditional, with fermentations in wood *cuves*, and storage in new oak barrels. The Château Gris is an enclave in the Premier Cru Aux Crots, not a Grand Cru as stated on some of the older labels. The new wood is very evident in recent vintages, but the wines should age well. The *négociant* wines seem most honourable, and their Savigny selections appear particularly successful.

Domaine Roger Luquet
See W&V, Mâconnais, Pouilly-Fuissé.

Lycée Agricole et Viticole
16 avenue Charles Jaffelin, 21207 Beaune. 19·3 ha (8·6 ha *en fermage*, 1 ha *en métayage*). Iᵉʳˢ Crus: Beaune: Les Bressandes, Les Champimonts, La Montée Rouge, Les Perrières, Beaune. Beaune (red and white), CÔTE DE BEAUNE, Puligny-Montrachet, Bourgogne Hautes Côtes de Beaune (Savigny) (red and white), Bourgogne Aligoté, Bourgogne Passe-Tout-Grains (red and rosé).
These are the wines made by the future guardians of the reputation of Burgundy, because so many growers' sons and daughters study here. The standard is high and great care is taken. They sell direct by mail order in France, and a little is exported to Belgium and Switzerland, but some goes *en vrac* (in bulk) to the local *négoce*. They make excellent Beaune Premier Cru, such as Champimonts,

Perrières and Montée Rouge. The Lycée Agricole et Viticole was founded in 1884.

Domaine Machard de Gramont
6 rue Gassendi, 21700 Nuits-St-Georges. 20 ha. (2·7 ha *en métayage*). I^{ers} Crus: NUITS-ST-GEORGES: **Damodes,** HAUTS PRULIERS, **Vallerots;** POMMARD LE CLOS BLANC; **Savigny-lès-Beaune: Vergelesses, Guettes;** BEAUNE LES CHOUACHEUX. **Chambolle-Musigny, Nuits-St-Georges, Aloxe-Corton, Savigny-lès-Beaune, Beaune, Pommard, Puligny-Montrachet, Bourgogne Rouge and Blanc.**
A comparatively new domain, which has gone through all the vicissitudes of Burgundian family troubles. But what remains of the estate is hardly insignificant, and the wines are models of what Burgundy should be all about. The emphasis is on fruit rather than acquired weight, and consequently there is always lovely Pinot Noir bouquet, not overwhelmed by alcohol. Vattings are long, with ageing in oak barrels, 30–50 percent of which are new. There is good *appellation* character here. The cellars are in Prissey, and the wines are widely exported.

Domaine du Duc de Magenta
Abbaye de Morgeot, Chassagne-Montrachet, 21190 Meursault. 12 ha. 1er Cru: Puligny-Montrachet Clos de la Garenne. AUXEY-DURESSES, **Chassagne-Montrachet Clos de la Chapelle,** MEURSAULT MEIX CHAVAUX.
Sole owner of the former monastic vineyard of Clos de la Chapelle beside the old abbey of Morgeot. The red Morgeot can last well but there are patchy bottles from this domain. Maison Louis Jadot now supervises both the making and the marketing of the domain's wines, so there is much greater consistency and quality here now.

Domaine Pierre Mahuet
See W&V, Mâconnais, Mâcon.

Domaine Maillard Père & Fils
2 rue Joseph Bard, 21200 Chorey-lès-Beaune. 17 ha. Grand Cru: Corton-Renardes. I^{ers} Crus: Aloxe-Corton, Beaune-Grèves. Aloxe Corton, Beaune, Savigny-lès-Beaune,

Chorey-lès-Beaune, Ladoix Les Chaillots, Côte de Beaune-Villages, Meursault.

Chorey-lès-Beaune which has a delicious red-fruit flavour.

Domaine de la Maladière
See W&V, Chablis.

Domaine des Malandes
See W&V, Chablis.

Domaine Michel Mallard & Fils
21550 Serrigny. Grand Cru: Corton Les Maréchaudes. Premier Cru: Ladoix.

Good wines, especially those from Ladoix.

Château de la Maltroye
Chassagne-Montrachet, 21190 Meursault. 16 ha. Grand Cru: Bâtard-Montrachet. 1ᵉʳˢ Crus: Chassagne-Montrachet (red and white); Santenay (red and white). Chassagne-Montrachet (red and white), Bourgogne Rouge and Aligoté.

There were some disappointments in the '70s and '80s, but this domain, where Jean-Luc Parent now makes the wine, is becoming an excellent source once again, predominantly for white wine, although the reds are good too.

Domaine Manciat-Poncet
See W&V, Mâconnais, Mâcon.

Château Mandelot
See W&V, Côte d'Or, Hautes Côtes de Nuits/Beaune.

Domaine Manière-Noirot
Vosne-Romanée, 21700 Nuits-St-Georges.
See W&V, Côte d'Or, Vosne-Romanée.

Domaine Marceau
See W&V, Côte Chalonnaise, Mercurey.

Traditional cellar work

Domaine Marchand Grillot
13 rue du Gaizot, 21220 Gevrey-Chambertin. 8 ha. Grand Cru: Ruchottes-Chambertin. 1ers Crus: Gevrey-Chambertin: Petite Chapelle, Perrières. Gevrey-Chambertin, Chambolle-Musigny, Morey-St-Denis.
Well-made, supple, forward and fruity Burgundies; drinkable with very little bottle-age.

P de Marcilly Frères
21200 Beaune.
A *négociant*, with small holdings in Chassagne-Montrachet and Beaune. Its best wines are the modest *appellation* Bourgogne Marcilly Première and Marcilly Réserve, which are usually velvety and oaky.

Jean Maréchal
See W&V, Côte Chalonnaise, Mercurey.

Domaine des Maronniers
See W&V, Chablis.

Domaine Maroslavac-Leger
21190 Puligny-Montrachet. 6·3 ha (1·5 ha *en fermage*). 1ers Crus: St-Aubin; Puligny-Montrachet. Auxey-Duresses, Meursault, Puligny-Montrachet, Chassagne-Montrachet (red and white), Bourgogne Rouge, Blanc and Aligoté.
Quality very up and down. I recently tasted a dull, one-dimensional '88 Puligny-Montrachet, but also a light, very pretty, honeyed '90 Premier Cru Les Folatières.

Domaine Maroslavac-Tremeau
21190 Puligny-Montrachet.
A pair of quite awful '89 Puligny-Montrachets (*village* and Premier Cru Champs Gains) suggests this source may be best avoided – at least in association with the Compagnie des Vins d'Autrefois!

Domaine Tim Marshall
47 rue Henri Challand, 21701 Nuits-St-Georges. 1·9 ha. 1ers Crus: Chambolle-Musigny: Les Cras, Les Feusselottes; Nuits-St-Georges: Argillat, Perrières. Chambolle-Musigny Les Athets, Bourgogne Rouge and Aligoté, Bourgogne Grand Ordinaire.
Tiny domain, but wines with very good *appellation* character. Until 1989, the wines were aged in 100 percent new wood, but from 1990 onwards only 40–50 percent will be used. Nicely wrought, elegant and clear-cut medium-weight wines with especially distinctive flavours from the Nuits-St-Georges.

Domaine Maurice Martin
See W&V, Mâconnais, St-Véran.

Les Vins Mathelin
See W&V, Beaujolais.

Domaine Jean Mathias
See W&V, Mâconnais, Pouilly-Vinzelles.

Domaine Joseph & Pierre Matrot

21190 Meursault. 18 ha. 1ers Crus: Volnay-Santenots;
MEURSAULT: **Blagny, Charmes,** PERRIÈRES**; Blagny La Pièce
sous le Bois;** PULIGNY-MONTRACHET: LES CHALUMEAUX**, Les
Combettes. Auxey-Duresses, Meursault, Bourgogne Blanc
and Aligoté.**

A typically Burgundian fragmented domain, with the biggest
parcel in straight Meursault, although the red Blagny La Pièce sous
le Bois is also made in significant quantities, and is well worth
finding. The red grapes are destalked, the amount varying between
60 and 100 percent according to the year. Vatting lasts for six to ten
days in enamel-lined *cuves* for the reds and the wines are matured in
oak barrels (with no new wood). The reds are fined with albumen,
the whites with bentonite, and both are filtered before bottling.
Sales in bottle are to private customers and restaurants in France, the
USA, England, Belgium, Germany, Holland, Switzerland, etc.
The wines do not show great breed, but often have full flavour and
character.

Domaine Prosper Maufoux

21590 Santenay. *Négociants-éleveurs* only. **Domaine St-
Michel: 1er Cru: Santenay. Côte de Beaune-Villages,
Puligny-Montrachet, Santenay, Bourgogne Rouge and
Aligoté. Château de Viré (Mâcon)** *monopole.*

This is a family firm of *négociants-éleveurs* based in Santenay.
Although the head of the firm, Pierre Maufoux, jointly runs the
Domaine St-Michel with Michel Gutrin, he is also dedicated to
selecting and maturing fine wines from all over the Côte d'Or. A
firm believer in wood-ageing, he matures his white wines in oak
barrels for 12–15 months, and the reds for a minimum of 18
months. Sales of red and white wines are equally divided – both last
well, and some of the whites are gloriously rich. Maufoux wines are
found throughout the world, and also appear under the name of
Marcel Amance.

Domaine Maume

56 route de Beaune, 21220 Gevrey-Chambertin. 4 ha.
Grands Crus: Mazis-Chambertin, Charmes-Chambertin.
1ers Crus: Gevrey-Chambertin: Les Champeaux, Lavaux

St-Jacques. Gevrey-Chambertin.
Big wines, sometimes rather inky and tannic, but they should last
well, especially the top *crus* of Gevrey-Chambertin Lavaux St-
Jacques and Mazis-Chambertin.

Domaine Mazilly Père & Fils
**Meloisey, 21190 Meursault. 12 ha. Iᵉʳˢ Crus: Beaune: Les
Cent-Vignes, Les Montrevenots, Les Vignes-Franches;
Pommard Les Poutures. Pommard, Monthélie Le Clou
des Chênes, Volnay, Meursault. Bourgogne Hautes Côtes
de Beaune: red, white, Le Clos, Clos du Bois Prévot.
Bourgogne Passe-Tout-Grains.**
This is principally a Hautes Côtes de Beaune domain, with small
parcels in grander *appellations*. Vinification is long and the wines are
tannic when young. The *élevage* lasts 12–18 months, with the wines
stored in barrels or bigger oak *foudres*. There have been generations
of Mazillys owning vineyards and making wine here, only now
they export half of their production. Some of the Hautes Côtes
wines are *Tastevinés* and are very pleasant at two to three years of
age; but quality can be rather patchy.

Domaine du Meix-Foulot
See W&V, Côte Chalonnaise, Mercurey.

Domaine Méo-Camuzet
**21700 Vosne-Romanée. 11·5 ha. (some vineyards still
partially *en métayage*) Grands Crus: Clos de Vougeot;
Corton; RICHEBOURG. Iᵉʳˢ Crus: VOSNE-ROMANÉE: CROS
PARENTOUX, Boudots, LES BRULÉES, Chaumes; Nuits-St-
Georges Murgers. Vosne-Romanée, Nuits-St-Georges.**
A domain with excellent vineyards and a reputation as one of
Burgundy's top sources. It is now managed by young Jean-Nicolas
Méo who carries out the vinification under the direction of Henri
Jayer, making impressive wines of similar depth of flavour and
impact of fruit, if without quite the breed of Jayer's own. Méo
attaches great importance to low yields, which accounts for the
concentration of his wines. He also uses, as Jayer did, 100 percent
new oak; and if the wines can be criticised at all it is because the new
wood sometimes seems to overwhelm the fruit. When tackled

about this, Méo simply says: 'On aime bien ça!', and there is clearly no shortage of people who would echo that.

Domaine Prince Florent de Mérode
Serrigny, 21550 Ladoix-Serrigny. 11·38 ha. Grands Crus: Corton-Bressandes, Corton Clos du Roi, Corton-Maréchaudes, Corton-Renardes. 1ᵉʳˢ Crus: Ladoix Hautes Mourottes, Aloxe-Corton. Ladoix Les Chaillots, Pommard Clos de la Platière.

There are certainly some 'prime sites' in this domain. It was a *maison forte* in the time of the Ducs de Bourgogne; the Château de Serrigny was rebuilt in 1700 by Pierre Brunet, president of the Chambre des Comptes in Paris. Since then it has always been inherited, never sold. The grapes are sorted on arrival, eliminating anything that does not come up to standard, and partially destalked. The domain itself considers that the wines should not be drunk before four to five years. In France and Belgium the wines are sold only through the Savour Club, a powerful force in mail-order sales. They are also exported to the principal markets. Maybe the wines could be more impressive. Achieving consistency is often a Burgundian problem, but is more serious when associated with a great domain.

Mestre Père & Fils
Place du Jet d'Eau, 21590 Santenay. 18 ha. Grand Cru: Corton. 1ᵉʳˢ Crus: Ladoix Clou d'Orge; Chassagne-Montrachet: Morgeot, Tonton Marcel *monopole*; Santenay: Beaurepaire, Clos Faubard, Comme, Gravières, Gravières Clos Tavannes, Passe-Temps (red and white). Ladoix Côte de Beaune, Aloxe-Corton, Chassagne-Montrachet, Maranges, Santenay.

An important Santenay domain, built up by the fifth generation of a family of vignerons. It is particularly strong on Premiers Crus. Vinification lasts eight to ten days with quite high temperatures and *remontages* twice a day. Ageing lasts 12–24 months in oak barrels, some of which are new. They particularly stress the fact that they bottle in strictly controlled, clean conditions, an imperative with all wines, but the Burgundian grape varieties are noticeably vulnerable to sloppy handling. Half of the crop is sold in bulk to local *négociants*, and half is now sold in bottle, divided between sales to the home market and export sales. In the past, some of the wines have appeared rather dry and tired at an early stage, with a marked lack of colour.

Domaine du Château de Meursault

21190 Meursault. 36 ha. 1ᵉʳˢ Crus: Savigny-lès-Beaune Peuillets; Beaune: Grèves, Cent-Vignes, Toussaint; Pommard: Clos des Epenots, Pommard; Volnay Clos des Chênes; MEURSAULT: **Charmes, Perrières,** CHÂTEAU DE MEURSAULT; **Puligny-Montrachet Champ Canet. Aloxe-Corton, Savigny-lès-Beaune (red and white), Beaune, Pommard, Meursault, Bourgogne Clos du Château, Bourgogne Rouge.**

This great domain is now owned by Patriarche, the very large Beaune *négociants*. But the estate side of things seems to me to be on a different level from the *négoce* business and the standard is impressive. They combine the modern (stainless steel, the latest presses) with the traditional (maturing in new oak casks). The white grapes are pressed and then fermented in new barrels (hence the stylish sheen to them) and the red grapes are crushed, partially destalked, fermented for eight to twelve days and then aged in new oak barrels. The domain sells direct, including to all those who visit the beautiful *caves*, or cellars, to restaurants and on the export market. Wherever one is, in far-flung countries or even on an airline (First Class!), a bottle of Château de Meursault is always rewarding to drink. In 1975, a park of eight hectares was replanted to vines, as it was two centuries ago, and now a Chardonnay white wine is produced: Clos du Château, AC Bourgogne. At this domain it is the white wines which stand out.

Domaine Gérard-Roger Méziat

See W&V, Beaujolais, Chiroubles.

Domaine Bernard Michel

See W&V, Côte Chalonnaise, Montagny.

Domaine Louis Michel/Domaine de la Tour Vaubourg

See W&V, Chablis.

Domaine René Michel
See W&V, Mâconnais, Mâcon.

Domaine Alain Michelot
**6 rue Camille Rodier, 21700 Nuits-St-Georges. 4·2 ha (3·5
en *métayage*). Iᵉʳˢ Crus:** NUITS-ST-GEORGES: **Les Cailles,** AUX
CHAIGNOTS, **Aux Champs Perdrix, Les Porets St-Georges,
La Richemone, Les St-Georges, Les Vaucrains; Morey St-
Denis Les Charrières. Morey-St-Denis, Nuits-St-Georges,
Bourgogne Rouge.**
M Michelot used to over-oak his wines, but this is no longer the
case. Quality leaped forward in the 1980s – his '88s will keep
beautifully. Real Nuits character shows throughout the spectrum.
Elevage lasts 20 months in barrel. The *villages* receive 40 percent new
oak, the Premiers Crus 50 percent.

Domaine Jean Michelot
Route d'Ivry, 21630 Pommard. Pommard, Meursault.
Correct wines which do not disappoint.

Domaine Michelot-Buisson
21190 Meursault. 20 ha (2 ha *en métayage*). Iᵉʳˢ Crus:
MEURSAULT: CHARMES, GENEVRIÈRES, PERRIÈRES. **Puligny-
Montrachet, Bourgogne Rouge, Blanc and Aligoté.**
Barrel-fermented white wines aged for 12 months in up to one-
third new oak. Excellent wines, some of my best Meursault
memories. The '83s were tasting beautifully at nine years of age.

Domaine François Mikulski
**5 rue de Leignon, 21190 Meursault. 0·35 ha. (5 ha *en
métayage*). Iᵉʳˢ Crus: Volnay Santenots; Meursault:
Caillerets, Charmes, Genevrières, Poruzots. Meursault
(red and white), Bourgogne Rouge, Blanc and Aligoté.**
François Mikulski is Pierre Boillot's nephew. He founded this new
domain in 1992 with a small inheritance of vines. If Domaine
Mikulski does not yet have a track record, it would appear that
François himself does, as he has been helping to make the wine at his
uncle's property since 1985. They will continue to work together
for some time to come.

Domaine Pierre Millot-Battault
7 rue Charles Giraud, 21190 Meursault.
Good wines, Meursault-Charmes especially.

GAEC René & Christian Miolane
See W&V, Beaujolais, Beaujolais-Villages.

Château de Mirande
See W&V, Mâconnais, Mâcon.

Maison P Misserey
3 rue des Seuillets, 21702 Nuits-St-Georges. 2·34 ha. Grand Cru: Corton Les Maréchaudes. 1ers Crus: Gevrey-Chambertin Lavaux St-Jacques; Nuits-St-Georges: Les Cailles, Clos des Corvées, Les Meurgers, Les St-Georges, Les Vaucrains, Les Vignerondes. Chambolle-Musigny, Vosne-Romanée, Pommard, Volnay, Côte de Nuits-Villages, Côte de Beaune-Villages.
'Big' but unexciting wines. Keepers, but don't hold your breath!

Domaine Moillard-Grivot
2 rue F Mignotte, 21700 Nuits-St-Georges. 44·47 ha. Grands Crus: Chambertin, Chambertin Clos de Bèze; Bonnes Mares; Clos de Vougeot; Romanée St-Vivant; Corton-Charlemagne, Corton Clos du Roi. **1ers Crus:** Vosne-Romanée: **Les Beaux Monts,** Les Malconsorts; Nuits-St-Georges: **Clos des Grandes Vignes,** Clos de Thorey, **Les Murgers, Les Porets St-Georges, Les Richemones;** Beaune Les Grèves. **Nuits-St-Georges: Les Charmottes, Les St-Julien. Bourgogne Hautes Côtes de Nuits.**
This is a large *négociant* firm as well as an important domain. The names of Moillard and Moillard-Grivot are interchangeable, although there is now a tendency to label the top domain wines Moillard-Grivot. Today's Thomas family is the fifth generation in charge. Fermentations are carried out partly in enamel-lined steel *cuves* and partly in stainless steel rotating *cuves* with automatic *pigeage*; they last five to eleven days, according to the type of *cuve*. The wines are subsequently stocked in a warm cellar to facilitate the

malolactic fermentation. Flash-pasteurization has been practised since the early part of this century, although there are now experiments with non-pasteurized wines. There is a large business in buying grapes and vinifying. I have not been very impressed by the *négoce* wines, but there seems to be distinct improvement in the domain wines (Thomas-Moillard), some of which combine structure with fat in quite a majestic way. Moillard wines are exported to 43 countries, in addition to sales in France.

Domaine André Moingeon
Gamay, 21190 St-Aubin.
See W&V, Côte d'Or, St-Aubin.

Mommessin/Clos de Tart
21220 Morey-St-Denis. 7·5 ha. Grand Cru: CLOS DE TART
Mommessin is first and foremost an important *négociant* firm dealing in wines from the Mâconnais and Beaujolais, as well as *vins de marque*. But the proverbial jewel in the crown is the Morey-St-Denis Grand Cru Clos de Tart, which it has owned since 1932. Founded in the 12th century by the Benedictines de Tart le Haut, this is the only *clos* in Burgundy which has never been divided since its foundation. Fermentations are carried out by the *chapeau immergé* system, where the skins are permanently in contact with the must – this is a rarity in Burgundy and results in big wines. Clos de Tart can age magnificently, with heady tastes and aromas. In the Beaujolais and the Mâconnais, Mommessin either owns or distributes a number of domains, such as the Domaine Bellenand in Pouilly-Fuissé and the Domaine de Champ de Cour in Moulin-à-Vent. Sometimes I find that a lighter touch here would be more attractive, as the fruit can be smothered by alcohol.

Domaine de la Monette
See W&V, Côte Chalonnaise, Mercurey.

Domaine Mongeard-Mugneret
21700 Vosne-Romanée. 20 ha (partly *en fermage*). Grands Crus: CLOS VOUGEOT; ECHÉZEAUX, GRANDS ECHÉZEAUX, **Richebourg. 1ᵉʳˢ Crus: Vougeot;** VOSNE-ROMANÉE: **Les Orveaux, Les Petits Monts,** LES SUCHOTS; **Nuits-St-Georges**

**Les Boudots; Savigny-lès-Beaune Les Narbentons. Fixin,
Vosne-Romanée, Nuits-St-Georges, Savigny-lès-Beaune,
Bourgogne Hautes Côtes de Nuits, Bourgogne Rouge and
Blanc, Bourgogne Passe-Tout-Grains.**
This domain is making better and better wines. There are some old
vines and chemical fertiliser is not used. Maceration is carried out
before fermentation, which lasts 13–15 days. Now, only natural
yeasts are used and fermentation temperatures can go high;
extensive *pigeage* always accompanies this stage. Half of the barrels
are new each year. The wines are incredible mouthfuls, if not the
ultimate in breed. The Grands Crus are immensely spicy and
concentrated, while Les Suchots often displays cherry notes.

Domaine Elie Mongénie
See W&V, Beaujolais, St-Amour.

Domaine de Mongrin
See W&V, Beaujolais, St-Amour.

Domaine Monnet
See W&V, Beaujolais, Juliénas.

Domaine Jean Monnier & Fils
**21190 Meursault. 17 ha. 1ers Crus: Beaune; Pommard,
Pommard Epenots Clos de Citeaux;** MEURSAULT: **Charmes,**
GENEVRIÈRES. **Meursault (red and white), Puligny-
Montrachet, Bourgogne Rouge, Blanc and Aligoté.**
An impeccably-run domain, which has been gradually increasing
in size through the acquisition of small parcels. In 1950, Jean
Monnier bought the Clos de Citeaux in Pommard Epenots – the
three hectares which once belonged to the monks of Citeaux.
Tradition is followed in the vinification, and all the wines, even the
petites appellations, are aged in oak barrels, with a certain proportion
of new *fûts*. The result is wines which have immense finesse and
style – it is always a treat to come upon a bottle from this estate.
They are sold in some of the best restaurants in France – 25 percent
of the production is sold in this way, 30 percent goes to the export
markets, and 45 percent to discerning private customers, who
obviously know a good thing when they find one.

Domaine René Monnier

**6 rue du Docteur Rolland. 21190 Meursault. 16 ha. 1ers
Crus: Beaune: Cent-Vignes, Toussaints; Volnay Clos des
Chênes; Meursault Charmes; Puligny-Montrachet Les
Folatières; Maranges Clos de la Fussière** *monopole.*
**Pommard Les Vignots, Meursault Les Chevalières,
Meursault Le Limozin, Puligny-Montrachet, Santenay Les
Charmes, Bourgogne Rouge, Blanc and Aligoté.**
This domain has been wisely built up through the acquisitions of
each generation of Monniers. White wines are vinified and aged in
barrels of three origins: Allier, Vosges and Nevers, with one-third
new barrels for each *cuvée.* The wines are bottled around June. The
reds undergo 12–14 days of fermentation, after about two-thirds of
the stalks are removed, varying with the year. Pigeage takes place
twice a day, after the must has started to ferment, with *remontages*
which cause the yeasts to multiply through the process of
oxygenation. The wines are then stocked in Limousin oak barrels
until the end of the malolactic fermentation. Exports are to 16
countries – the UK, USA and Switzerland are the most important
recipients – and the wines are also to be found in a number of starred
restaurants.

Domaine Jean-Pierre Monnot

Place des Marronniers, 21190 Puligny-Montracht.
See W&V, Côte d'Or, Puligny-Montrachet.

Domaine Monrozier

See W&V, Beaujolais, Fleurie.

Domaine Monternot

See W&V, Beaujolais, Beaujolais-Villages.

Domaine de Montgenas

See W&V, Beaujolais, Fleurie.

Château de Monthélie

Monthélie 21190. 10 ha. 1ers Crus: CHÂTEAU DE MONTHÉLIE-
MONTHÉLIE SUR LA VELLE**; Rully Meix Caillet. Rully Agneux.**
The red wines here are aged for 18 months in 25–30 percent new

oak, the white sees much less new wood and for a year only. The red
Château de Monthélie needs, and repays, keeping.

Domaine Monthélie–Douhairet
**21190 Monthélie. I^{ers} Crus: Pommard Fremiets; Volnay
Champans; Meursault Santenots (white); Monthélie Les
Duresses. Monthélie, Bourgogne Aligoté.**
A new cellar manager and the advice of André Porcheret mean that
these wines are both cleaner and less rustic than they used to be. The
Meursault Santenots is a light but honeyed wine and the '88
Champans is perfumed and gently oaky. The domain's Aligoté
can be good too.

Domaine de Montille
Volnay, 21190 Meursault. 7 ha. I^{ers} Crus: POMMARD: **Grands
Epenots,** PÉZEROLLES, RUGIENS; VOLNAY: CHAMPANS, MITANS,
TAILLEPIEDS. **Bourgogne Rouge.**
Tight, concentrated, tannic wines which need years to mellow but
which are worth the wait. Hubert de Montille makes the wines by
long *cuvaisons*, temperatures over 30°C, and ageing for 18 months
to two years in 25 percent new wood. *Vins de garde* are his aim.

Domaine de Montmain
21700 Villars-Fontaine.
See W&V, Côte d'Or, Hautes Côtes de Nuits, Bernard Hudelot.

Domaine de Montmeron
See W&V, Beaujolais, Beaujolais-Villages.

J Moreau & Fils
See W&V, Chablis.

Domaine Bernard Morey
Chassagne-Montrachet, 21190 Meursault. 8·7 ha. I^{ers} Crus:
BEAUNE LES GRÈVES; **St-Aubin Charmois;** CHASSAGNE-
MONTRACHET: LES CAILLERETS, LES EMBRAZÉES, **Morgeot,** LES
BAUDINES; SANTENAY GRAND-CLOS-ROUSSEAU. CHASSAGNE-
MONTRACHET (RED **and white), Bourgogne Rouge and
Blanc.**

Excellent wines; the whites above all, but the reds are good too. Both are aged in 25 percent new wood, the reds for 18 months, the whites for 12 months.

Domaine Jean-Marc Morey

21190 Chassagne-Montrachet. 6 ha (2 ha *en métayage*). 1ers Crus: Beaune Grèves; Chassagne-Montrachet: Caillerets, Clos St-Jean (red), Champs Gains (red and white), Les Chaumées, Chenevottes; St-Aubin Charmois; Santenay: Grand Clos Rousseau, Les Cornières. Chassagne-Montrachet (red), Bourgogne Rouge, Blanc and Aligoté.

Bernard Morey's brother Jean-Marc makes soft, full and perfumed white Burgundies which spend one year in 20 percent new wood.

Domaine Marc Morey

21190 Chassagne-Montrachet. 8.75 ha. Grand Cru: Bâtard-Montrachet. 1ers Crus: Puligny-Montrachet Les Pucelles; Chassagne-Montrachet: Chenevottes, Morgeot (red and white), Verindot; St-Aubin Charmois. Beaune, Chassagne-Montrachet (red and white), Bourgogne Rouge, Blanc and Aligoté.

Marc Morey is a cousin of Jean-Marc. Excellent Bâtard-Montrachet, and good quality whites, without quite the polish of Bernard's or Jean-Marc's wines. The whites spend one year, and the reds 15–18 months, in 25–30 percent new oak.

Domaine Pierre Morey

9 rue Comte Lafon, 21190 Meursault. 3 ha (5 ha *en métayage*). Grand Cru: BÂTARD-MONTRACHET. 1ers Crus: Meursault; Pommard Grands Epenots; Monthélie, Meursault (red and white), Bourgogne Rouge, Blanc and Aligoté, Bourgogne Passe-Tout-Grains.

Pierre Morey's holdings have diminished considerably as a result of various *métayage* arrangements coming to an end – with Domaine Comtes Lafon amongst others. This was the principal reason for his starting to work for Domaine Leflaive in 1989. His wines still combine fruit and oak in a lovely mouthful.

Domaine Albert Morot

Château de la Creusotte, 21200 Beaune. 7 ha. 1ᵉʳˢ Crus:
Beaune: Bressandes, Cent-Vignes, Grèves, Marconnets,
Teurons, Toussaints. Savigny-Vergelesses La Bataillère
*monopole***.**

The house of Albert Morot is both *négociant* and domain owner, as
is often the case in Beaune, only this *négociant* business is on a very
small scale. There is no departure from the vinification in oak vats/
élevage in oak barrels formula and the resulting wines really are very
good. The cellars, on two levels, are beside the vineyard. Although
it does export, there is a strong clientele of private customers.

Alphonse Mortet/Les Fargets

See W&V, Beaujolais, Moulin-à-Vent.

Domaine Denis Mortet

22 rue de l'Eglise, 21220 Gevrey-Chambertin. 4·6 ha.
Grands Crus: Chambertin; Clos Vougeot. 1ᵉʳˢ Crus:
Gevrey-Chambertin: Les Champeaux; Chambolle-
Musigny Les Beaux Bruns. Gevrey-Chambertin, Gevrey-
Chambertin Clos Prieur; Bourgogne Rouge, Blanc and
Aligoté, Bourgogne Passe-Tout-grains.

From 1992, this domain will be divided between the sons Denis and
Thierry Mortet. Not a lot of tasting experience, but in general the
wines have plenty of colour and extract. The Premier Cru Les
Champeaux does well in blind tastings. The Chambolle-Musigny
Premier Cru Les Beaux Bruns is sturdy for the *appellation*, and the
straight '90 Gevrey-Chambertin Clos Prieur is elegant, perfumed
and persistent. Delightful quality.

Clos du Moulin-à-Vent

See W&V, Beaujolais, Moulin-à-Vent.

Château du Moulin-à-Vent/Domaine des Héritiers
Tagent

See W&V, Beaujolais, Moulin-à-Vent.

Moulin-à-Vent des Hospices

See W&V, Beaujolais, Moulin-à-Vent.

Domaine Gérard Mouton
See W&V, Côte Chalonnaise, Givry.

Société Civile de la Moutonne
See W&V, Chablis.

Domaine Mugneret-Gibourg/Domaine Georges Mugneret
Vosne-Romanée, 21700 Nuits-St-Georges. 1·24 ha (1·73 ha
en métayage). **Grands Crus: Ruchottes-Chambertin; Clos-Vougeot;** ECHÉZEAUX. **1ers Crus:** CHAMBOLLE-MUSIGNY LES FEUSSELOTTES; **Nuits-St-Georges: Les Chaignots, Les Vignes Rondes. Vosne-Romanée.**
There are six families called Mugneret at Vosne-Romanée, all wine-producers, so this becomes complicated. The names of Mugneret-Gibourg and Georges Mugneret are both associated with the same domain. Since Dr Georges Mugneret's death in 1988 the wine has been made by his eldest daughter, Marie Christine (a qualified oenologist) who had been helping her father for some time already. Methods owe nothing to modernization – open *cuves*, vattings of about 15 days, first racking after the malolactic fermentation, then two others before bottling at 18 months to two years – *élevage* is in oak barrels, one-third new. Fining is with egg whites (six for a barrel of 228 litres). The wines are very well made, stylish and perfumed, with good keeping potential.

Domaine André Mussy
21630 Pommard. 6 ha. 1ers Crus: Beaune: Epenottes, Montremenots; Pommard: Epenots, Pézerolles, Saucilles. Pommard, Volnay, Bourgogne Rouge.
Reputation seems higher than my experience of the wine bears out. Some tastes of old casks.

Philippe Naddef
21160 Couchey. 4·5 ha. Grand Cru: Mazis-Chambertin. 1ers Crus: Gevrey-Chambertin: Cazetiers, Champeaux. Gevrey-Chambertin, Marsannay (red and white).
Good quality, fairly rich, oaky wines. Being wary of 'snap' judgements, I shall watch evolution in bottle with great interest.

Domaine Naudin
Magny-lès-Villers, 21700 Nuits-St-Georges.
See W&V, Côte d'Or, Hautes Côtes de Nuits/Beaune.

Michel Niellon
21190 Chassagne-Montrachet. 4 ha. Grands Crus: Bâtard-Montrachet, Chevalier-Montrachet. **1ᵉʳˢ Crus: Chassagne-Montrachet: Clos St-Jean, Clos de la Maltroie, Les Vergers.** Chassagne-Montrachet.
Taut, elegant, concentrated wines, aged in 25 percent new wood.

Domaine Ninot-Cellier-Meix-Guillaume
See W&V, Côte Chalonnaise, Rully.

Domaine Gilles Noblet
See W&V, Mâconnais, Pouilly-Fuissé.

Domaine Charles Noëllat
This domain was bought by Domaine Leroy (qv) in 1988.

Domaine Jean-Paul Paquet
See W&V, Mâconnais, Pouilly-Fuissé.

Domaine Michel Paquet
See W&V, Mâconnais, St-Véran.

Domaine du Paradis
See W&V, Beaujolais, St-Amour.

Domaine Parent
21630 Pommard. 12 ha (4 ha *en métayage*). Grand Cru: Corton-Renardes. **1ᵉʳˢ Crus: Ladoix La Corvée;** Beaune: **Les Boucherottes,** Les Epenottes; Pommard: **Les Arvelets, Les Chanlins, Les Chaponnières,** Le Clos Micault *monopole*, Les Epenots, **Les Fremiers, Les Pézerolles, Les Rugiens; Monthélie Le Clos Gauthney** *monopole*. **Volnay: Le Clos des Chênes, Les Fremiets. Bourgogne Rouge.**
There are no departures from traditional methods here, as befits a former supplier of Thomas Jefferson. The wines are usually perfect

examples of their *appellation* and an exercise in the charms of the Pinot Noir. Just occasionally, when the year has given high yields, there is a lack of definition (especially vexing at high prices), but their Premiers Crus Pommard Les Epenots and Le Clos Micault always give great pleasure.

Parigot Père & Fils
21190 Meloisey. 1ᵉʳˢ Crus: Beaune-Grèves; Pommard; Savigny. Savigny-lès-Beaune, Beaune, Pommard, Volnay, Meursault, Bourgogne Hautes Côtes de Beaune, Bourgogne Rouge, Blanc and Aligoté, Bourgogne Passe-Tout-Grains.
There are some good buys at this domain.

Domaine Jean Pascal & Fils
Puligny-Montrachet, 21190 Meursault. 6 ha (9 ha *en métayage*).
Bland and disappointing wines.

Pasquier-Desvignes
See W&V, Beaujolais.

Domaine Georges Passot
See W&V, Beaujolais, Chiroubles.

Domaine Guy Patissier
See W&V, Beaujolais, St-Amour.

Domaine Jean Patissier
See W&V, Beaujolais, St-Amour.

Patriarche Père & Fils
Couvent des Visitandines, 21200 Beaune. 40·46 ha. 1ᵉʳˢ Crus: Château de Meursault; Beaune.
A huge concern, fuelled by the sales of a non-*appellation* sparkling wine. But they are also the owners of the magnificent estate of the Château de Meursault (qv), where quality is high. The *négociant* wines are dull.

Baron Patrick
See W&V, Chablis.

Domaine Jean-Marc Pavelot
21420 Savigny-lès-Beaune. 4·43 ha (10·7 ha worked), half in the 1ᵉʳ Cru vineyards of the slopes. 1ᵉʳˢ Crus: Pernand-Vergelesses Les Vergelesses; Savigny-lès-Beaune: **La Dominode, Narbantons, Aux Gravains,** Aux Guettes, **Peuillets.** Savigny-lès-Beaune **(red and white).**
Growers in Savigny since 1640. The red wines are very good with a lovely 'red cherry' fruit character to them.

Domaine André Pelletier
See W&V, Beaujolais, Juliénas.

Domaine Pernin-Rossin
21700 Vosne-Romanée. 1ᵉʳˢ Crus: Chambolle-Musigny; Morey-St-Denis Les Monts Luisants; Nuits-St-Georges Les Richemones; Vosne-Romanée: Les Beaumonts, Champs-Perdrix. Morey-St-Denis, Vosne-Romanée.
Guy Accad is the consultant oenologist here. A domain that needs to prove its worth over the distance, to use racing parlance.

Domaine Paul Pernot
Place du Monument, 21190 Puligny-Montrachet. 1ᵉʳ Cru: Puligny-Montrachet Les Folatières.
A wide range of white wines from the Côte de Beaune, Puligny-Montrachet especially. Rich, smoothly-textured, elegant wines, beautifully crafted.

Maurice & Gilles Perroud
See W&V, Beaujolais, Régnié, Château du Basty.

Domaine du Petit Pressoir
See W&V, Beaujolais, Côte de Brouilly.

André Philippon
See W&V, Chablis.

Piat
71570 La Chapelle-de-Guinchay.
A large, quality firm.

Domaine des Pillets
See W&V, Beaujolais, Morgon.

Domaine Fernand Pillot
Les Champs Gains, 21190 Chassagne-Montrachet.
Honorable, straight, white Chassagne-Montrachet and quality is improving here.

Domaine Paul Pillot
21190 Chassagne-Montrachet. Chassagne-Montrachet Morgeot.
Lovely, lush, white wines.

Domaine Pinson
See W&V, Chablis.

Domaine Pitoiset–Urena
1 rue Velle, 21190 Meursault.
A very small estate making classy, concentrated Meursaults.

Château de Pizay
See W&V, Beaujolais, Morgon.

Domaine du Point du Jour
See W&V, Beaujolais, Fleurie.

Château de Pommard
21630 Pommard. 20 ha.
The largest domain in one single parcel in the Côte d'Or, producing 60,000 bottles per annum; the best barrels are kept back after tasting and sold under the exclusive label of the Château de Pommard. An impressive property, with the Château in the middle of the vineyard, which is entirely surrounded by walls. Traditional vinification, with two years' ageing in 50 percent new oak casks before bottling. Big, tannic and beefy wines, much beloved by the

general public (mostly French, Swiss, German and Belgian), who buy direct. M Laplanche says a good winemaker should be able to make good wine in any year. Beautiful bottle and label.

Maison Pierre Ponnelle
See Jean-Claude Boisset.

Domaine Ponsot
Morey-St-Denis, 21220 Gevrey-Chambertin. 7 ha (3 ha *en métayage*). Grands Crus: CHAMBERTIN, **Chapelle-Chambertin;** GRIOTTE-CHAMBERTIN; LATRICIÈRES-CHAMBERTIN; CLOS DE LA ROCHE, **Clos St-Denis. Iᵉʳˢ Crus: Morey-St-Denis Monts-Luisants, Chambolle-Musigny Les Charmes. Gevrey-Chambertin, Morey-St-Denis.**

Spicy wines of great breadth and richness in fine vintages, though they can be surprisingly weak in lesser ones (overcropping?). Grapes harvested very ripe, long *cuvaisons*, high fermentation temperatures, frequent *pigeages*, mainly old wood for ageing and no filtration make these splendid wines. Ponsot also makes a white Morey-St-Denis – Monts-Luisants – from Chardonnay, Pinot Blanc and Aligoté. This is a curiously 'flat' wine; I have never seen a memorable bottle, and wonder why they make it.

Château Portier/Michel Gaidon
See W&V, Beaujolais, Moulin-à-Vent.

Domaine Pothier-Rieusset
Route d'Ivry, 21630 Pommard. 7·5 ha. Iᵉʳˢ Crus: Beaune-Boucherottes; POMMARD: **Charmots,** EPENOTS, RUGIENS, CLOS DE VERGER, **Pommard. Pomard, Volnay, Meursault, Bourgogne Rouge and Blanc.**

Usually very good Pommards; *vins de garde* which need years to show their best.

Domaine de la Poulette
Grande Rue à Corgoloin, 21700 Nuits-St-Georges, 15 ha (2 ha *en métayage*). Iᵉʳˢ Crus: Vosne-Romanée Les Suchots; Nuits-St-Georges: Les Brûlées, Chaboeufs, Les St-Georges, Les Poulettes, Les Vallerots, Les Vaucrains. Côte

de Nuits–Villages (red and white), Bourgogne Rouge,
Rosé and Aligoté, Bourgogne Passe–Tout–Grains.
A domain where all the traditions are followed, including treading
(after the treaders have showered, says M Lucien Audidier!). But
modern innovations of improved presses and temperature control
are also in evidence, as befits the cellars of a distinguished Ingénieur
Agronome. There is a strong following for these wines in France,
but Switzerland is also an important market. The domain dates
back to the 18th century and has been in the family since that time.

Château des Poupets
See W&V, Beaujolais, Juliénas.

Domaine de la Pousse d'Or
**Volnay, 21190 Meursault. 13 ha (0·4 ha *en métayage*). 1ᵉʳˢ
Crus: Pommard Les Jarollières;** VOLNAY: CAILLERETS CLOS
DES 60 OUVRÉES *monopole*, CLOS DE LA BOUSSE D'OR *monopole*,
Clos d'Audignac *monopole*, **En Caillerets;** SANTENAY LES
GRAVIÈRES, CLOS DE TAVANNES.
Gérard Potel, an Ingénieur Agronome and oenologist, runs this
domain with admirable precision; the principal proprietor, M Jean
Ferté, is a noted connoisseur of fine wine and food. There is little
destalking, vinification in open vats, with *pigeage* every day and a
vatting of 10–15 days. *Elevage* takes place in oak barrels with about
20–30 percent new wood. 70 percent of the production is exported
around the world, with the 30 percent sales to the French market
being divided between private customers and top restaurants. The
wines combine fruit and *appellation* character together with a long,
emphatic aftertaste. The top *crus* last beautifully in bottle.

Domaine Jacques Prieur
**21190 Meursault. 14 ha. Grands Crus: Chambertin,
Chambertin Clos de Bèze; Le Musigny; Clos Vougeot;
Chevalier–Montrachet, Montrachet. 1ᵉʳˢ Crus: Beaune Clos
de la Feguine; Volnay: Champans, Clos des Santenots;
Santenots; Meursault–Perrières; Puligny–Montrachet Les
Combettes. Meursault Clos de Mazeray (red and white),
Bourgogne Rouge and Blanc.**
This is a famous domain, with excellent vineyards on both the Côte

de Nuits and the Côte de Beaune. In order to avoid the break up of the domain on his death, Jacques Prieur formed it into a Private Company in the early 1960s and the Prieur family now owns 50 percent of the shares. In 1988, the Mercurey firm Antonin Rodet purchased ten percent of the shares as well as the right to distribute 50 percent of the domain's production, and that year also saw another signal change when Martin Prieur (Jacques' grandson) took over the management of the property. Martin is a qualified oenologist; young, energetic and dedicated to putting this domain right back amongst the top Burgundy properties. Just where it ought to be, given its enviable array of vineyards. After a number of years, during which the wines have been noticeably below par, the Prieur/Rodet combination looks like achieving this renaissance. 1990 was the first vintage where the changes really began to show, with the Meursault-Perrières, Volnay Clos des Santenots and Le Musigny, to note three of the best, tasting wonderful in cask.

Domaine Prieur-Brunet

21590 Santenay. 20 ha. Grand Cru: Bâtard-Montrachet. Iers Crus: SANTENAY: Comme, MALADIÈRE; Pommard Les Platières; Volnay-Santenots; Meursault-Charmes; Chassagne-Montrachet: Les Embazées, Morgeot (red). Santenay Clos Rousseau, Santenay (red and white); Beaune Clos du Roi; Meursault (red and white). Bourgogne Rouge and Blanc.

Distinctive and reliable wines, with good *appellation* character. Both the reds and the whites are aged in ten percent new wood, with the Chardonnay wines being fermented in barrel as well.

Domaine du Prieuré

See W&V, Mâconnais, Mâcon.

Domaine du Prieuré (Armand Monassier)

See W&V, Côte Chalonnaise: Rully, Mercurey.

Domaine Maurice Protheau & Fils/Domaine François Protheau & Fils

See W&V, Côte Chalonnaise, Mercurey.

Domaine Henri Prudhon & Fils
Place l'Eglise, 21190 St-Aubin.
These wines are also sold under the label Gérard Prudhon, Henri's son. Well-made, stylish red and white Sᴛ-Aᴜʙɪɴ: intensely strawberryish reds, and delicious whites, marked by vanillin and clean oak and with a honeyed finish.

Domaine Michel Prunier
Auxey-Duresses, 21190 Meursault. 5·4 ha (8·5 ha *en métayage*). Iᵉʳˢ Crus: Beaune Les Sizies; Volnay Caillerets; Aᴜxᴇʏ-Dᴜʀᴇssᴇs Cʟos ᴅᴜ Vᴀʟ, **Auxey-Duresses. Meursault,** Aᴜxᴇʏ-Dᴜʀᴇssᴇs **(red and white). Bourgogne Hautes Côtes de Beaune (red), Bourgogne Aligoté.**
A lovely range of wines: supple, textured, fruity and harmonious reds, and stylish whites. 30 percent new wood for 18 months is the norm for the Premier Cru wines, 20 percent for one year for the *village* and regional wines.

Domaine des Quatre Vents
See W&V, Beaujolais, Fleurie.

Domaine Charles Quillardet
18 route de Dijon, 21220 Gevrey-Chambertin. Grand Cru: Chambertin. Iᵉʳ Cru: Gevrey-Chambertin Les Champeaux. Rosé de Marsannay, Fixin, Gevrey-Chambertin, Côte de Nuits-Villages, Bourgogne Les Grandes Vignes, Bourgogne Rouge Montre Cul.
This is something of a puzzling domain. Occasionally there are good wines with liquorice and cassis overtones, but at other times real disappointments, with clumsy, coarse wines which lack Pinot Noir frankness. M Quillardet says he vinifies *à l'ancienne*, with partial destalking according to the vintage. Half of the production is exported, half is sold direct, which must be easy, as the domain is right on the Route Nationale. There is also a Bourgogne Rouge, called Montre Cul, produced at Larrey in the suburbs of Dijon. The label is in execrable taste, but apparently it is a traditional name for the site – the slope is so steep that the *vendangeuses* showed more than they perhaps should have. It would be better if they wore jeans for picking, I would think.

Quinson
See W&V, Beaujolais, Fleurie.

Domaine Ragot
See W&V, Côte Chalonnaise, Givry.

Domaine André Ramonet
Chassagne-Montrachet, 21190 Meursault. 17·6 ha, half white, including: Grands Crus: LE MONTRACHET**, Bâtard-Montrachet, Bienvenues-Bâtard-Montrachet. 1ᵉʳ Cru:** CHASSAGNE-MONTRACHET: LES CAILLERETS, LES RUCHOTTES. **Chassagne-Montrachet. Half red, including: 1ᵉʳˢ Crus: Clos de la Boudriotte, Clos St-Jean. Chassagne-Montrachet.**
André and sons Noël and Jean-Claude have a cult following. I have done complete tastings, thanks to Bipin Desai, and the wines are remarkable. Try Les Caillerets for value. They are keepers. *Quite* different in style from Leflaive. There is a disturbing lack of consistency, however, in bottles of the prized Le Montrachet.

Château de Raousset
See W&V, Beaujolais, Chiroubles.

Domaine Rapet Père & Fils
Pernand-Vergelesses, 21420 Savigny-lès-Beaune. 16 ha *en fermage.* **Grands Crus: Corton-Charlemagne; Corton. 1ᵉʳˢ Crus: Pernand-Vergelesses: Vergelesses, Ile des Vergelesses; Beaune. Pernand-Vergelesses, Côte de Beaune and Côte de Beaune-Villages (Pernand), Aloxe-Corton, Savigny-lès-Beaune, Beaune, Bourgogne Rouge and Aligoté.**
Good to very good wines, with the test of time behind them. The Grands Crus are not really imposing examples, however, and the *village* and Premier Cru wines are the best value from this property.

Domaine Gaston & Pierre Ravaut
21550, Ladoix-Serrigny.
Sturdy red wines that often seem to have rather too much tannin for their underlying fruit.

Domaine François & Jean-Marie Raveneau
See W&V, Chablis.

Domaine Henri Rebourseau
10 place du Monument, 21220 Gevrey-Chambertin. Grands Crus: Chambertin, Chambertin Clos de Bèze, Charmes-Chambertin, Mazis-Chambertin; Clos de Vougeot. 1ers Crus: Gevrey-Chambertin: Fonteneys, Perrière. Gevrey-Chambertin.

There have been wonderful bottles from this estate in the past, but current form is very patchy. A pity – considering the quality of the vineyards!

A Régnard & Fils
See W&V, Chablis.

Domaine de la Reine Pédauque
BP10, 21420 Aloxe-Corton. 38 ha (mostly *en fermage*). Grands Crus: Corton-Charlemagne; Corton Clos des Langres, Corton-Combes, Corton-Pougets, Corton-Renardes; Clos Vougeot. 1ers Crus: Aloxe-Corton; Savigny-lès-Beaune: Les Clous, Les Guettes, Les Peuillets. Ladoix, Aloxe-Corton, Savigny-lès-Beaune, Bourgogne Rouge and Aligoté.

This is both domain and large *négociant-éleveur*, owned by Pierre André, another name under which they trade. I am afraid I find their red wines to be somewhat jammy and burnt-tasting, right across the range, but the whites are more palatable. The reds go through the *chapeau immergé* method of vinification, a rare occurrence in Burgundy, for ten days and the *grands vins* are matured in oak barrels, a third of which are renewed each year. The Corton-Charlemagne is vinified in new oak barrels. They bottle early as they believe this conserves the maximum fruit.

Remoissenet Père & Fils
21200 Beaune. 2·4 ha. 1ers Crus: Beaune (including Grèves and Toussaints).

Both domain owner and important *négociant*. The white wines, particularly the top *appellations*, can be very good – their Corton-

Charlemagne for example. The reds, however, are much less consistent; while their 'big' style enables them to keep well they don't have much AC character.

Michel Rémon
See W&V, Chablis, A Régnard & Fils.

Domaine Henri & Gilles Remoriquet
25 rue de Charmois, 21700 Nuits-St-Georges. 5·5 ha (2·5 ha *en métayage*). 1ᵉʳˢ Crus: Nuits-St-Georges: Les Bousselots, Les Damodes, Rue de Chaux, Les St-Georges. Nuits-St-Georges, NUITS-ST-GEORGES LES ALLOTS, Hautes Côtes de Nuits, Bourgogne Aligoté, Bourgogne Passe-Tout-Grains.
This is a small domain which has been slowly built up this century and where the wines are made with great care and respect for true taste and flavour. The grapes are half destalked and vatting is quite lengthy. *Elevage* is in oak barrels renewed 'as often as possible'. Bottling takes place at 22 months, after a fining with white of egg. The wines are good, without being special.

Domaine de la Renarde
See W&V, Côte Chalonnaise: Rully, Givry.

Domaine Armelle & Bernard Rion
8 Route Nationale, 21700 Vosne-Romanée. 7 ha (1 ha *en métayage*). Grand Cru: Clos Vougeot. 1ᵉʳˢ Crus: Chambolle-Musigny; Vosne-Romanée Les Chaumes; Nuits-St-Georges Les Murgers. Chambolle-Musigny Les Echézeaux, Vosne-Romanée, Nuits-St-Georges, Bourgogne Rouge and Aligoté, Bourgogne Grand Ordinaire.
There has been a big improvement at this domain, now under the management of son Bernard. Long *cuvaisons* and manual *pigeage*, followed by 100 percent new oak for the Clos Vougeot, 50 percent for the Premiers Crus and 30 percent for the *villages* make for dark, sturdy, concentrated wines. Armelle and Bernard Rion are also 'fresh truffle' producers from October to January – plan your visits accordingly!

Domaine Daniel Rion & Fils

Prémeaux, 21700 Nuits-St-Georges. 15 ha (0·7 ha *en métayage*). Grand Cru: CLOS DE VOUGEOT. 1ers Crus: Chambolle-Musigny Les Charmes; VOSNE-ROMANÉE: LES CHAUMES, LES BEAUX MONTS; NUITS-ST-GEORGES: **Aux Vignerons**, CLOS DES ARGILLIÈRES, HAUTS PRULIERS, **Nuits-St-Georges (red). Chambolle-Musigny, Vosne-Romanée, Nuits-St-Georges Vignes Rondes, Côte de Nuits-Villages (all red); Bourgogne Rouge, Blanc and Aligoté, Bourgogne Passe-Tout-Grains.**

Wines that combine class with quite delicious fruit. This domain had a string of notable successes in '88, '89 and '90. The Vosne-Romanées are full of seductive black cherry and spice flavours, while the Nuits-St-Georges are marked by the *appellation's* particular *goût de terroir*.

Domaine Patrice & Michèle Rion

8 rue de l'Eglise, Prémeaux, 21700 Nuits-St-Georges. Chambolle Musigny Les Cras, Bourgogne Rouge Les Bons Bâtons.

Daniel Rion's son Patrice has bought some land with his wife, separate from the family domain. The '90 Bons Bâtons (first vintage) was very strong in black cherry flavour, with just a touch of oak; sturdy without being coarse, and at a quality level much above its *appellation*.

Domaine de Roally

See W&V, Mâconnais, Mâcon.

Domaine Guy Robin

See W&V, Chablis.

Domaine de la Roche

See W&V, Beaujolais, Brouilly.

Domaine Joel Rochette

See W&V, Beaujolais, Régnié.

Antonin Rodet
See W&V, Côte Chalonnaise, Mercurey.

Domaine Rollin Père & Fils
21420 Pernand-Vergelesses. 7 ha (11 ha *en métayage*). Grand Cru: Corton-Charlemagne. 1er Cru: Pernand-Vergelesses Ile de Vergelesses. Aloxe-Corton, Savigny-lès-Beaune, Pernand-Vergelesses, Pernand (white), Bourgogne Hautes Côtes de Beaune, Bourgogne Aligoté.
A mixed bag here. The white wines are lean (young vines, early picking, overcropping?), even the Corton-Charlemagne lacks depth and breadth for the AC. The reds are better with a good pure Pinot character, if not a great deal of charm. However, the '90 Ile de Vergelesses Premier Cru shows that Rémi Rollin can make reds with scent, richness and length. A new *cuverie* is planned, so things may be looking up.

Domaine de la Romanée-Conti
Vosne-Romanée, 21700 Nuits-St-Georges. 25·54 ha. Grands Crus: ECHÉZEAUX, GRANDS ECHÉZEAUX, RICHEBOURG, ROMANÉE-CONTI, ROMANÉE-ST-VIVANT **(rented *en fermage* from the Domaine Marey-Monge),** LA TÂCHE; LE MONTRACHET.
The vineyard holdings are fabulous, some of the best sites in Burgundy. The policy is for late picking, to achieve maximum possible ripeness. The domain says it always practises rigorous grape selection in years where there is rot. Partial destalking according to the vintage, and very long fermentations are also features of DRC practice. There is, naturally, the finance to use new oak barrels every year and racking and filtrations are kept to a minimum. The domain aims for great longevity in its wines.
　　The domain is owned by the de Villaine and Leroy families. While I have criticised some wines of the 1970s, the 1980s saw an enormous improvement, largely due, I feel, to the increasing influence of the modest and talented Aubert de Villaine. Even the 1984s are now showing exciting gamey tastes, and the great vintages of '85, '88, '89 and '90 are the stuff of dreams. The '87s are tight, concentrated and small-yield. Some '83s are shedding their 'hail and rot' dryness (amazingly enough) and the '82s are drinking

deliciously now. The sheer heady quality and persistence of flavour of DRC wines is unequalled.

Domaine André Ronzière
See W&V, Beaujolais, Brouilly.

Ropiteau Frères
21190 Meursault. Grands Crus: Clos Vougeot; Echézeaux. Iers Crus: Beaune: Grèves, Genevrières, Perrières; Puligny-Montrachet. Chambolle-Musigny, Pommard, MONTHÉLIE, **Volnay, Meursault.**

A *négociant* house with some estate wines. The whites are better than the reds; their Meursaults, for which they have always been known, are the best of the whites.

Domaine Michel Rossignol
21190 Volnay.

Some good wines, although I suspect the owner is more suited to growing grapes than making wine.

Domaine Philippe Rossignol
59 avenue de la Gare, 21220 Gevrey-Chambertin.
See W&V, Côte d'Or, Gevrey-Chambertin.

Domaine Régis Rossignol-Changarnier
21190 Volnay.
See W&V, Côte d'Or, Volnay.

Domaine Rossignol-Trapet
Rue de la Petite Issue, 21220 Gevrey-Chambertin. 12·5 ha. Grands Crus: Chambertin, Latricières-Chambertin, Chapelle-Chambertin. Iers Crus: Gevrey-Chambertin: Clos Prieur, Petite Chapelle, Gevrey-Chambertin; Beaune Teurons. Gevrey-Chambertin, Morey-St-Denis, Savigny-lès-Beaune, Beaune. Bourgogne Rouge and Blanc, Bourgogne Passe-Tout-Grains.

This new domain derives from the division of Domaine Louis Trapet where, broadly speaking, the holdings were simply halved (the other new property is Domaine Jean Trapet). It is too early to

make any judgements about quality here, but the '90s had more
extract and oak than the Louis Trapet wines had, and of course
many of the vineyards are exceptional, so the potential is there.

Domaine Joseph Roty
**24 Mar de Lattre de Tassigny, 21220 Gevrey-Chambertin.
7 ha. Grands Crus:** CHARMES-CHAMBERTIN, **Griottes-
Chambertin, Mazis-Chambertin. 1er Cru:** GEVREY-
CHAMBERTIN LES FONTENYS. **Gevrey-Chambertin: La
Brunelle, Champ Chenys, Clos Prieur, Marsannay,
Bourgogne Rouge.**
Small but good grower – prices positively at 'boutique' level.
Wines with an abundance of ripe fruit and an almost Port-like
concentration in good vintages – and plenty of new oak as well.
Mostly very good quality rather than 'fabulous'.

Domaine Marc Rougeot
Rue André Ropiteau, 21190 Meursault.
Marc Rougeot's white wines are better than his reds. The Meursault
Charmes is rich in good years, but his Meursault Monatine is his
best value and most reliable wine. If rarely very concentrated, it is
always elegant and stylish.

Domaine Emanuel Rouget
**37 rue Charmois, 21700 Nuits-St-Georges. Grand Cru:
Echézeaux. 1ers Crus: Vosne-Romanée: Les Beaumonts,
Cros Parentoux. Vosne-Romanée, Nuits-St-Georges,
Bourgogne Rouge.**
Emanuel Rouget is Henri Jayer's nephew and his uncle's influence is
clear for these are rich and flavoury wines. Not yet Henri Jayer . . .
but the '90s are splendid, especially the Cros Parentoux.

Domaine Guy Roulot
1 rue Charles Giraud, 21190 Meursault. 12·5 ha. 1ers Crus:
MEURSAULT: CHARMES, PERRIÈRES. **Monthélie; Auxey-
Duresses; Meursault: Les Luchets, Les Meix Chavaux,
Tessons; Bourgogne Rouge, Blanc and Aligoté.**
This is an admirable domain, ably managed by Madame Guy
Roulot, with the wines now made by her son Jean-Marc. They

were amongst the first growers in Meursault to vinify the different *lieux dits* separately. Guy Roulot, who so sadly died in November 1982, developed the domain to what it is today. For me, these are wines of finesse and breed. Vinification is in oak barrels with a proportion of new wood, varying between one-third and one-quarter for the Meursaults. Bottling takes place, on average, after 10–11 months. The results have texture and length on the palate.

Domaine Georges Roumier
21220 Chambolle-Musigny. 13·7 ha *en fermage*, 0·81 ha *en métayage*. Grands Crus: Charmes–Chambertin, RUCHOTTES–CHAMBERTIN; BONNES-MARES, MUSIGNY; CLOS VOUGEOT; **Corton-Charlemagne. 1ers Crus:** MOREY-ST-DENIS CLOS DE LA BUSSIÈRE ***monopole***; CHAMBOLLE-MUSIGNY AMOUREUSES. **Chambolle-Musigny, Bourgogne Rouge.**
Christophe Roumier now makes the wines with his father. Fermentation temperature is not allowed to exceed 30°C, there are one to two *pigeages* a day, and the wines are aged in a maximum of one-third new oak. The Ruchottes- and Charmes-Chambertin will appear under Christophe Roumier's own label in future. Wines of purity and great class.

Domaine Armand Rousseau
21220 Gevrey-Chambertin. 13·3 ha. Grands Crus: CHAMBERTIN, CHARMES-CHAMBERTIN, CHAMBERTIN CLOS DE BÈZE, CHAMBERTIN CLOS DES RUCHOTTES, MAZY-CHAMBERTIN; MOREY-ST-DENIS CLOS DE LA ROCHE. **1ers Crus:** GEVREY-CHAMBERTIN: **Les Cazetiers,** CLOS ST-JACQUES, GEVREY-CHAMBERTIN. **Gevrey-Chambertin.**
Apart from being one of the most engaging and generous characters in all Burgundy, Charles Rousseau is also a gifted winemaker. The heritage of this estate is awe-inspiring, but present-day standards bow to no-one, and many are the tastings where, in my opinion, Rousseau wines come out top. Most of the wines are aged in 25–30 percent new oak, except for the straight Gevrey, which is put into old wood only, and the Chambertin and Chambertin Clos de Bèze which mature in 100 percent new barrels. Most people would agree that the Clos St Jacques is a Grand Cru in all but name. These wines are the very spirit of Burgundy.

Domaine Roux Père & Fils
St-Aubin, 21190 Meursault. 18 ha (8 ha *en métayage*). 1ᵉʳˢ Crus: ST-AUBIN: LA CHATENIÈRE, **Les Frionnes, La Pucelle; Meursault Clos des Poruzots; Chassagne-Montrachet Clos St-Jean;** SANTENAY. **St-Aubin, Puligny-Montrachet Les Enseignères, Chassagne-Montrachet (red and white), Bourgogne Rouge and Aligoté, Bourgogne Passe-Tout-Grains, Bourgogne Les Grands Charmeaux.**

A very good domain; the Roux family also started a *négociant* business two years ago. There is no destalking and the *élevage* is done in oak barrels which are renewed by one-third every three years. The wines are perfect examples of their different *appellations*.

Domaine Bernard Roy
21190 Auxey-Duresses.
Patchy quality, apart from Le Val which is a real keeper and worthy of the *cru*.

Domaine Roy-Thévenin
See W&V, Côte Chalonnaise, Montagny.

Domaine Ruet
See W&V, Beaujolais, Brouilly.

Château de Rully
See W&V, Côte Chalonnaise, Rully.

Domaine de Rully St-Michel
See W&V, Côte Chalonnaise, Rully.

Domaine de Ruyère
See W&V, Beaujolais, Morgon.

Domaine Fabien & Louis Saier
See W&V, Côte Chalonnaise, Mercurey.

Domaine Francis Saillant
See W&V, Beaujolais, St-Amour.

Domaine Jean-Louis Santé
See W&V, Beaujolais, Chénas.

Domaine de l'Abbaye de Santenay/Louis Clair
21590 Santenay
See W&V, Côte d'Or, Santenay.

Domaine PBI Sarrau
See W&V, Beaujolais, Juliénas.

Robert Sarrau/Caves de l'Ardières
See W&V, Beaujolais, Beaujolais-Villages.

Château de la Saule
See W&V, Côte Chalonnaise, Montagny.

Domaine Roger Saumaize
See W&V, Mâconnais, Pouilly-Fuissé.

Domaine Etienne Sauzet
Puligny-Montrachet, 21190 Meursault. 7·5 ha. Grands Crus: Bâtard-Montrachet, Bienvenues-Bâtard-Montrachet. 1ᵉʳˢ Crus: PULIGNY-MONTRACHET: Champ Canet, LES COMBETTES, Les Perrières, Les Referts. Puligny-Montrachet, Chassagne-Montrachet, Bourgogne Blanc and Aligoté.

Impeccably-made wines under the management of Gérard Boudot, Etienne Sauzet's son-in-law. The wines are aged in one-third new wood and bottled after about 14 months. The oak seems to show on these wines more than on Vincent Leflaive's (though it is eventually absorbed) and occasional bottles have had reductive bouquets. I have had a few disappointments – '87s and '88s were not as good as expected – but the '89s and '90s were back on form, and there have been some glorious bottles from this property. The domain's size decreased by nearly a third in 1991, when Jean-Marc Boillot took his 'share' of the vineyard holdings. All the original Sauzet wines will still be available – in smaller quantities – except for La Truffière (0·25 ha) which went to M Boillot in its entirety.

Domaine Savoye (Pierre Savoye)
See W&V, Beaujolais, Morgon.

Domaine René Savoye
See W&V, Beaujolais, Chiroubles.

Domaine Seguin
**Rue Paul Maldant, 21420 Savigny-lès-Beaune. 3·5 ha.
Iᵉʳ Cru: Savigny-Lavières. Savigny Godeaux, Savigny-
lès-Beaune.**
Pierre Seguin (whose grandfather invented the *wagon-citerne*, or
road tanker) is both a domain owner and a *négociant*. The domain
wines are fermented in oak *cuves* in a 14th-century Cistercian
cuverie, and the aim is to make wines which will keep well. But that
does not mean heaviness – the wines have bouquet and supple fruit.
The Seguin family has owned the house, cellars, *cuverie* and the
vineyards since the 18th century.

Domaine de la Seigneurie de Juliénas
See W&V, Beaujolais, Juliénas.

Domaine Daniel Senard
**21420 Aloxe-Corton. 8 ha (15 ha *en métayage*). Domaine D
Senard: Grands Crus: Corton-Charlemagne (red); Corton,
Corton-Bressandes, CORTON CLOS DES MEIX, Corton Clos du
Roi. Iᵉʳˢ Crus: Aloxe-Corton Valozières; Beaune Les
Coucherias. Aloxe-Corton. Domaine Terregelesses: Iᵉʳ
Cru: Savigny-lès-Beaune Les Vergelesses (red and white).
Savigny-lès-Beaune (red), Chorey-lès-Beaune (red and
white), Beaune (red).**
Philippe Senard now makes the wines, the fourth generation of
vignerons. The 14th-century cellars were built by the monks of the
Abbaye de Ste-Marguerite and were forgotten for several centuries. Methods are traditional, but with great emphasis on automatic
temperature control at the time of fermentation/vatting. There are
both wooden *cuves* and enamel-lined steel vats, and *élevage* is in oak
barrels, with 25 percent new wood. These were nearly always
wines for long keeping, bottled after two years and tannic, even
rustic, when young. However, since the late 1980s Guy Accad has

been the consultant oenologist here and we have yet to see how that will affect the style, *typicité* and keeping potential of the wines; however they promise much from cask.

Domaine Christian Serafin
5 rue Caron, 21220 Gevrey-Chambertin. Grand Cru: Charmes-Chambertin. Iers Crus: Gevrey-Chambertin: Les Cazetiers, Les Fontenys. Gevrey-Chambertin Vieilles Vignes, Gevrey-Chambertin.
Limited tasting experience has shown the domain's reputation might be running ahead of performance.

Domaine Bernard Serveau
21220 Morey–St-Denis. Iers Crus: CHAMBOLLE-MUSIGNY, LES CHABIOTS; MOREY-ST-DENIS LES SORBETS.
Winemaking with real respect for the material and the AC.

Domaine Michel Serveau
Larochepot, 21340 Nolay. 8 ha. Chassagne-Montrachet, St-Aubin, BOURGOGNE HAUTES CÔTES DE BEAUNE (red and white), Bourgogne Aligoté, Bourgogne Passe-Tout-Grains.
Michel Serveau makes particularly good Hautes Côtes de Beaune.

Domaine Servelle-Tachot
21220 Chambolle-Musigny.
Chambolle-Musigny and Les Amoureuses in a refined vein.

Simonnet-Febvre
See W&V, Chablis.

Pierre Siraudin/Château de St-Amour
See W&V, Beaujolais, St-Amour.

Domaine Robert Sirugue
Rue Neuve, 21700 Vosne-Romanée. 9·5 ha. Grand Cru: GRANDS ECHÉZEAUX. Chambolle-Musigny, Vosne-Romanée Les Petits Monts, Vosne-Romanée, Bourgogne Rouge.
Good Bourgogne Rouge, remarkable Grands Echézeaux.

Domaine de la Sorbière
See W&V, Beaujolais, Beaujolais-Villages.

Paul Spay/Domaine de la Cave Lamartine
See W&V, Beaujolais, St-Amour.

Château de St-Amour
See Pierre Siraudin.

Domaine St-Michel
See Domaine Prosper Maufoux.

Domaine St-Sorlin
See W&V, Beaujolais, Beaujolais-Villages.

Domaine Ste-Claire
See W&V, Chablis.

Domaine de Suremain
See W&V, Côte Chalonnaise, Mercurey.

Domaine Talmard
See W&V, Mâconnais, Mâcon.

Domaine Jean Taupenot-Merme
33 route des Grands Crus, 21220 Morey-St-Denis.
See W&V, Côte d'Or, Gevrey-Chambertin.

Domaine Philippe Testut
See W&V, Chablis.

Louis Tête
See W&V, Beaujolais, Beaujolais-Villages.

Société Civile du Domaine Thénard
See W&V, Côte Chalonnaise, Givry/Côte d'Or, Puligny-Montrachet.

Jean Thévenet/Domaine de la Bon Gran
See W&V, Mâconnais, Mâcon.

Domaine René Thévenin-Monthélie & Fils
**St-Romain, 21190 Meursault. 16 ha. 1ᵉʳˢ Crus: Monthélie;
Volnay Clos des Chênes.** ST-ROMAIN (WHITE), **Côte de
Beaune (St-Romain) (red), Beaune, Monthélie,
Bourgogne Rouge, Bourgogne Passe–Tout-Grains.**
This domain is principally known for its white St-Romain, which is
a more than honourable wine, deserving to be better known. It is, as
they say, for those 'in the know'.

Domaine Thévenot-le-Brun & Fils
**Marey-les-Fussey, 21700 Nuits-St-Georges. 26 ha.
Bourgogne Hautes Côtes de Beaune (red);** BOURGOGNE
HAUTES CÔTES DE NUITS: **red, white, Clos du Vignon (red
and white), Les Renardes; Bourgogne Aligoté, Bourgogne
Grand Ordinaire, Bourgogne Passe-Tout-Grains.**
Father and two sons work this property, and they are particularly
proud of their Clos du Vignon, revived after the vines had been
completely abandoned. I have liked the red better than the white.
There is rather a special Bourgogne Aligoté, Perles d'Or, which is
bottled straight off the lees to give some fresh *pétillance*.

Château Thivin
See W&V, Beaujolais, Côte de Brouilly.

Domaine Girard Thomas
**21190 St-Aubin. 6 ha. 1ᵉʳˢ Crus: Meursault-Blagny;
Puligny-Montrachet La Garenne; St-Aubin: Murgers des
Dents de Chiens (white), La Chatenière (white), Les
Frionnes (red); Puligny-Montrachet; St-Aubin (red and
white). St-Aubin, St-Aubin Côte de Beaune, Bourgogne
Rouge and Blanc.**
The whites are better than the reds; the Premier Cru Puligny-
Montrachet, Meursault-Blagny and St-Aubins are worth trying.

Thorin
See W&V, Beaujolais, Moulin-à-Vent.

Domaine de Thurissey/Les Vieux Ceps
See W&V, Mâconnais, Mâcon.

Martine & Jean-Luc Tissier/Domaine des Crais
See W&V, Mâconnais, St-Véran.

Domaine Tollot-Beaut & Fils
Chorey-lès-Beaune, 21200 Beaune. 18·3 ha (21·88 ha *en fermage*). Grands Crus: Corton-Charlemagne; Corton, Corton-Bressandes. 1ᵉʳˢ Crus: Savigny-Lavières; BEAUNE: **Blanches Fleurs, Clos du Roi,** GRÈVES. ALOXE-CORTON, SAVIGNY-LÈS-BEAUNE CHAMP-CHEVREY, **Savigny-lès-Beaune,** CHOREY-LÈS-BEAUNE, **Bourgogne Rouge, Blanc and Aligoté.**
This is a renowned family domain – the first vines were bought in 1880 – and now the fifth generation is starting to work. The age-old Burgundian formula is followed here: vinification in open wood *cuves* with a floating *chapeau* of skins, constantly in contact with the fermenting must, all with the aim of producing wines of good colour, aromatic in their bouquet and with real potential for longevity. In the main, Tollot-Beaut succeed admirably, with some gloriously heady wines. The Chorey-lès-Beaune is a wine with a good *rapport qualité/prix*, a distinct asset to those on a budget. Two-thirds of the production is exported.

Domaine Tollot-Voarick
21200 Chorey-lès-Beaune.
See W&V, Côte d'Or, Chorey-lès-Beaune.

Domaine Tortochot
12 rue de l'Eglise, 21220 Gevrey-Chambertin. 11 ha. Grands Crus: Chambertin, Charmes-Chambertin, Mazis-Chambertin; Clos de Vougeot. 1ᵉʳˢ Crus: Gevrey-Chambertin: Champeaux, Lavaux St-Jacques. GEVREY-CHAMBERTIN: **Champerrière, Les Corvées, Les Jeunes Rois, Gevrey-Chambertin, Morey-St-Denis, Bourgogne Grand Ordinaire.**
A well-respected domain, run by M Gabriel Tortochot. Half of the production is sold to local *négociants* in barrel, half in bottle direct

from the domain – Switzerland and Belgium are good customers, and private clients calling in are given a warm welcome. Grapes are destalked, and fermentations are long, up to 14 days. One-tenth of the barrels are bought new each year. The wines tend to be big, sometimes slightly rustic; but there are grand bottles when aged.

Château de la Tour/Domaine Pierre Labet
Clos de Vougeot, 21640 Vougeot. Château de la Tour: 5·50 ha. Grand Cru: Clos Vougeot. Domaine Pierre Labet: 6 ha. 1ers Crus: Beaune Coucherias; Savigny-Vergelesses (white). Beaune Clos des Monsnières (red and white), Bourgogne Rouge.
Guy Accad has been advising on the vinification here since 1987 and there has been a marked improvement in the wines since that vintage. The Clos Vougeot stresses finesse rather than power, and the '87 was already drinking well at five years of age. We shall have to wait and see how the wines develop in the long term.

Domaine de la Tour du Bief/Comte de Sparre
See W&V, Beaujolais, Moulin-à-Vent.

Château de la Tour Bourdon
See W&V, Beaujolais, Régnié.

Domaine Louis Trapet
This domain ceased to exist in 1990 (*see* Domaine Rossignol-Trapet). *See also* W&V, Côte d'Or, Gevrey-Chambertin.

Domaine Gérard Tremblay/Domaine des Iles
See W&V, Chablis.

Trenel & Fils
See W&V, Mâconnais, Mâcon.

Domaine Jacques Trichard
See W&V, Beaujolais, Morgon.

Domaine des Trois Coteaux
See W&V, Beaujolais, Beaujolais-Villages.

Domaine Truchot-Martin

43 Grande Rue, 21220 Morey-St-Denis. 7 ha. Grands Crus: Charmes-Chambertin; Clos de la Roche. 1ᵉʳˢ Crus: Chambolle-Musigny Les Sentiers; Morey-St-Denis Clos Sorbés. Gevrey-Chambertin, Chambolle-Musigny, Morey-St-Denis, Bourgogne Rouge.

Moderately extracted wines aged in 25 percent new wood for the Premiers Crus, a bit more for the Grands Crus. These are very clean, frank wines, pure in their fruit flavours and supple in texture. They are good rather than great, with the Grands Crus lacking a little scope for really top quality. They lack for nothing in immediate appeal though, and they are typical of their *terroirs*.

Domaine Jean Vachet

See W&V, Côte Chalonnaise, Montagny.

Château Varennes

See W&V, Beaujolais, Beaujolais-Villages.

Domaine des Varoilles

11 rue de l'Ancien Hôpital, 21220 Gevrey-Chambertin. 11·9 ha (2 ha *en métayage*). Grands Crus: Charmes-Chambertin, Mazoyères-Chambertin; BONNES MARES; CLOS VOUGEOT. 1ᵉʳˢ Crus: GEVREY-CHAMBERTIN: Champonnets, La Romanée, CLOS DES VAROILLES, Clos du Couvent, Clos Prieur, Clos du Meix des Ouches, Gevrey-Chambertin.

Both the domain and the *négociant* business are now owned by the Swiss group Hammel SA. Great '90s at the domain.

Domaine Bernard Vaudoisey-Mutin

Rue du Mont, 21190 Volnay. 6 ha. (5 ha *en métayage*). Pommard, Volnay, Meursault, Bourgogne Rouge and Blanc.

Sturdy *village* red wines that will keep. Half M Vaudoisey's wine is still sold to *négociants*.

Domaine de Vauroux

See W&V, Chablis.

Domaine Alain Verdet
21700 Arcenant, Nuits-St-Georges. 8 ha. Bourgogne Hautes Côtes de Nuits (red and white), Bourgogne Aligoté.
The red wines undergo a long *cuvaison* and are aged in 30 percent new oak for two years; the white wines spend 12–15 months in wood. M Verdet's labels proudly proclaim his 'organic' methods: 'Domaine en Agrobiologie depuis 1971 – Culture sans produit chimique ni de synthèse'. Both reds and whites have plenty of flavour; the bouquets can be problematic – 'organic' odours?

Domaine Lucien & Robert Verger
See W&V, Beaujolais, Côte de Brouilly.

Verget
71960 Sologny.
The *négociant* business started by Jean-Marie Guffens (qv) in 1990. He buys grapes from growers whose vineyards he has helped supervise during the year, and pays a premium for the quality of the fruit as judged by yield, sugar-acid balance, health and cleanliness. So far he only makes white wines, in a purpose-built winery at Sologny in the Mâconnais. The wines start their fermentation in stainless steel vats and finish in barrel. For *négociant* wines, first results look very promising indeed. They are fresh and clean, with plenty of flavour and good *typicité* for blends within an *appellation*.

Domaine Patrick & Martine Vermorel/Domaine de la Fully
See W&V, Beaujolais, Brouilly.

Charles Viénot
5 quai Dumorey, 21700 Nuits-St-Georges. 4·83 ha (0·75 ha en *métayage*). Grands Crus: Charmes-Chambertin; Musigny; Clos de Vougeot; Bonne Mares; Corton. 1ers Crus: Nuits-St-Georges: Les Corvées Paget, Les Damodes; Gevrey-Chambertin Bel Air. Gevrey-Chambertin, Bourgogne Rouge, Bourgogne Blanc Clos Le Village.
Traditional methods produce full, slightly sweet wines. Charles Viénot is also a *négociant-éleveur* in Nuits, and I have liked the firm's

Côte de Nuits-Villages. They have taken a leaf out of the New World notebook, and now put very informative back labels on their bottles. Viénot belongs to Jean-Claude Boisset.

La Maison des Vignerons à Chiroubles
See W&V, Beaujolais, Chiroubles.

Eventail de Vignerons Producteurs
See W&V, Beaujolais: Chiroubles, Brouilly, Beaujolais-Villages.

Domaine Thierry Vigot
21220 Messanges. Grand Cru: Echézeaux. 1er Cru: Vosne-Romanée Les Gaudichots. Nuits-St-Georges, Hautes Côtes de Nuits.
A promising domain using a modest proportion of new wood. Supple and pleasing Hautes Côtes de Nuits and good, rather than great, Vosne-Romanée and Echézeaux. Pretty wines with ripe-cherry Pinot flavours, but occasionally the old wood 'shows'.

A & P de Villaine
See W&V, Côte Chalonnaise, Bouzeron.

Henri de Villamont
Rue du Docteur Guyot, 21420 Savigny-lès-Beaune. 9·5 ha. Grand Cru: Grands Echézeaux. 1ers Crus: Chambolle-Musigny; Savigny-lès-Beaune Clos des Guettes. Chambolle-Musigny, Savigny-lès-Beaune Le Village, Bourgogne Rouge.
An important Swiss-owned *négociant*. The Savigny wines can sometimes be most pleasant. In 1969 they bought the Barolet business, but of course the recent wines have nothing to do with the great collection of wines built up by the late Dr Barolet which are now, unfortunately, mostly happy memories.

Domaine Vincent
See W&V, Mâconnais, St-Véran.

Domaine Bernard Virely-Rougeot
21630 Pommard. 8 ha. 1ers Crus: Pommard Clos des

Arvelets, Pommard; Meursault Charmes. Beaune,
Meursault, Pommard, Bourgogne Rouge.
Usually dependable.

Union des Viticulteurs Romanèche-Thorins at Chénas
See W&V, Beaujolais, Moulin-à-Vent.

Société Coopérative des Viticulteurs de Saône et Loire
See W&V, Mâconnais, Mâcon.

Domaine Michel Voarick
21420 Aloxe-Corton. 5 ha (4 ha *en fermage*). Grands Crus:
Romanée-St-Vivant; Corton-Charlemagne; Corton-
Bressandes, Corton Clos du Roi, Corton-Languettes,
Corton-Renardes. PERNAND-VERGELESSES, Aloxe-Corton.
Amongst the vines tended by this domain is the famous 2·5 ha
Hospices de Beaune vineyard, Cuvée Corton Docteur Peste. The
old Burgundian rules are followed to the letter here, including a
policy of no destalking. The resulting wines usually last very well
and make fine, sturdy bottles, though the style is really not 'me'.

Domaine Robert Vocoret & Fils
See W&V, Chablis.

Domaine Comte Georges de Vogüé
21220 Chambolle-Musigny. 12 ha. Grands Crus: BONNES
MARES, LE MUSIGNY; Musigny Blanc. 1er Cru: CHAMBOLLE-
MUSIGNY LES AMOUREUSES. Chambolle-Musigny.
Marvellous vineyards and some very fine wines in the past. Most of
the '70s and '80s lacked the magic associated with the best from this
property, but the '90s suggest things may be looking up.

Joseph Voillot
Volnay, 21190 Meursault. 8 ha (2 ha *en métayage*). 1ers Crus:
Pommard: Clos Micault, Epenots, Pézerolles, Rugiens;
Volnay: Caillerets, Champans, Frémiets; Meursault Cras.
Pommard, Volnay, Meursault Chevalier, Bourgogne

Rouge and Aligoté.
The Voillot family have been vignerons in Volnay since the 14th century, which certainly displays fidelity to one's origins! They support warm fermentations, and one-third new oak barrels are used for the domain-bottled wines; two-thirds of the production is sold in bulk, either to Beaunois or Swiss *négociants*.

Domaine Leni Volpato
21220 Chambolle-Musigny.
A domain with a good reputation for its Passe-Tout-Grains.

Domaine de la SCI du Château de Vosne-Romanée
Vosne-Romanée, 21700 Nuits-St-Georges.
See W&V, Côte d'Or, Vosne-Romanée.

Domaine de Vuril
See W&V, Beaujolais, Brouilly.

Index

Wine estates, domains, etc and their proprietors are listed in the A–Z of Burgundy Producers (pages 222–336). Figures in italics indicate maps or tabulated material.